i

MAKING AN ENTRANCE

The biography of Gerard Gould

Margaret Martin

Published by
D.R.Green, Oxford
October 2010

Publisher's agent
David Martin
Exeter, Devon, UK
Email: dave.g.martin@btinternet.com

© Margaret Martin

ISBN 978-0-9538455-1-4

9 780953 845514 >

Printed and bound by:
Short Run Press Limited, Exeter, UK
www.shortrunpress.co.uk

Contents

Dedication

To all those who died in concentration camps and for whom there was no biographer to tell their story. We honour them.

Margaret Martin

ii

Acknowledgements

I would like to thank all those who have contributed to the writing of this book and who have supported its production by their good wishes and helpful suggestions. In particular:

Those who were interviewed by me or provided written passages for inclusion:

Anne Vessey	Liz Whitaker
Belinda Beasley	Margaret Tyzack
Cate Fowler	Martyn Read
Catherine Hartley	Mary Stuck
Derek Turner	Msgr. David Botrill
Elizabeth Martin	Nick Rawlinson
Father Peter Cornwall	Nick Woolfrey
Geoffrey Goodall	Nigel Cooke
Gillian Thorne	Norman Lilley
Graham Thomas	Pat Chantry
Hal Fowler	Peter More
Ian Waite	Philip Quartermain
Jackie Keirs	Tish Francis
Jennifer Thorne	Tom Hassall

Those who helped with the photographs and artwork:
Clare Harris   David Green

Those who spent hours proof reading:
Amy New   Mary Batten-Stevens

David Green who gave invaluable help with preparing the book for publication.

And finally the biggest thank you of all goes to my husband, David, for putting up with me while I wrote it and for preparing what I have written for publication.

A timeline to show key dates in Gerard's life

Year	Event
1922	Gerard born on 26th August
1932	Gerard attends Johannes Gymnasium
1933	Hitler becomes Chancellor of Germany
1934	Gerard's last trip to Marienbad Gerard attends Jewish Synagogue school
1935	Gerard's Bar Mitzvah (Jewish ceremony for the initiation into manhood at 13 years) Gerard's sister Margot has a son
1938	Gerard's sister Gerda marries Kurt and they emigrate to New Zealand Kristallnacht
1939	In May Gerard comes to England on *Kindertransport* and goes to live with Mr and Mrs Pease Gerard enters 5th form at Oxted County School at the age of 16
1940	Gerard does agricultural war service at Watlington
1942	Margot and Max sent to concentration camp with their son
1945	War ends in Europe Gerard first dramatic production in England - 'The Mask' at Watlington Gerard takes up assistant teaching post at Rotherfield Peppard Secondary Modern School
1947/ 8	Terrible winter. Gerard gets pneumonia and pleurisy
1950	Gerard appointed Head of English and Drama at Wheatley Secondary Modern School and meets Eileen
1952	Gerard and Eileen marry

1957	Gerard appointed head of English and Drama at Lord Williams's Grammar School, Thame
1959	Gerard takes school production of 'Twelfth Night' to Germany
1964	Gerard's twinning mission to Germany
1966	Gerard takes a sabbatical from teaching to investigate involving professional actors in education
1972	Gerard and Eileen buy property in Dordogne
1976	Gerard leaves LWS and takes up post as Educational Advisor
1984	Gerard retires form full-time employment
1988	Gerard converts to Catholicism
1996	Eileen dies
1996	Gerard retires from his position as foundation governor of LWS
2004	Gerard last drama production -'The Merchant of Venice' with the Oxford Theatre Group
2005	Gerard is honoured with a surprise tribute evening at the Oxford Playhouse
2009	Gerard and Margaret Martin meet for the first time

PREFACE

Among the many occasions to celebrate the 450th anniversary of Lord Williams's School in Thame we had a garden party in July 2009. It was a particular pleasure to meet again David Martin who, in the nineteen-fifties, had a distinguished career as a scholar, school actor, musician, rugby player, all crowned by a place at Exeter College in Oxford. David, his wife Margaret (known as Matty) and I sat at the same table at the garden party. Conversation flowed easily. On our second meeting a few weeks later at the New College dinner Matty suddenly asked me for my permission to let her write my biography. Nothing could have been more surprising. My first reaction was a volley of laughter. Unusual and varied though my life has been, I did not think it would be of sufficient interest to attract readers beyond an inner circle. I had not taken Matty's energy and determination into account. Within a few days she submitted an outline of such a book. I was kept busy for several weeks compiling a list of names and addresses of family, friends, former students and actors with whom I have worked. My thanks to all those who took so much trouble to recall souvenirs of events in their lives. All our lives were deeply enriched by these contacts with theatre and literature. Special thanks to Matty for her enthusiasm in this task.

Gerard Gould
September 2010

Making an Entrance!

Prologue   The Butterfly Touch

A few months ago I'd never even heard of the man known as Gerard Gould. The first merest hint of a wing brushing my consciousness was when my husband, David, was going through some souvenirs of his days at Lord Williams's School, Thame. I was busy reading a novel with a complicated plot at the time, but he managed to catch my attention with an earnest appeal to 'look at this'. He showed me a photograph of the performance of 'Twelfth Night' in which he played the part of Feste.

"Handsome fellow!" I remarked.

But David looked more wistful, verging on serious, than my comment could account for.

"The man who taught us drama really inspired me."

"Is he still alive?"

"I think so. I could easily find out."

"Why don't you try to see him again?" I replied with a hint of finality before returning to my book.

This was the first gentle 'butterfly touch.'

Nothing more was said on the matter for some weeks until we received information about the Lord Williams's School's forthcoming 450th Anniversary Celebrations on July 1st 2009.

"I might go up for that," David announced. I didn't show any interest and it sat in the pending tray. Then, in a rare de-cluttering of his study, David came across an old letter that was to have a profound effect on us both. He was reading it when I happened to come in with tea.

"You know, he was such a wonderful teacher. I've got a letter here he wrote when I graduated." Tears welled up in his eyes as he spoke to me. I drew up a chair, realising at once which particular teacher he meant.

"Tell me about him," I said. "What's his name?"

"Gerard Gould. Well, that was the name he changed to. He was a German Jew. He came over here when he was a boy. He was an amazing teacher. He started off with a bunch of ordinary boys with no particular interest in drama and turned us into performing players. Some were inspired enough to go on to RADA."

"You need to see him again."

"He might be going to the anniversary celebrations – I could find out."

I was becoming intrigued by this mysterious teacher who could move a grown man to tears.
"I'd like to meet him," I said.

It was the second butterfly touch.

Arrangements were made to attend the July 1st get-together. David assured me that I could go along too, but he was rather concerned that I'd be bored.

"I can take a book and read it under the table" was my rejoinder. I had no intention of being bored. It was like asking a child if he or she would like to miss Christmas. If there was any chance of seeing Mr Gould, I wanted to be there to meet the man who has such a profound effect on people.

"Have you asked if Gerard Gould's going?" I queried and, much to my irritation, David was in an enigmatic mood.

"No, I haven't. But if he's alive, he's bound to be there."

I was becoming the human equivalent of Kipling's Elephant's Child, filled with 'satiable curiosity'!

Lord Williams's School, Thame, Oxfordshire. July 1st 2009.

As soon as I entered the marquee, I was aware that the focal point of energy in the room was in a small area to my right. David's attention was drawn there too, which is remarkable in that the drinks were over to the left.

"He's here!" he exclaimed with obvious joy.

I saw an elegantly dressed man sitting with what looked like splendid ease on a very ordinary wooden chair as if it were a throne. His face shone with pleasure as one old pupil after another came up to greet him. The air around him positively pulsated with his vibrant charisma. It was enchanting to watch the meeting of old teacher and old boy, as my husband greeted him.

A long drawn out and beautifully choreographed 'Ah' came from Gerard, as he set eyes on David and slowly stretched out an arm towards him. Then he turned quite naturally to touch my arm as if he had always known me, and said, "He was my Feste, you know!" On seeing the old photograph of Feste in the album that David was holding, he turned to me with a mischievous stage whisper that was intended to be heard quite clearly by all in attendance.

"Lovely thighs, lovely thighs!" I agreed with him entirely! From the beginning, I felt very comfortable and at ease with this man.

David Martin showing Gerard the photographs of 'Twelfth Night' at the Quatercentenary celebrations at LWS Thame

On the way home I was aware of intrigue cementing into compulsion. I had to have that man's story because, if it remained untold, the world would have lost something rare and irreplaceable. It was energy working with energy to produce an inevitable result. I think quantum physics is now confirming such phenomena, thus endowing 'weirdness' with credibility and respectability!

After a few days I threw it out to David, in an off the cuff sort of way.

"I want to write Gerard Gould's biography."

The seed was sown, and like parsley, it took a while to germinate.

The notion did not entirely leave my head – it just lay dormant until David booked for us both to go to the follow-up event in the celebrations, a 450th Anniversary dinner at New College in the autumn. It would make sense for me to see Gerard then and ask him, but he needed to be prepared. At the last minute, I found a card depicting young lads bathing by the river to send to him, and launched into a funny quip about their thighs not being a patch on Feste's – that was the easy bit. I resorted to feminine wiles, deciding that a little intrigue would not go amiss, and boldly announced that I had a proposition to make to him. I would fill him in about it in a few days.

The scene switches to New College, Oxford.

On the evening of September 21st in the gardens of New College a little drama is taking place.

To set the scene: - It is a dry, but bleak and cloudy, evening. People are gathered with stiff upper lips, undaunted and determined to enjoy the champers and nibbles and good company. The ladies are doing their best not to shiver and possibly wishing that they had had the presence of mind to put on thermal underwear beneath their evening dresses. Fortitude is on display – the British at their best. They have formed standing groups and are chatting animatedly with old pals, perhaps not seen for years, catching up on news. And maybe, just as when Icarus fell from the sky, the drama about to be enacted will go entirely unnoticed.

Gerard Gould is sitting on a garden bench near the entrance when I arrive and has only one person standing talking to him. I sit down next to him with what I hope is seen as an air of definite purpose. Gerard makes several attempts to speak to me, but the man does not pause for breath. When he finally takes the hint that it is someone else's turn, we immediately get to business.

"Do you remember me?" I blurt out feeling nervous now the time has come.

"Yes, yes," Gerard smiles broadly, turning sideways on the bench to face me. I am already facing him.

"You got my card?" I am hoping he is plugged in and knows what I am on about.

"Yes, yes! Now, I **want** to know what it is! I've been thinking about it all the time and wondering **what** it can be!"

He looks intrigued and very curious, almost like a little boy. I am so glad there is energy to work on. I seize my moment of power and grin at him, saying nothing, happy to tease him a bit longer.

"You're not going to tell me **now**, are you?"

I shake my head, playfully.
"No, I'm waiting till you're well oiled and then you'll say 'yes' to anything."
Gerard throws back his head and laughs loudly.

"But I'm only having one glass of wine with dinner. I'm driving, you see."
My moment of power dissipates with the immediacy of a burst balloon.

"Oh! That means I've got to tell you **now**, then."

Gerard nods with what I can only describe as an impish expression in his eyes, and he chuckles infectiously. My cold feet are not entirely due to the inclement British weather. I take a deep breath and blurt it out. There is a distinct feel of the confessional about it.
"I love stories. I want your story."

He does not seem in the least disconcerted.
"Yes," he says encouragingly. "Not tonight, though."

"Oh no, not tonight. You see I want the whole story."
There is a pregnant pause while I remember to breathe. "I want to write your biography."

There is no pause from Gerard. As always, he knows his lines well. His reply is immediate.
"Yes".

My jaw drops in a most unladylike way – not to put too fine a point on it, I gawp!
"You mean that's it? You agree."
My voice has gone up several octaves.

"Yes!"
Here, he roars with laughter at my incredulity. I still cannot quite take it in.

"You mean we have a deal, then?" I look at him intently.

"Yes, we have a deal!" There is another roar of laughter and we shake hands.

At this point the gong sounds for dinner. Gerard and I let the world stream past us in the fast lane. We saunter along taking a detour down memory lane at the same time. It is a beautifully natural yet polished little anecdote about his arrival in England. We are comfortable. We gel and the butterfly flutters around our heads in a dance of jubilation.

Scene 1
Childhood in Germany between the Wars

There are two relative strangers talking on the telephone linking Oxford and a village in the West Country. They are setting off on a journey together, back in time to 1920's Germany.

This is the first time that Gerard and I speak together by telephone in order to work. I am surprised it goes quite so smoothly. I expect some initial awkwardness until we get used to each other. But, right from the start, it is an easy process and we settle into a natural rhythm, just as old friends do. I am aware that there will be very sensitive areas and I am anxious to let him know that we need not deal with them until he is ready.

In the hours before Gerard was born, his Father is recorded as making the following pronouncement: 'If it's a girl I shall go into the office by the back door. (*He already had two girls.*) If it is a boy, I shall enter through the front door.' On the day Gerard was born, he made an entrance through the front door. Gerard has inherited this particular set of genes. He always '**makes an entrance**'.

M "Gerard, I'm leaving it to you where we start. As far as I'm concerned we can start anywhere and move backwards, forwards or sideways from that. It doesn't have to be chronological or linear. So, tell me, have you been thinking about any particular period in your life in the last few days?"

G "Well, yes, as it happens, I have. I've been reading reviews of the play, 'The Class' – do you know it? It's set in the Ukraine and it reveals how a group of Polish children who played and learned alongside Jewish pupils before the war turned out to be holocaust perpetrators in their adult lives. It made me think about my own school days in Germany, you see." (*So, quite naturally, we start at the beginning.*)

M "Tell me about it. What are your earliest memories?"

G "My childhood was an exceptionally happy one and it was destroyed. When I think about the photograph that was taken of me standing in front of the grandfather clock, it was a very happy child standing there. I was about 6 years old." (*Here, it is appropriate to include an excerpt from something Gerard started to write some years ago .Unfortunately, the photograph is missing.*)

'I am looking at the photo of a tubby little boy standing in front of a massive grandfather clock. The smiling face looks confidently at the camera, unafraid of the explosive flash which would, at any moment, be triggered off by the photographer hidden underneath a black hood. The child's hands are clutching the mouldings of the clock as if the familiar solidity of this piece of furniture would give him all the reassurance he might need to face this particular operation. There is some faded writing on the back of the photo: Günter am fünften Geburtstag 1927 (*on fifth birthday*). Who is Günter? It takes me a little while to remember that this was the name given to me by my parents at birth – that I was Günter for the first sixteen years of my life. No one has ever called me by this name for well over fifty years. The name does not evoke any response in me. Günter was wiped out of my existence.'

(*This is obviously what Gerard feels to be true at the time of writing this, when he was in his seventies. Whether it is the whole truth or not will be revealed in due course.*)

G "You must understand we considered ourselves to be German. We were totally assimilated into German life. My Mother's family had been living in Breslau since the 18th Century.

Gerard's Mother aged about 52 in the mid-1930s

Gerard's father in the mid-1930s

My Father was a textile merchant in Breslau and had a factory in the Upper Silesia region. He was not affected by the economic crisis between the two world wars – anyone who had anything to sell survived. My father was not very political, but he was interested in current affairs. I remember he always came home for a main meal midday, one to three, and we all sat around the big table and we talked. I, being the youngest, was able to pick up all kinds of adult conversation of course."

M "I can imagine!"

G "One day he announced very, very gloomily that a politician had suddenly died of a heart attack - Stresemann – he was still quite young. He was a highly intelligent and liberal minister. He had negotiated with the allies on behalf of Germany for a reduction in the huge fines imposed in the Treaty of Versailles after the First World War that were now crippling the country. Germany was simply not capable of paying and it caused utmost poverty and that, of course, fired an anti-Semitic attitude in Germany. Most Jews were in the medical, legal and commercial professions so they were quite prosperous at this time, whilst many Germans, particularly ex-soldiers, were living on the poverty line. Daily we had well-spoken beggars at our door begging for food and money – **terrible**. Stresemann was respected by the allies and he was about to get a big reduction in the debt when he died. This made a deep impression on me."

M "But, Gerard, you were only five years old when this happened. It's amazing you were at all interested."

G "Oh but I **was**, you see. It made a very deep impression on me indeed." (*From his response it is clear that his memory is indeed accurate and that the young Günter was not only keen to know, but was also endowed with perception way beyond his tender years.*) The gradual increase in the Nazi movement was so clear to us at this time – they were allowed to march, as were the communists. Every day there were street marches. At every election the Nazi party gained more and more votes. I was not aware of any anti-Semitism amongst our friends – a lot of my parents' friends at this time were either Protestant or Catholic. But things were changing slowly. My older sisters came home with stories."

M "When did you start school?"

G "Normal intake is at six. My birthday is in August and the yearly intake is in April, which would have made me nearly seven by the time I got in. My Mother, who was **very, very** ambitious for me, was determined to get me in when I was **only five**! (*Here there is a slight pause while Gerard chuckles*!) That, of course, also meant that at the other end I would have been well over ten, nearly eleven to get to the Secondary School. When that time came, my Mother used a special device that she'd worked out. The secondary school she wanted me to get into was called Johannes Gymnasium, where they took boys from ten to nineteen years up to the final exam. The year was 1932, when I would have been ten in August. Well, my Mother was determined that I should start at Easter when I was only nine, as I would have completed my four years at primary school. You know what she did? You had to go to the local authority and that of course was **terribly officious**, German. Well, you can imagine, can't you?"

M "Yes, I can imagine very well!"

G "She was not going to be fobbed off with seeing clerks or faceless underlings. Only the top man would do. So she dressed herself up in a very sort of German hausfrau costume - the skirt with a white top – a white blouse with a jabot – you know we used to have these jabots -you know what a jabot is?"

Mother all dressed up with her hat and jabot

M "No, tell me."

G "Well, it's a bow in the front, a sort of..."

M "Oh, I know. I've seen them in the old films."

G "It comes from the French. I don't know whether we have the word in England, perhaps we do. (*I notice that although he is absorbed in his German past, he used 'we' when speaking of the English.*) Anyway, and a hat and gloves and so on and she made an appointment to see the chief education officer. I think he was duly impressed! (*hearty laugher here from both of us*) The result was that I was **permitted,** (*pregnant pause here for dramatic effect*) given **special** permission, to start the Johannes Gymnasium at the age of nine. **Imagine the Germans doing this**! And it was **1932** - already hotting up!

It was in the city - we were living just outside the city on a tram route. My Mother was determined that I should be safe for already it was a little bit tricky for a young Jewish boy to be on his own." (*I suspect that 'little bit tricky' is an understatement and a half.*)
M "Because of anti-Semitism, you mean?"

G "Yes. She came with me, but on the tram she deliberately sat a little way away from me so I wouldn't be embarrassed by her."

(*Gerard has a little chuckle here. In this delightful thumbnail sketch he brings to life vividly for a few moments a woman that is long since dead. I feel that I know her. She displays a marked firmness and determination, but this is combined with a sweet sensitivity of touch. Gerard's conversation is peppered with the words 'wonderful' and 'delightful' when describing others. He clearly has a great love of people and the ability to see the best in them. He delights in what makes them their unique selves so that, for Gerard, meeting someone new is like a child being*

*given an unexpected and mysterious present in a box. People
are important to him and he remembers individuals who came
into his life briefly and insignificantly with as much clarity as he
does family and close friends. What makes him so special is that
he also has the ability to paint magic pictures for others, so we
too can see these characters in our mind's eye and enjoy their
uniqueness. Realising that he has got ahead of himself in his
story, he goes back to his primary school days.)*

G "The first school I went to was run by two very aristocratic
spinsters. (*chuckle here*) They **really were** spinsters too! Right
from the start there was wonderful teaching. I don't remember
much about those first four years, except that the teaching was
good. I enjoyed going to that school. It was about twenty
minutes walk away from our house - lovely part of the city - and
we learnt a great deal."

M "Did you have many friends in the school? Did you make
friends easily?"

G "Oh yes, yes. Yes, yes."

M "And were you able to keep any of those friends when you
went to the Gymnasium?"

G "No. Real friends came later in the Jewish school. You know,
after about thirteen, that's when you begin to make real
friendships. (*Much of his schoolboy excitement and enthusiasm
is recaptured in the telling. I am sure there is a sparkle in his
eye and certainly a lift in his voice. Even at the other end of a
telephone his joy is evident.*) Oh, there was wonderful teaching
at the Jewish School. But I didn't find the first one we had for
English so hot! She was another spinster – a real spinster, you
know what I mean, named Seekel and she spent the whole term
giving us phonetics – utterly boring, but it laid a good
foundation. Then Fräulein Foerder took over and we were off.

She was marvellous – highly intelligent woman. But what happened, you see, and this also is quite amusing – in Germany, even in highly academic schools, teachers were expected to offer at least three subjects. Hers were mainly German and English – she was a **wonderful** German teacher. This is where I got my love of literature. I fell in love with her!" (*laughter from both of us*)

M "Now, refresh my memory as to how old you are at this point."

G "I was about fifteen or so. She'd been teaching my sisters too at the girls' school. My middle sister Gerda was a bit of a tomboy! She was a very attractive girl, but she was very, very tomboyish. And my Mother was sent for frequently (*pause for raucous laughter here*) by these lady teachers who were grieved! Well, I fell in love with Fräulein Foerder and at home I described her as 'piquant'! Gerda nearly hit the roof! She had some awful stories about Fräulein Foerder, you see. I shouted, 'No, no!' We were fighting each other about her! (*laughter break, before he continues*) I loved her because I was her star pupil!" (*These light-hearted memories are so full of fun – it makes me forget where we are. They have a timeless, 'everyman' quality about them.*)

M "I was going to ask if you had any problems with school, but it sounds as though you took to it right from the start!"

G "I did! We read Oscar Wilde's 'Canterville Ghost' and I found it so funny. She told us to 'read, read, read in the language' and not look up every word – to be able to read Oscar Wilde, just imagine!"

M "It's really amazing that you were reading it so young, and in a foreign language too!"

Gerard's sister Gerda aged about 21

G "Oh I loved it. In the third year at the Jewish school we read 'Macbeth' and that started my love of Shakespeare. (*At this point Gerard says that he wants to dwell on the English.*) I loved English from the word go."

M "Well obviously! You're very much at home with it!"

G "My first intimation of what England and the English were, did I tell you?"

M "No, not yet."

G "Well, you see, our summer holidays were usually spent in that wonderful Bohemian spa, Marienbad – Czechoslovakia - very famous Victorian spa, very elegant and lovely. It's in the Sudetenland over which there was a lot of trouble later on. My Father was recommended by his doctor to take a cure – because he was very overweight. And for three weeks he did a very Spartan cure there - did a lot of walking and lost a bit of weight, which he immediately put on again as soon as he got home! (*Again, this sounds very typical of the way things go in families – very human.*) You know, I have **wonderful** memories of Marienbad. The only thing was, when I was very small, I was put to bed early and then they all went **off** on the parade, walking up and down! (*laughter here*) Very, very elegant place."

M "Were you annoyed?"

G "Very! I remember the place so well. You went along the main promenade, which was about two or three kilometres and at each end there was the famous source, which was the waters. All the people had their own glasses with their names on and they filled them. Then they had the whole promenade to consume it while they walked to the other end and left the glass there. The only thing was, the next day they had to remember where they should start!

All along one side there were some very, very smart boutique shops – it was a kind of Vichy, you see – and there was a tourist office. My Father was interested in that. He used to go in.
'Who has arrived?'
Everybody who had arrived for the holiday or a cure had to enter his or her name. And one morning we went in – the lady behind the counter - she knew my father very well – looked animated.
'The **English** have arrived! Now the tone will improve!' she announced. (*Raucous guffaws from both of us here, and he pauses for dramatic effect.*)
Now that made a **colossal impression** on me. **Could you believe it!** And I sort of said, '**Who are these English?**' (*more hilarious laughter*)
And of course, you know who the English were? – The Prince of Wales used to go there long before I was born – he went every year, along with famous actors. It was people of that calibre, you see.
'The English have arrived!" (*guffaws*) When the English came on the first day … the English colony! (*more and more guffaws from both of us – we are verging on hysteria*) "**Isn't it lovely! Absolutely lovely!**"

M "It's a perfect gem!"

G "The last journey we could take to Marienbad was in 1934, which was already one year after Hitler had come to power. The train station in Marienbad was outside the town, like it was in all these spas. We had to hire a horse-drawn carriage to take us to the hotel. And the cab driver – it was quite a long, lovely journey and wonderful arrival of course - turned round to us and said, 'Humph, it's high time we had a Hitler here.'"

M "Oh!"

G "Yes. (*slight pause here*) It was '34, and … err … and we realised we wouldn't be … err … you see, Germany had been sanctioned, and the exchange rate was bad. It was very, very difficult. We realised that we would not be able to come again." (*I note all the hesitations and sense his discomfiture.*)

M "What were your feelings and the family's feelings about that sort of statement – 'It's high time we had a Hitler here'?

G "There are too many Jews. (*This is said so quietly, almost under his breath and I find it hard to hear.*) The poison had spread."

M "Yes, that's what these people meant by it, but how did you feel about that?"

G "Very sad. (*Gerard moves swiftly to the safer ground of calculating the ages of siblings.*) But you see my sisters, now let me see, Margot – now she was already married so she didn't come – and Gerda, now let me see – she was just nineteen to twenty, just eight years older than I was and she still had a very good time – yes, a very good time there. But I sensed that things were not as my parents had always had it … We continued to have a good time at Christmas for a while. My Father was a Freemason and they had a big house in the South towards Bohemia – lovely place. We all celebrated Christmas and New Year there."

M "What was a Jewish family doing celebrating Christmas?" (*He answers with a chuckle.*)

G "It was all part of the social life of the Masons – we were accepted there. As soon as we arrived, my Father was elected as social secretary. He was very good at that. Well, Christmas Eve

– they had a lot of staff there – and Christmas Eve was for the domestic staff. They had to work hard so they were given this treat. Always on the menu was a carp – it was a Czech, Polish recipe I think – beautifully cooked, swimming in a thick sauce ..."

M "So speaks the gourmet!"

G "Ha, ha, ha! Think of the thickest sauce you can imagine, swimming in sultanas and butter – lovely! It was wonderful! And carp is really so tender. There was a kind of ice pudding – nothing like Christmas pudding. I didn't know **that** until I got here."

M "You don't need to know it!"

G "Ha, ha! But I'm deviating a lot, aren't I? (*I assure Gerard that his deviations are permissible and indeed highly desirable little gems! He then very neatly reverts to speaking about his secondary education in Johannes Gymnasium.*)

"I was telling you about the Gymnasium school. We started at eight in the morning and ended at one – lots and lots of homework, starting with Latin and then Greek. We had two lessons of Latin a day and Saturday morning school, of course. English began in the third year. By that time I had been thrown out of the school."

M "**Why?**"

G "We all had."

M "Oh, I see."

G "You see as soon as 1933 came - I think this is an important point I am now making - all Jewish teachers were dismissed.

Jewish doctors were allowed to go on practising, but they were not allowed to treat what were called 'true Germans' – as if we weren't **true** Germans! (*a wry laugh here*) If my father had been an academic or in the medical profession, he would have emigrated long, long ago, but because his business continued, with some interference – I'll come to that later – he did not see the necessity. He'd built it up from scratch and did not want to let it go.

'But we're **Germans**. We were born here', he said. He couldn't see it. He just **could not** see it, to my Mother's great distress. She wanted him to sell up and leave. A big price to pay." (*This is said in such matter of fact sort of way that I am unsure what he means – is he referring to the business man's sense of loss or the concentration camps? I am not going to ask him – it will be left as an enigma. It is however followed by a clearing of the throat and a 'where was I?' – a rare occurrence in this normally word-perfect man. I learn to take note of such needs for a prompt.*)

Anyway, where was I?"

M "You were talking about your secondary education in the Gymnasium."

Here I feel it is appropriate to include an excerpt from a newspaper article that Gerard wrote about this time.

The day the friendly colonel stopped saying "Guten tag"

'Hier sind die Mittagsnachrichten!' (This is the midday news.) 'State President von Undenburg has appointed Adolf Hitler, leader of the National Socialist Party, chancellor of Germany.' It was Monday, 30th January 1933, in Breslau, capital of the German province of Silesia. My parents, two sisters and I had just started lunch. First to break the stunned silence was my father. 'He won't last long. He doesn't have a majority. Let's finish our meal.'

I didn't really understand the full significance of the news. I knew that General von Schleicher, the Chancellor, had resigned two days before and that we had no government. But that was nothing unusual. There had been one government crisis after another. Suddenly, I caught sight of something on the balcony of the house opposite. We lived on the first floor of a large apartment house and, although the street was wide and the other side seemed far away, I could see a huge flag being raised on the balcony. The swastika was unmistakable. Surely, flags other than the official national black, red and gold one were banned?

I rushed out onto our balcony. The air was crisp. A sharp frost during the night had given way to a few hours of sunshine out of a cloudless blue sky. Soon the street was festooned with swastika flags, some suspended from poles attached to balconies, others draped over window sills and long expanses of wall. Only the sound of trams and a few passing cars penetrated the usual midday quiet. It was too cold to stay on the balcony. Deep down I was disappointed that so momentous an announcement had not been met with clamours of jubilation or protest. A sea of scarlet flags with black swastika crosses and silence, that was all.

I was in my first year at St John's Gymnasium, an old and very traditional school. My Mother insisted on accompanying me there: street brawls were common in the last years of the Weimar Republic and the school was in the centre of the old town where the narrow streets and small squares were an ideal battleground. Nazi Brownshirts would march down one street and confront Communist Party members parading down another. The police were powerless to halt the fighting that inevitably followed.

Jewish children were particularly vulnerable, but the school was tough enough for the 10-year-old boy I was then, without the indignity of being called a sissy as well. My Mother and I reached a compromise. We travelled in different parts of the tram, ignored each other and walked the last stretch on opposite sides of the road. At midday she would wait at a grocer's near the school and follow me home.

That Monday had followed the same pattern as other weekdays. But then came the news announcement, and the flags. Suddenly, the telephone rang. My sister answered it. I can hear my father saying: 'Be careful; the lines may be tapped.' Why should they be tapped? I don't think I even knew what that meant ... We all returned to our 'normal' afternoon activities. For me, that meant homework. Afterwards, as usual, I went to a friend's house. On the staircase I met the friendly colonel who lived above us.

'Guten Tag, Herr Oberst' I said. This time, unusually, there was no reply.

I arrived at my friend's house to find chaos: he and his mother and younger sister were all packing cases and bags as though for a long journey. His father, a professor at Breslau University, was lecturing in France. I knew that he was an active member of the Communist Party and had often taken part in street rallies.

'I am joining my husband in Dijon for a while,' his mother said. 'Dieter and his sister are going to stay with their grandmother until all this has blown over. The children will be safe there.'

Only then did I begin to realise that everything was different.

Gerard now continues speaking about his time at the Gymnasium.

G "Our Form master looked like Himmler! He had the same sort of face and was totally unsmiling. You know what I mean by pince- nez?"

M "Yes."

G "Well he had a pince nez. We had him for Latin and we had him for German – **terrible!** He terrified me. He **absolutely** terrified me. (*I know from personal experience what it is like to be afraid of an adult in power, and I remember the agony it causes in the psyche of a child. But Gerard, as I have come to expect, glosses over this anguish to dwell on something much more positive - his love of learning. From what comes later, I see that for him this passion for knowledge has helped him through the most dire circumstances.*) But I learnt a lot of Latin. I loved Latin. I wasn't any good at Mathematics and Science. I was there for about two years and ... umm ... one day I was mugged. And ... umm ... I've still got the scars." (*This is said in a very matter of fact tone of voice. He is simply informing me, along with the duration of his stay. I notice the hesitations, and*

28

realise from the way his voice falls at the end of the sentence that no more is forthcoming. I decide to press him a little.)

M "Can you tell me any more about that?"

G "Well, a group of senior boys set on me – non Jewish of course – it was anti-Semitic attack... And err, you know, it was quite painful." (*the understatement of the century*)

M "How old were you? About ten?"

G "About ten and a half."

M "Can you talk about what they did and said?"

G "They set on me. I can't remember all the details, but the scar is still on my cheek. There's a scar on my left cheek."

M "You must have been very frightened."

G "Very frightened, yes."

M "Did you have any time off school?"

G "No, no, no, no. (*This is said in a very low key, matter of fact sort of way, which signals that there is nothing more to be said. I am left to imagine the horror of his parents and the bravery involved in their sending him straight back the next day – they were not raising a namby-pamby. The mind boggles at the thought of what that poor little boy went through in his bed that night, knowing he had to return and face his attackers the next day. I struggle with righteous indignation at the thought of how many blind eyes must have been turned in that establishment. It is so painful for me to move on and just leave all these things unsaid, but I have to follow Gerard's lead. If he has the dignity to leave them unsaid, then I have to find it as well. After only a couple of seconds he continues, giving me an explanation of the way in which German headmasters differ from the English ones.)* You see, the German headmaster is not as powerful as the English headmaster, but he is more of a manager. It's very often a political appointment – we're talking of the Weimar Republic now."

M "Yes, I understand."

G "And that headmaster who allowed me to come **early**, he was not Jewish, but he was dismissed anyway. He was a socialist. I can't remember much about the new head ... Anyway, that was the determining point for my parents to take me away, before we were actually thrown out.

Meanwhile there were a lot of Jewish teachers out of a job. They formed themselves into a new school at the liberal Jewish Synagogue - very gifted teachers as you can imagine. The only thing was the school was not allowed to have public exams or teach academic subjects such as Latin – all that was held against the Jews, you see. They were too academic. And so the teachers found a solution to this – they opened the school from ten o'clock in the morning to three o'clock in the afternoon, which was the official time. For those who wanted to do the academic subjects it started at eight o'clock and went on after three. It worked. It worked beautifully. We had Latin, English, French, physics, etc. you see. We got it all in. They were excellent teachers. The only thing was, of course, that bit by bit they emigrated and the pupils too. It was a diminishing factor. But it was an excellent school."

M "Were you a boarder or a day pupil?"

G "A day pupil. Boarding was not an option."

M "So, when you went home and said, 'Another teacher's left' or 'Another pupil's left', you must have been aware of the ongoing and ever more pressing conflict between your parents on the issue of emigration?"

G "Oh yes, yes. My Mother begged my Father. (*Now comes a neat bit of fielding from Gerard.*) Meanwhile, my older sister, who was thirteen years older than I was, became engaged and married to a delightful man, Max Hirsch. My Father took him into his business."

M "What was your sister's name?"

G "Margot - a very beautiful girl. I loved her dearly."(*With hindsight, I am surprised how level and gentle his voice remains here, as if it is the easiest thing in the world to reminisce about such matters. However, the multiple hesitations that follow betray the effort involved in steering himself through to safer waters. He does not continue, so after a pregnant pause I ask a question that I hope will be uplifting*)

M "Did she look after you when you were little?"

G "Yes ... yerrrs! (*This is said with a little chuckle. I hope for some stories about that, but it is not to be.*) We also had a live-in help who was originally my nanny, until she had to ... in 1935 the Nuremberg Laws were kicking in which forbade any Jewish family to live with a non-Jewish person. So Clara had to leave us. But she kept in touch. She really saved my Father's life for us, but that comes later." (*The last three sentences are full of hesitations as he begins to reconnect with that time. We pause, which is a signal to me to move things where I think they should go.*)

M "Going back to your parents' disagreement – it's obviously upsetting for a young child when there's conflict."

Margot and her husband Max in the early 1930s

G "It was very sad. My Father was a very jovial person, very, very jovial – big and delightful person, absolutely delightful. Everybody loved him - brilliant at his business, socially very acceptable. And my Mother was really the driving spirit behind it all! You see, she was the eldest of five!" (*He laughs here. There is a long pause again, so I take the lead.*)

M "You were obviously very intelligent – you were thinking about all these things and didn't miss much in the conversations. Did it make you confused when your Mother wanted one thing and then your Father said 'no, no, no', because a child doesn't like taking sides?"

G "Yes, yes. You know the Passover? We were not in any way religious, but we kept the holy days and the feast days, you see. My Father came from a very religious family – so did my Mother as a matter of fact - but they had both become very, very liberal in adult life. And at the Passover, the father, the master of the house, presides over the prayers. It's a very, very pleasant occasion. At one moment the youngest always has to say something. Instead of going to a Sunday school, I went to a Hebrew school and I learnt Hebrew and loved it – I loved it. The youngest has to conclude the whole thing in Hebrew, you see, with 'And next year in Jerusalem!' (*He laughs so much here he can hardly get the punch line of the story out!*) **Me, being me**, with a **very loud voice** came out with '**And next year in London**!' (*More loud laughter follows, the sort to fill a theatre.*)

M "I see, you were making a point!"

G "Exactly. 'Next year in London...'" (*His voice is still strained and high pitched with holding back laughter.*)

M "So what happened when you said that?"

G "My Mother was very upset, my Father laughed, I think, and my sisters told me off! '**I want to be in England**!'" (*The latter is said with a boyish whine followed by laughter again!*)

There would be several more Passovers, several more years of fear and anguish before that young boy would have his wish granted.

This account of early childhood and boyhood experiences uses his exact words, as I record his reminiscences and astute observations. He speaks for just over an hour with just a few prompts from me. From somebody of Gerard's mature years, one would forgive a certain amount of rambling and confusion, but not a bit of it. He is lucid, dynamic and succinct throughout and I come away dazed by his powerful delivery. Yes, there is a lot of hearty laughing on his part, but in between the funny anecdotes is a serious and informed analysis of the historical, political, social and ethical situation during those years. I can see why Gerard makes such a profound impression on people. I have had no direct experience of what happened in pre-war Germany, but he is able to paint the picture for me with a few swift brushstrokes and then bring it alive with pinpoints of fine detail. I am there living it with him. I see what he's seeing and know the people that he knows. It is a privilege.

Scene 2

Germany 1934 - Living with Fear and Constriction

The same two characters are centre stage, telephoning each other. Their journey takes them into the turmoil of Germany in 1934.

M "Shall we continue where we left off, with your transfer to the Jewish Synagogue School?"

G "Yes, yes."

M "You were so clever, you must have been top of the class! (*This provokes hilarious laughter before we have even started*!)

G "Oh no! No, by no means." (*more guffaws*) "We were all very bright and keen to learn. I had to work very **hard**. (*drawn out and pronounced haaaard*) English was fantastic for me – I loved it from the word 'go' to the extent that, as soon as I could, I would just read and read and read! I had no notion at the time that I would become an Englishman! - no notion. It was **amazing!**"

M "And of course, you did it perfectly, Gerard. You became the perfect Englishman."

G "Yes, you see, anything English - even to the extent of a daily trip to the newspaper kiosk not very far away. In the afternoon they got the continental version of the '**Daily Mail**'. I had no idea, you know, what a rubbishy paper it was! I went (*voice rises in pitch for dramatic effect.*) **every afternoon** to get a copy of it! (*He pauses so we can have a really good laugh. Humour is never far away with Gerard.*) It was printed in Germany so it was a very grown up sort of thing. But it was

English! And we didn't know any English people. We were far away from it, you see."

M "So how did the political situation affect you at this time? You were still living together as a family?"

G "Yes. (*There is the slightest of pauses before he launches off ad-libbing his next section virtually seamlessly. He is able to shift smoothly from something light-hearted and very comical to something profoundly serious and moving.*) 30th January 1933 the Nazis came to power – that day is deeply printed in my mind. The midday news told us that Hitler had become chancellor. What was amazing was that we were sitting as a family round the table having our midday meal. I was sitting with my back to the balcony window and I happened to look round. The whole of Kaiser Wilhelm Street was full of flags. Swastika flags flew from every balcony **immediately**. They'd stored them away, you see, ready for the occasion. I've never forgotten it. My Mother was very upset. (*He does not elaborate on this statement, and it would be brash of me to ask him to do so. That simple understatement made with a quiet dignity says a great deal.*)

The first of April was a day when all the Jewish businesses in the city were covered with graffiti and had SA troops outside preventing people going in. It was a day's boycott - the shape of things to come. After that, people like my Father were pretty much left alone. It was a shock for us at first. It took time for us to become aware of the radical changes taking place in our lives. Meanwhile all lawyers, teachers and university lecturers who were Jewish were dismissed, which meant, of course, that they made an effort to emigrate at a time when it was still relatively easy."

M "And still your Father wouldn't."

G "No. No, he thought there was no need to. He said, 'They won't last'. He was optimistic, you see. Little did he know the Germans. (*Again, a powerful understatement. We both know that, if his Father had let his Mother have her wish to emigrate, all the agony that followed simply would not have happened on a personal family level. Any emotional response to this is kept under wraps with a quiet dignity and an explanation of the sudden rise in popularity of the Nazi party. He is then ready to speak of the terrible Night of the Long Knives.*) In 1934 Hindenburg died and Hitler made himself number one to tumultuous cheers. June that year was the Night of the Long Knives when Hitler demolished in one blow his beloved SA - that was the Brownshirts - Storm Troupers. Röhn had been with Hitler from the start in the '20s, so Hitler owed him a great deal of loyalty. But Hitler shot him that night along with others. He found them in bed with pleasure boys. The whole lot of them were caught like that and he shot on sight – no trial – it was mass murder - it was **terrible.**

Now on the Saturday evening when the news broke it was hot. My parents had gone to the club and Clara was still with us - '34 - it was later she had to leave us because of new laws. On hot evenings we sometimes leant out of the windows - put a cushion on the ledge. We just talked. There was **a red sky**, I remember that. It was almost as if there was a fire burning. (*pause for reflection*) Afterwards, when the news came through, we thought that the red sky had been very appropriate. News was heavily censored of course. One didn't really know what was going on - terrifying. It was **absolutely** terrifying."

M "Did you cry?"

G "No." (*There is a longer pause than normal*) "No, no, no, no. In a way I felt a bit more secure with Clara." (*The four denials are not vehement, but trip off the tongue like demi-semi quavers.*)

M "All this was going on in your life - didn't it give you nightmares?"

G "I don't know. I can't remember. I was still sleeping in the same room as my parents – that may have been a contributory factor why I didn't have nightmares. The only nightmare I remember was when I was seven or eight. After a History lesson I dreamt we were being asked to make sacrifices and hand over, silver for the national cause to help in the war effort against Napoleon. I was sleepwalking – I went about the house collecting all the metal I could carry, taking it to bed with me. I stood up in bed holding it all out. I was selling metal for **my country**! (*Wry chuckle here at the irony of a young Jew being so keen on assisting in the German war effort. This young boy is profoundly affected by the appalling irrationality and brutality of Hitler's actions, so much so that this night still haunts him all these decades later. The fact that he is sleepwalking at seven years old suggests that he is deeply disturbed, even at this early stage in the hideous proceedings that were to follow. Here it is appropriate to include an excerpt from an article written by Gerard for 'The Independent'*)

When Hitler killed his Nazi ally: After 60 years, Gerard Gould remembers the storm-threatened Night of the Long Knives

SATURDAY 30 June 1934 was one of those sultry days that would end in a thunderstorm and bring at least temporary relief from the sweltering heat. I was then 11 years old and living with my parents and sister in an apartment on a main street linking south with north Breslau, capital of Silesia in south-east Germany (now the Polish town Wroclaw).

All day long we had heard rumours of terrible events taking place among the top Nazis, their party having come to power one year previously. Since dawn an operation aimed at massacring the leaders of the Nazi SA Corps (Sturmabteilung - Storm Section) had been personally put into force by Hitler. This militia force had been set up by Ernst Röhm, Hitler's closest friend since the foundation of the Nazi party, shortly after the First World War. No wonder such news was beyond belief.

My parents and my sister went out, as was usual on Saturday evenings, to a Jewish club, which was still allowed to function, or to friends. As evening drew on, the oppressive heat made the rooms in our apartment even more stifling. So Clara, our faithful domestic help, who was like a member of the family, decided that we would indulge in one of her favourite pastimes. Placing cushions for comfort on a sill, we leant out of an open window to watch the passing scene on the street below.

Normally on a summer evening there was plenty going on. That Saturday evening, not only was there not a breath of air, not a leaf stirring on the chestnut trees lining the broad avenue, but an eerie silence hovered over the street. Motor traffic was still sparse in 1934. Occasionally, the clanking sound of a passing tram disrupted the silence. It was usual for people to sit in their front gardens, gather at street corners, parade up and down the street. Not that evening. Neither did we see a single uniformed person, whether police or SA.

In the west, storm clouds were gathering; thunder began to roll in the distance. I remember a strange reflection in the sky. Clara muttered: 'You mark my words, there will be war.' The events of the day, the approaching storm, Clara's forebodings, all played on my imagination. I was half afraid, half excited.

We listened to the evening news. After keeping the population deliberately in the dark about the day's events, the propaganda machine supervised by Joseph Goebbels went into overdrive. Oozing with oral indignation at the betrayal and depravity of the leaders of the SA, Goebbels, who was in charge of the state broadcasting stations, announced how poor Hitler had found his former friend Ernst Röhm and his followers in bed with Lustknaben and had ordered them to be immediately executed.

'Clara, what are Lustknaben?' I said. Poor Clara! In the darkening light, I couldn't see that I had made her blush. 'Oh, they are boys hired to wait at table at great feasts.'

I didn't pursue the matter. Thanks to a good grounding in the Bible and the Classics, I already had some notion what Lustknaben or 'boys for pleasure' might be. What I couldn't understand was their connection with Röhm and the SA. My picture of Röhm was of an obese, coarsely featured creature strutting about in a brown shirt and breeches which outlined an enormous posterior and obscenely protruding stomach. I could not imagine that there would be room for anyone else beside him in bed.

The full irony of Hitler's discovery that this most trusted of his chiefs should have turned out to be a sexual pervert struck me only years later. The party had always preached German purity in both racial and moral senses.

The news broadcast had also told us that Henlein, the Gauleiter (District Leader) of the Breslau area, and his brother had both been found guilty of treason against Hitler and shot in their own apartment, not far from where we lived. Clara's comment stuck in my memory: 'Poor Frau Henlein, losing both sons like that.'

Once Hitler had become Chancellor of Germany, in 1933, it was inevitable that a great power struggle would ensue between the SA and the SS. Hitler knew that his own survival hung in the balance. President Hindenburg, who had appointed Hitler Chancellor as a bulwark against Communist attacks, made it quite clear that his patience was exhausted by these internal feuds. And Hindenburg still commanded the respect of most Germans. Hitler was on probation, and time was running out.

Hence the massacre of 30 June 1934, known as 'The Night of the Long Knives'. It permanently shattered the SA, which continued only as a small internal party-police organisation. The SS now became a powerful and much-feared organisation. Hindenburg sent Hitler a telegram congratulating him on having 'nipped treason in the bud' and saved the German nation from serious danger.

The scene shifts to Germany 1935 when the Nuremberg Laws are passed.

M "How did these laws affect your family?"

G "Clara, our beloved and faithful maid had to leave us – you see non-Jews could no longer work in Jewish homes unless they were old and past having children. We missed her very much. And of course Jews could only work with Jews. Margot was all right working for my Father and Gerda worked as a typist for a Jewish widow."

M "Were you able to enjoy social lives like you did before?"

G "No. Jews were forbidden to go to the theatre – it was a great deprivation for my Mother. She loved the theatre. My Father was a Freemason and they began to go more and more to the social club."

M "Wasn't it difficult with no Clara to sit with you when they were out?"

G "Yes, they had quite a busy social life. My Mother was very fond of playing cards. The only trouble was she would not leave me alone in the house in the evenings so I had to go with them to the club."

M "Did you enjoy that?"

G "No."

M "You hated it?"

G "I was bored to tears. (*There is a pause and then he adds a droll comment.*) It led to a permanent hatred of cards." (*Loud laughter from me at the thought of this precocious young lad sitting there, looking disdainfully around him when his nose was not in a book.*)

M "Was it hard to get hold of literature at that time?"

G "Well, you see, my parents had to send me to the only remaining Jewish school. It was a very high-powered and academic school – strictly orthodox. That's why I wasn't sent there from the beginning. They didn't approve of that. I went to the new school in '36 and even then I had to sit a test before they let me in!"

M "I'm sure you did very well."

G "It was a terrific school, it **really** was. I thrived in certain areas. We had this brilliant woman, Fräulein Foerder, for German, German literature and English Literature. I mentioned her earlier, didn't I?"

M "Yes. The one you were in love with!"

G "Now, she was sort of peachy, you see. Let me give you an example, shall I? The headmaster, I still remember his name - Harry Abt - very orthodox - youngish - **highly** intelligent - an excellent teacher. Oh my goodness! He took us for Hebrew at first. Hebrew was a great feature – old Hebrew, you know, the bible Hebrew. Fräulein Foerder began reading a modern play with us by a great German author Stephan Zweig - great, great novelist – Jewish. Have you heard of him? (*Following my reply in the negative, he gives me a quick resume of the writer, not to stress my ignorance and his knowledge, but rather to make sure I understand and feel at home with what he has to say. There is an underlying consideration for the listener combined with a genuine love of expanding knowledge in others throughout his communications.*)

The play was based on Jeremiah, in a modern style. Well, Fräulein Foerder read that play with us in German – **a magnificent play!** Well, when Abt came to hear of it he immediately switched into Jeremiah, the biblical Jeremiah. So we had two **absolute** opposites. That's the kind of teaching we had. I just loved it. You see, that is education – I learnt a lesson that I never, never forgot. It was **brilliant** - exciting. And would you believe it, a few years ago, a very, very dear friend of mine here, alas no longer with us, found – he was a great hunter in second hand bookshops – he **found** a copy of Zweig's Jeremiah and gave it to me. Wasn't that wonderful!" (*His enthusiasm throughout this brief sketch of his new school is almost electric down the telephone. It is typical of Gerard not to indulge in a long monologue – his narration is interspersed with short asides to keep the dialogue alive and elicit some response from the listener. The whole experience is then shared in a very intimate way.*)

M "It was amazing!"

G "That was the kind of teaching that we had. And then another example – can I give you another example?"

M "Yes, of course."

G "A young Rabbi - very gifted – took us for Hebrew as well. And one day, quite out of the blue, in front of the whole class, he said to a friend of mine and to me, 'If you two are prepared to work on the first 25 chapters of Samuel Book 1, you will get Grade 1 in the report!' Ha, ha! Would you believe it? That was an incentive. We took it!"

M "I expect you did! You like a challenge!"

G "Coming to today, teachers wouldn't be allowed to do it – (*Gerard's voice goes up in pitch*) **immediately** there would be an outcry, '*ELITISM! ELITISM*!' But we did it! There was nothing else to do – we worked and worked for pleasure – it was a pleasure. You see, our minds were stretching, stretching. It was just the right time. Under the influence of that school I became Orthodox. In '35 – you know what Bar Mitzvah is? – a very, very important ceremony – you stand in front of the whole synagogue and read from the Talmud in Hebrew. And of course there is always a feast afterwards. My parents, with only the one boy, gave me a wonderful Bar Mitzvah. Meanwhile, I had become Orthodox – which meant that I kept the Sabbath very strictly. I wouldn't travel or write and I ate only kosher food. This went on for quite some time, this Orthodox period."

Here I include an excerpt from Gerard's own writing, 'Intimations of Jewishness'. The photograph that he refers to is missing.

I am remembering a photo taken in 1935. A very serious boy, still in short trousers but a tallis round his shoulders and a cap on his head, stands beside an elderly matriarchal figure sitting in a chair - Grandmother with her oldest grandson on the occasion of his Bar Mitzvah. What did this initiation into adulthood mean to a thirteen - year old boy growing up in Nazi Germany? What, indeed, did being Jewish mean?

By the time I celebrated my Bar Mitzvah in 1935, two and a half years after the Nazi party took command in Germany, I had become painfully aware that being Jewish implied an existence well beyond a religious observance. Painfully aware, because it hurt having to accept the limitations, restrictions, abuse and terrors that were inflicted on Jews in Germany. Many of my peers belonged to Jewish youth clubs where Zionism and a return to the 'home land' of Palestine were held up as ideals. I had no wish whatsoever to 'return' to Palestine. England, whose marvellous language I had just begun to learn, offered an irresistible attraction.

M "On reflection, Gerard, can you work out why this sudden religious fervour happened – why it was important to you at this point?"

G "Why it was important? - I took to it - I loved Hebrew. I loved languages. If things had been different I might have become a linguist. It was a very, very beautiful language, particularly in the biblical sense. And we were to a certain extent indoctrinated with it."

M "You said it went on for some time. I was wondering if it gave you some rigid structure that was missing during those years because life was so precarious."

G "Yes, yes, I'm sure it did. And it didn't dawn on me till quite a bit later that, to my Mother, this was welcome because, in a way, she was hoping and thinking that this might be a very good diversion from sexuality. And to a certain extent it was, but only because literature took over. English took over and it's going on still!" (*He roars with laughter here. He is certainly not yielding up any dark secrets at this juncture and I feel he is rather enjoying the thought of what I might be speculating.*)

M "Was it a mixed school or all boys?"

G "It was a mixed school. And of course theatre had raised its head, you see. That's a separate chapter!" (*a big chuckle here*)

M "I think it raised its head never to lower it again! (*There is a pregnant pause between us here so I take the lead.*) So, you are a very strict Jew at this time, you're busy learning, your life is very full, but you're still presumably aware of everything that's happening outside?"

G "Very much. One had to be so careful. We had very strict instructions not to talk to anyone or stand in groups anywhere. We had to come to school and go straight home at the end." (*Gerard's voice is so quiet here that I can hardly hear him, as if he is back again amongst all the fear and need for circumspection.*)

M "It sounds quite a sad time really, in spite of all the thrill of what was happening in school."

G "At school I was very happy – year after year it came top of all the schools in Breslau. (*neat fielding here*) It irritated people and it didn't help us. In the end permission to sit exams was taken away. (*All this is related in the quiet voice that is so contained and is followed by what I have come to recognise as a nervous clearing of the throat.*) And that school was burnt down and destroyed in Kristallnacht." (*'Crystal Night' or 'The Night of Broken Glass', was an anti-Jewish pogrom in Nazi Germany and Austria from the 9th until the 10th November 1938.*)

M "We haven't got that far yet, have we? That's for later." (*I sense we should back off - not something to be talked about on the phone.*)

G "Yes, later." (*second nervous clearing of the throat*)

M "So, continue in a chronological way. You are very happy in the school, in spite of what's going on outside."

G "I'd got a lot of friends – a lot of warmth – we had the time, you see. We were pretty much of the same level as far as our parents were concerned and our intellects."

M "Were these friends just boys or were there girls too? Did you have any girl friends?"

G "Oh yes. Oh yes, yes, yes."

M "Do you want to tell me?" (*chuckle from Gerard here.*)

G "We were doing a lot of drama. The drama helped me. That was approved of – it had the imprimatur of the head! It was quite proper." (*Here Gerard manages to sound like a character out of Jane Austen – quite the English gentleman, apart from the tremendous guffaw that follows!*)

M "So this was a very satisfying time for you."

G "It was. Sometimes I think about it and I think, 'my goodness, what a school. It gave me so much to aim for.' I think my wish to become a teacher was already burgeoning then. I thought, **'next year London'!**"

M "So tell me how the years were before you were moved to England. Tell me how it built up, in other words."

G "Well, it was taken up – you see, school was from eight o'clock in the morning until about two o'clock in the afternoon. Then there was oodles and oodles of homework. I came home and had nothing else to do except to do the homework and read, nothing else. We were not leading normal lives and much of mine was spent sitting around. My mother made me take regular exercise – she even put some gym equipment in the house - you know the sort of thing. She was very concerned that I wasn't getting enough exercise! (*neat gear change follows*) By that time, 1935, I had become a young uncle. My sister Margot had had a child – a boy."

M "What happened to Gerda? Was she still working for the widow?"

G "Gerda married a doctor in 1937. What was so **embarrassing** to me was ... he had happened to be the boyfriend of my best friend's sister, before he met Gerda. Of course, I took the part of my friend's sister! (*mischievous chuckle from Gerard here*) It was very naughty, wasn't it!"

M "It was a bit! Tell me more!"

G "Well, I **teased** him about Vera, that was her name."

M "Did that make Gerda very angry?"(*much merriment on Gerard's part*)

G "I was loyal to my friend's sister and to my sister! He was a clever bloke - his name was Kurt – brilliantly all round clever. He knew that I was hopeless at Maths so he gave me private lessons. He was the only one who ever made me understand Mathematics."

M "He must have forgiven you then!"

G "Oh yes! I thought very highly of him in the end. Then he spoilt it all by questioning my taste in reading and in music! I was deeply into Alexander Dumas – I just loved 'The Three Musketeers'. He just dismissed it as 'Oh, it's all very inferior stuff and in a few years' time you'll not even look at it.' I went off him at once! We were great friends later though, until they emigrated to New Zealand. He played the oboe, quite professionally, and introduced me to Beethoven. In retrospect, 1937 was the last year of more or less normal family life. We got used to Hitler screaming about the Jews. Margot's best friends were non-Jewish and they stayed together."

M "Shall we stop now, Gerard? You must be tired."

G "Yes, I am a little and it is getting near to lunch time."

We make arrangements for our next phone call, for which he is always precisely on time and ready for action. On reflection, I must admit to feeling some relief on hearing this admission of Gerard's – 'hopeless at Maths'! At last there is one thing he is no good at! This man is amazingly talented and able in so many areas. He has comprehension of seven, perhaps eight, languages for a start. It would be very easy to feel intimidated by his vast learning. But with Gerard there is no one-upmanship, no superiority or pleasure in putting people down. He is so natural about his abilities and even resorts to making little jokes about how precocious he must have sounded as a young lad. One is always at ease with him, knowing that he is not judgmental or critical. On the contrary, he is always supportive and concerned with eliciting the best out of others, especially when they themselves are unaware of just how much 'best' there is to be brought out.

Scene 3

Germany 1936-8 via Britain, Denmark and New Zealand - The Family Splinters

The same two people are still communicating only by telephone. The journey is becoming dangerous to handle in this way. They need to meet. They have to make detours. Gerard begins in true British style.

G "Hello. Have you got this very beautiful day?"

M "We have. It's absolutely amazing."

G "Lovely, isn't it."

M "Absolutely lovely. (*After a suitable pause I tell him I want to divert from our linear path.*) Gerard, I think we should leave Kristallnacht till we meet face to face."

G "Yes, I agree."

M "I thought, this morning, we could get you to England – when you first set foot on English soil. How does that sound?"

G "England? Yes, good!" (*He sounds very perky at the prospect!*)

M "So, you're sixteen years old, and you came over on the boat."

G "Yes. And my sister, Gerda, - she had married in 1938 and her husband was completing his housemanship in Hanover. His younger brother had gone to New Zealand to farm. He didn't get on very well with his stepfather at home and (*pause*) ... he decided that he wanted to go sheep farming. (*The pace is slow and so leisurely. I am beginning to think that I am being led away from the personal action in Gerard's life because it is too emotional to speak about. Little did I know that, as ever, Gerard is on the ball, and busy providing me with all the details I need to appreciate the fantastic consequences of seemingly unrelated events.*) He'd heard of New Zealand, and of course, at that time, New Zealand was a dominion of Great Britain. The only way to get to New Zealand was via Britain."

M "Yes."

G "And also, he was expected to have a little bit of farm training – he was a town boy. So he went to Denmark to do training on a farm, which was quite possible. And from there via England – he had to do another training on an English farm before he could get his visa to New Zealand. (*Now I **know** I am being drawn a long way from 1936 Germany.*) All that was fixed up, and the farm that he went on was in Surrey."

M "Yes."

G "And he got off the train at a very little, peaceful, country halt called Hurst Green."

M "Yes." (*I am thinking we will be meandering in the backwaters of Surrey for the rest of the session!*)

G "He knocked at a house to find the way to the farm where he was expected. And an elderly lady opened the door … (*pregnant pause here for dramatic effect*) saw him … and nearly fainted on the spot! (*Side-track it might be, but Gerard has beguiled me with his magic. He has me totally gripped now. What's more, I am sure he knows it!*) He was the **spitting image** of one of her twin sons who got killed in the First World War."

M "Ah!"

G "Now, I've seen a portrait of that young man, and I can vouch for it. It is an astonishing likeness - quite astonishing. So of course she was interested in him immediately and she gave him directions to the farm he was looking for and said, 'Look'. She showed him the portrait of her son in the drawing room. He became a permanent guest of honour in the house and used to go to lunch every Sunday. When the time came for him to apply for a visa to enter New Zealand, this lady, Mrs Rheam, said, 'Well there is a lady living just across the valley here, a Mrs Pease. She's a very influential person, a County Councillor and also a Justice of the Peace. To get a visa you have to get a Justice of the Peace's signature. I know her vaguely – I haven't met her properly – but I'll get in touch and see if she will see you.' (*I have a strange déjà vu feeling at this point. It is not until later that I trace it back to reading Dickens where one is drawn into subplots of great intricacy and you just have to go along with them until he decides to get back to the main business in hand. And just like Dickens, all these minor characters and details are in fact forming vital links with the protagonist, only one cannot see it at the time.*) Well, that was arranged, and Heinz, that was the name of my brother-in-law's younger brother, was a charmer."

M "I can imagine!"

G "He managed to charm Mrs Pease as well and had no problem getting a visa. And out he went to New Zealand to go on a sheep farm. Well, as soon as he was there, I think I am talking now about the year 1936-37 it must have been, he set into motion getting a visa for his brother and his young wife, my sister. All that worked, and they went out in September '38 ..." (*long pause for dramatic effect*)

M "Yes."

G "...via England. And they stayed with Mrs Rheam ..."

M "Ah!" (*a chink of light becomes apparent*)

G "… and Mrs Pease and all that."

M "Amazing! (*I begin to see where all this is leading. There's a little chuckle here from Gerard. I think he's delighted to have astounded me*). Isn't it amazing, Gerard?"

G "Yes, and they did a long trip on the water – they went the long way round from Liverpool to a Canadian port on the Empress of Britain, which of course was sunk during the war. Then they took the train – a lovely train ride and went from the east of Canada right across to Vancouver in the west. It was a present from my Father to them, you see – a lovely ride across the Rocky Mountains to Vancouver and then by boat again, eighteen days down to New Zealand – Hawaii, Fiji and all that. (*This is an idyllic scene that he has just painted for me, and I have to remind myself that they were not just off on holiday. Yes, it was a journey of hope and new beginnings, but at a terrific price. Most members of the family they would never see again.*)
And my brother-in-law, although he was a fully qualified doctor, was not accepted in New Zealand – he had to start **all over again.** It was reduced a little bit – four years training – so my Gerda was the breadwinner all that time. And she was quite skilful at making things, gloves and hats etc. and set up a little shop...they were in Dunedin, right in the South Island."

M "Yes, I know it."

G "They had a tough time, but they were free.

(*The picture on the next page shows a happy mother and child on the steps of their home in Dunedin. Gerda hides her problems well.*)

Gerda and her daughter safe in New Zealand in 1944

Meanwhile we had the Kristallnacht. When that happened Gerda and my brother-in-law were very anxious about me and his younger sister, who was a little bit older than I was, and the two ladies decided they would each take one of us."

M "Which two ladies? The one's in England?"

G "Yes. Then with an English person's guarantee it made it very easy, you see. And I was lucky enough to be taken in by Mr and Mrs Pease, and Mrs Rheam took Inge, my brother-in-law's sister. It was on the second of May that I left Breslau on the Kindertransport and arrived in Harwich early on the fourth, in the morning. (*Kindertransport is the name given to the rescue mission that took place nine months prior to the outbreak of World War II. The United Kingdom took in nearly 10,000 predominantly Jewish children from Nazi Germany, and the occupied territories of Austria, Czechoslovakia, Poland and the Free City of Danzig. The children were placed in British foster homes, hostels, and farms.*) Umm … now, do you want me to go further?"

M "Yes please." (*I am wondering how much we have glided over – the agony combined with joy of his parents – surely his Mother must have known at that point that they themselves would not get out, even if his Father was still in denial. I am wondering how Gerard felt himself – a young lad leaving his family and all that is familiar to go to the unknown. In spite of all his love of English and his burning ambition to get to England, it must have been very frightening when it was actually happening. What a brave face his Mother must have put on and what it cost her beggars belief. I am finding it hard to shake off strong feelings of empathy with her, which are not helpful here.*)

G "Oh, right!" (*I think Gerard is aware of my dissatisfaction because he chuckles here.*)

M "**Much further!**" (*Then I laugh too. He has got himself out of Germany, though, and he is not eager to put himself back there at this point. As ever, England calls him and he is ready to launch into amusing and fascinating anecdotes. The nitty gritty of Germany will have to wait till we met face to face.*)

G "Am I going too fast for you?"

M "No, no. I'm ok. I've caught up with you."

G "Tell me if I'm speaking too quickly."

M "No, no. It's lovely. It's just right." (*Having settled all that we are well and truly away from Germany!*)

G "We landed in Harwich at five o'clock in the morning. We had a medical test to make sure we didn't have any disease and then we were taken to Liverpool Street Station, London. And I found a sort of **slowish** (*drawn out and emphasised*) train. It stopped at **various** (*also elongated*) stations along the way. (*I sense from the slow, deliberate pace of his speech that an amusing anecdote is in the air. I can feel he is building up to it, rather like an angler – I am the fish on the end of the line, thoroughly hooked.*) Every station had a big label called 'BOVRIL' And I thought, 'Is every station called Bovril?' I'd never heard of Bovril before, you see! But it was explained to me later. (*We have a good laugh about this to shake off the heaviness of his departure from the family.*)

At Liverpool Street Station there was, of course, a big crowd, with a huge committee looking after things. A friend of Margot's, who'd been living in London, had come to receive me, which was nice of her – a face that looked familiar. When we were through all the formalities and the customs, Home Office requirements, etc. etc. they transferred us out of London. Mrs Pease couldn't come that day. She was on some committee or other – couldn't come and meet me – she was going to meet me in Oxted instead. And I was transferred to Victoria Station and from then on I was on my own. I remember I knew about Victoria Station by then, because of course by that time I had fully acquainted myself with Oscar Wilde's 'The Importance of

Being Earnest' in which that station plays an important part. (*He makes me laugh with this, as he knew he would. I am certainly not going to be allowed to wallow in the uncertainty, fear or apprehension of a poor young lad who was left to find his own way around a strange country, even if that country was England! But maybe that is a girl thing, and boys only feel the adventure and allure of the 'out there'.*) I was all excited, you see. There was a little incident there that I shall never, never forget. By that time, I was on my own. I was put in a train – a little old Southern railway – you remember the old Southern railway?"

M "I think I might. I remember the old steam trains."

G "A door in every compartment, you see. Anyway, I am there and looking out of the window and a very English lady came up to me – a total stranger – I had my sign on my neck - my identification - etc. etc. And she said to me – now I thought she said, 'Good luck to the sun'. I'd never heard that expression before. It might have been 'good luck, my son.'"

M "Yes."

G "I thought she said, 'good luck to the sun'. Have you ever heard of that?"

M "No. She said, 'Good luck, my son', I'm sure."

G "But I was so touched by that – it was a wonderful welcome, you know – to a total stranger, coming from that terrible place called 'Germany'. (*He gives a wry little laugh here.*) It never would have happened there, even in the good days. 'Good luck, my son!' (*Gerard allows himself a wistful millisecond before ploughing on. It was a butterfly touch for Gerard from an old lady who could have no idea how profoundly her few words would affect the young lad for the rest of his life.*)

Anyway, the journey from Victoria to Oxted was via Croydon – not very far – about fifty minutes or so. As it got nearer and nearer Oxted I got more and more excited. As we got there, on the platform stood what was obviously Mrs Pease, stately – very tall, very elderly, little bit lame, very distinguished-looking, and very Scottish. (*Gerard laughs here as he recalls her. With these few deft brush-strokes I feel that I know her already! It is just as though she has walked into the stage set.*) And I got a very, very nice welcome from her.

The Peases sitting outside their home, 'The Pendicle', in Lympsfield, Surrey in 1939

The car was outside the station, and we then drove to Limpsfield
– lovely countryside – absolutely lovely country. And their
house – they built it themselves in 1900 - a huge garden - it
sloped down and had a wonderful view of the South Downs."

M "Oh, lucky you!"

The house in the South Downs that gave Gerard refuge. His bedroom
is top left.

G "A beautiful view towards Edenbridge, Kent and Kent
Woods. It was very near Kent – the Kent border, East Surrey,
Sussex and Kent Woods in that sort of triangle, you see. (*Having
composed this stunning set for his little drama, Gerard is ready
to introduce the next character, but keeps him an up-staged
mystery for the moment.*) Saw an elderly man in the garden,
working there - very quiet, very peaceful. It was excellent –
they'd given me their best guestroom – lovely windows towards
the South Downs."

M "Ooh!"

G "Lovely view, absolutely lovely."

M "It sounds like heaven."

G "I felt at home immediately. And my parents had sent some of my things – they could do that in advance, luggage could be sent in advance. It had arrived, and there I was. (*There is a natural little pause here for a gentle settling.*) It was a May morning, and midday was very light lunch. And I met Mr Pease.
Mrs Pease said, 'He **is** deaf. He'll hear you if you shout'. (*chuckle here*)
And like a lot of deaf people he was shouting himself! (*more laughter*) He sounded much fiercer than he was – he was the **kindest** person you could meet. I knew he had been a founder of the Fabian Society – I knew that and I had to find out quite a bit about the Fabians."

M "Before you got there?"

G "Yes."

M "Ah, you did your homework!"

G "Yes. He showed me the garden – I wanted to help him, because I'd never had any garden. I think I was flattering myself because I am wholly impractical! He had a home-made sort of sacking where he packed weeds, etc. It was bound up with rope ready to take to the fire - what do you call it?"

M "Bonfire."

G "Yes, bonfire. And I threw the whole sack and everything on the bonfire!"

M "Oh no!"

G "Yes! (*a lot of laughter here!*) Not a good start! Well then, after the evening meal - they were always busy writing letters galore – I helped in the kitchen and all that sort of thing. Mr Pease washing up and Mrs Pease drying up or the other way round - I can't remember (*This admission of a possible inaccuracy about something so minor goes to show how careful Gerard is to be accurate in all he tells me. We can be sure we are getting his truth.*) Then, of course, dear Mr Pease wanted to make some sort of conversation. By then, I was beginning to feel sorry for both of them, having to put up with something – they didn't know me at all. You know, where do you begin? (*At the age of sixteen, most boys are so wrapped up in themselves that very few would have the empathy that Gerard reveals here.*) Mr Pease went, 'Ha, ho – I had a very, very amusing letter today from somebody you've probably never heard of before.'
And I said, 'Oh.' I knew 'oh' and 'ah' worked quite well. (*Laughter from me as he slowly builds up to the punch line of his story and I can feel the tension.*)
'Ho! It's a very famous author called Bernard Shaw!' announced Mr Pease triumphantly. (*There is chuckling from both of us, as Gerard takes off the old man, complete with accent.*)
'Well, yes, I do know – I **have** heard of Bernard Shaw... In fact, I've read a lot of his plays, you see!' (*the laughter in his voice here is so contagious*)
'Ho, ho, ho!' (*One can picture Mr Pease so well – this quick pen sketch gives us the essence of him and he comes to life as a very Dickensian oddity.*)
And so we had a conversation going. I explained to him – since my school was destroyed in Kristallnacht, I had no schooling whatsoever and nothing to do except read. And I read and read right through my Father's library. And I loved Shaw, you see, so we had a lot to talk about." (*I cannot help thinking here how*

fortunate it was that these books were available to Gerard because I am quite sure they kept him sane.)

M "Yes, I can see that."

G "And my stock went up! – obviously, you see! (*I chuckle over this little nugget that sums up a whole situation in a succinct and very clever way and, of course Gerard, the entertainer, loves me to love it.*) And then from there we got on to the Webbs - most notably Beatrice, whom I hadn't heard of before, who played a very important part - they were the co-founders of the Fabian Society – and all sorts of other people, obviously famous names, but not like Shaw. Oh, H.G.Wells featured. He joined the Fabians. Shaw joined after it had been going for some time. H.G.Wells even later. And he was a very destructive influence. Wells and Shaw would debate in public and contradict each other. Shaw would win every time. Mr Pease was the first secretary of the Fabian society – he was the unpaid secretary for many, many years – 30 odd years or so. And he immediately showed me the book that he'd written about the Fabians, which I read within a day or two. It was wonderful!" (*Gerard is obviously enjoying talking about all these famous people – not in order to name drop and impress the listener, but because they enthralled him as a young and impressionable lad. He was interested in them, not just on a 'film star' level, but as people with influence who could shape the way society was moving. Most teenagers would find such a tome exceedingly stuffy, especially if it was written in a language that was not his or her mother tongue. It says a lot about the nature of Gerard's mind.*)

"Well, that was **day one**! ..." (*He pauses to allow for my reaction. This last little quip tickles me no end, as he knew it would. It is almost unbelievable – in fact, if it was written in a novel one would say it was an unrealistic plot that stretches the reader's 'willing suspension of disbelief' too far! He simply* *could not have landed anywhere more suitable to his particular needs – he would get all the stimulation he needed and more.*)

M "It's unbelievable, Gerard! It could only happen to you!"

G "That was Thursday! Friday was **day two,** and in the morning Mrs Pease took me to Oxted County School, where I was expected to go from Monday, to meet the headmaster. (*Gerard knows not to overplay the 'hype' and a very powerful and amusing anecdote is followed by something more ordinary – this is not planned or rehearsed in any way. He does it quite naturally in a constant stream of consciousness - we ad-lib our way through most perfectly.*) What's his name? - I can find out his name ..."

M "That's all right."

G "I wasn't impressed by him at all!"

M "Oh dear! That's why you don't remember his name!"

G "Now Mrs Pease was a governor of the school. He was very, very polite to her, but he was shouting at me. (*chuckle here*) He was a mathematician, which of course put me off immediately! (*pause for my reaction, which he gets*!) Anyway, he showed me round the school for a little bit – lovely to be in a school again – an English school. I was very proud of that. It seemed very organised, very pleasant and all that. Then **Friday afternoon,** (*This is drawn out to give me the vital clue that something is building up again.*) was the time for one of Mrs Pease's tea parties. She would give tea parties every afternoon at 4-15 on the dot. And she made real Scottish scones."

M "Yummy! You'd really fallen on your feet!"

G "The front entrance of the house led to a dining area. There was a huge oak table there. It looked all very Victorian. The drawing room was made out of two rooms – books all everywhere – everywhere books, books, and yet more books. (*This is a veritable paradise for Gerard! The scene is set for the entry of the* guests.) And that afternoon, Litvinov, who was the Russian ambassador at St. James's, and his wife, Ivy, came to tea, driven by the chauffeur. And they brought with them Walter Nash who was the finance minister of the first Labour government of New Zealand. (*I let him know that I am impressed and he laughs with gusto.*) **That was the first tea-party!**"

M "Gosh! That is **absolutely** amazing!" (*What impresses me even more is that he should remember the names of these bigwigs. People are important to Gerard, irrespective of whether he meets them for an hour or knows them for years.*)

G "Of course, I absorbed it all! It was manna from heaven, it was. It really was. And – I'm sorry – I mustn't forget that very important point – I wrote immediately to my parents of course – I wrote to my parents every day in great detail (*I think of how much it must have consoled his parents that he was not only safe but well-landed. In the months to come when they hid from him the horrors in Germany, the fact that he was having fun as a young lad must have been manna from heaven for them as well.*)

M "It must have made them so happy to get those letters."

G "Ah, yes, yes, yes, yes, yes. That was the Friday. (*said in a very deadpan sort of* way) On the Saturday – oh amongst the luggage my parents had sent on in advance was my old bike – that had also arrived. On the Saturday, Mrs Pease sent me on the first of many, many, many messages. And this was into the Kent Woods, a couple of miles away. (*Gerard has set the scene at a leisurely pace, which makes me suspicious that something is brewing*!) And before I went I got the whole history of the lady I would go and see. Her name was ... **Constance Garnett**!"

M "**Oh yes, yes, gosh!** (*Here Gerard laughs with great pleasure because I am so impressed.*) Our famous translator from Russian!"

G "Yes, yes – a great friend of Mrs Pease! They were great buddies, you see. Her husband at that time had already died, Richard Garnett, the great publisher. Now, Mr Pease was a very outspoken man, with a dry sense of humour. Quite frequently, he would go about the house proclaiming, 'The country's in a funk!'
On this occasion, he warned me, 'She's got a son, David, and she's **utterly spoilt him**. He's a **brat**!' (*I hope if David is still alive he will forgive this, which he certainly will, if he has ceased to be a brat!*)
Anyway, David wasn't there, and Mrs Garnett was on her own – everybody called her 'Aunty Connie'. And of course **again**, I had to show off! **Oh dear!**"

M "Oh, Gerard!" (*much merriment at this point*)

G "Of course, I knew she was a famous translator – she was the first person to translate the Russian authors.
I said, 'Yes, I've read Tolstoy and Turgenev! (*Here his voice goes up several octaves as he tries to get the words out over the laughter. Having got them out he collapses into guffaws of merriment and so do I.*) Oh dear, dear! It must have sounded so precocious, I mean, **really**! (*His voice is weak and strained with holding back laughter – after more guffaws he makes a strangled attempt to continue.*) But I couldn't help it, could I?"
(*I am laughing so much that my voice has taken on the same strangled timbre when I try to reply.*)

M "Oh you were sweet!"

G "And there was Aunty Connie, and she looked like she was the typical English governess (*His voice is relaxed now, with only a hint of the former strain, as we move into calmer waters for a while.*) You know, she looked quite neat. She wore a blouse – a lace blouse taken in at the waist and a long skirt with a belt round it. She was the typical governess. She was **charming**. She was **lovely**.

She was very, very interested in what I had to say. I told her that in those months between November and my leaving Germany a friend of mine and I got together and taught ourselves a bit of Russian – a teach-yourself method. She gave me a Russian/English dictionary, a Russian grammar and a sort of vocabulary book – three books.
She said, 'This is how I began.'

Originally, she went out there – didn't speak a word of Russian - to be a governess to a sort of Romanov family. She was very sympathetic. Mrs Pease had told me that she had taken a Russian family into her home in England. (*Gerard is annoyed with himself for not being able to remember their name, but assures me he might be able to get it from Mrs Pease' grandson! I feel I am being led far away from Gerard's personal life at this time, but I am a willing captive because I am enchanted by his stories and amazed by his vivid recall of events that took place decades ago.*)

It was an aristocratic family and in 1905 he had assassinated one of the princes or dukes or whatever it was and he had to flee from Russia. Meanwhile, his wife – she was the first Russian woman allowed to go to university – took medicine for her degree and became a doctor. She had brought a sister over and Constance Garnett took them in. She gave them what was quite a pleasant sort of summerhouse in the garden and they lived there. Meanwhile – oh, I wish I could remember his name … (He *mutters to himself with some irritation. He is trying to go back seventy years and remember people he met briefly, en passant as it were. He is hard on himself!*) They got to England, and he was a dreamer - a charming dreamer, according to Mrs Pease. I think Mrs Pease fell in love with him, as did Constance Garnett. I think they would have been horrified if somebody had told them that, but I bet they were in love!

He would go for long walks, daydreaming. There was a little railway line running near her house there and he didn't see or hear a train coming – he crossed over and got caught by the train – that was his end. Sad, after having been right in the middle of the Russian Revolution. Of course it left his wife and her sister very much alone, but Constance Garnett took charge of them. And there they were in that summerhouse. They took in every stray cat they could find – living in a wood there were lots of stray cats. There was a samovar on the table – like a little Chekhov play."

M "Yes, yes, it's enchanting." (*This is 'Arabian Nights' take two!*)

G "The samovar was simmering away all day long and it was boiling hot inside the house, (*chuckle here*) boiling hot. And we talked a lot - it was like meeting Chekhov characters. Straight out of Chekhov – extraordinary! Well, after that I saw Constance Garnett quite frequently. Mr Pease wasn't very enchanted with her - I think he couldn't cope with dreamers. Mrs Pease and Constance were great buddies – that Russian fellow was a great bond between them, you see. (*The young Gerard has a great deal of empathy and is capable of some very astute observations of the female psyche!*)

That was day two!" (*This is said in a very droll way and I burst out laughing.*)

M "Sorry, but this is fantastically unbelievable!"

G " At Sunday's tea party a very English lady came, whose husband was a great explorer – he was on an expedition so she was on her own. Every day there was a tea party. Now, on Monday of course, I started school. And I was put into the fifth form, who were, in May, already doing revision for the School Certificate they were going to take in June, so it was a little bit difficult for me. (*This is a massive understatement, I should think - no leeway for adjusting to new life – no social worker or counselling, just straight in at the deep end.*) I mean, I wasn't ready to do School Certificate at that time. It was a total change from the German school – couldn't have been more different. Splendid French teacher woman, Marguerite Morris, a very tough Yorkshire lady – I was by far the best in French! (*belly laugh here*) It boosted my confidence a bit."

M "Yes, absolutely. Just what you needed!"

G "She was thrilled to bits to have somebody who appreciated French! (*chuckle*) It was a mixed school – everybody was very, very nice and kind to me. There were two other refugee boys in other classes there so I wasn't the only one."

M "That must have helped."

G "Then it came to the Latin lesson. Only a few took Latin - Miss Jenkins was the teacher. I'd already been told by Mrs Pease that Miss Jenkins was a great League of Nations person (*chuckle*) – a good point at that time!
She said, 'Well, you won't be doing Latin. Have you got some homework you can do? Sit at the back of the classroom.'
All those who didn't do Latin got on with their homework.
And of course a little voice said, 'I **do** know Latin'.
'Oh, I was told you didn't.' (*chuckle here*)
'I've been doing it now for five years!' (*more chuckling*) So she allowed me in."

M "I should hope so!"

G "And she soon discovered that not only did I **do** Latin, but I got 'A' results. There was one other boy who was good at Latin and she was very glad that he at last had a competitor, you see. Ha! I made great friends with Miss Jenkins. She was a lovely person – lovely person. Wonderful physics teacher, Router-Callard, but useless to me because physics and I never ... (*Because I intimate that I understand, he sees no need to complete the sentence. We have already talked over a meal about our mutual inability to deal with Maths or physics!*)

The English, I soon discovered was dreadful. The teacher was the deputy head – Miss Dean – and we all called her Dixie! She was very snobbish and middle class and hopeless – hopeless at teaching! She was always in with the Headmaster, which wasn't very good for the rest of us – buddies together they were. I'm ashamed to say, we played her up! I remember one incident when we were in the Sixth Form and reading Chaucer. Now she wasn't very good on that so she used a very boring crib and we were all getting cheesed off! I was the leader!"

M "Oh, really!"

G "We were in the library and I climbed several chairs or something – anyway, as high as I could go, and threw the book behind the bookshelves! Naughty ..."

M "Shame on you!"

G "Yes, the poor woman searched high and low for it and never found it and we all sat there with straight faces! I am not proud of it ... Ha, ha! And I told you, the Head took us for Mathematics!" (*I groan in sympathy here.*)

M "Oh no!"

G "He used to come in to the classroom with his gown halfway down and shout, 'I know you're here! You, you, you and you!' (*loud guffaw*)

Oh dear, dear, dear! Of course, I then started to report back to Mrs **Pease**, and she had never heard a **quarter** of this before! It wasn't a good school, but at least it had one or two very good teachers. The rest were pretty low calibre, but I was very grateful to be there. The history teacher, Mr Mumford I think his name was, was very solid and knowledgeable. He'd always sit at his desk with his notes in front of him. And I felt that history was fascinating, you see. I loved history and this was English history, which I didn't know. He set me work and I caught up. I read and read and read English history. And, of course, Mr Pease had all the books I wanted. Churchill lived not very far from us – Chartwell was very near where the Peases lived. You see, Mrs Pease was anti-Chamberlain, virulently anti-Chamberlain. Politics featured very commonly in their conversation. What I learned - what I picked up – at this time was summed up in a warning letter from my brother-in-law in New Zealand.
He said 'Be careful – don't talk too much. There are spies around.' Every day I wrote to my parents – my Mother was very worried ...
What more do you want? Shall I carry on?" (*This is a neat movement away from an emotional subject, which doesn't go unnoticed on my part. But I feel it will not be appropriate for me to press the point. There is a swift summing up in order to get back to safe ground*)

M "Yes, please do, if you are not too tired."

G "By the end of the first week my pattern had been formed. I would be telling a lie if I said I wasn't happy. I took to the

English life as if I had been born here. I mean I was lucky – extraordinarily lucky. And dear Mrs Pease, she wanted me to keep in touch with old friends and quite often she invited Inge, my brother-in-law's sister, to come. My best school friend – he was in London with his sister – was not as lucky as I was with his billeting. He was sent out to work. He came on a Sunday.

Meanwhile, I made friends with a lot of schoolmates and they were all **so** nice to me – unbelievable. (*It has been bothering me for some time that the most vivid characters in this presentation are all mature adults. They are the ones who are painted, in costume and down-staged, even if their role is extremely minor. We see them clearly in the mind's eye and feel we know just what they are like. His peer group, if mentioned at all, is grey and amorphous. We are told about a 'best friend' but he has no name. They are up-staged to the extent that they are mere ghosts. What is being unsaid is very significant here. On a superficial level all seems well. This teenager is friendly, personable and good to know, but alas too different from the peer group to fit in with ease – he has seen and known too much. He is an adult far beyond his years and in a sense he 'has put away childish things.' Deep down, there must have been a great loneliness and sense of the lost innocence of childhood that was wrenched from him too soon. Yes, he is happy, but that happiness has a price. He is not an ordinary boy.*)

Then, of course, the problem was, what are they going to do with me, because – I mean the head said, 'Oh, you must repeat this year' – he didn't have any vision. It would have been much better if I had gone straight into the sixth form. But I had to get the School Certificate. In August, this was '39 now, I remember the Sunday when the news broke that Germany and Russia had formed a pact, which was **absolutely staggering** – communism and fascism, utter enemies, and there they were together. Mrs Pease couldn't believe it. She was particularly upset because she felt an affinity with the ideals of communism. Her great interests, apart from general politics, were social ones. She was the first person to set up soup kitchens, teas and things, in the local area, so that the children from poor families could have a proper meal. Now that was something for which she should have had recognition – nowadays she would have had an award for that. (*It is amazing for this young boy to be growing up in this environment. Experiencing such acute social awareness and active compassion is just what he needs to counterbalance all the negative input from pre- war Germany.*)

You see, in 1931 a number of famous British people had planned a journey to Russia. The party was led by Bernard Shaw. It included other people of that calibre like Lady Astor. Mrs Pease was going to join them, but her sons stopped her. It was dangerous, socially and politically. She never forgave them for that! It was a famous journey. So she never got to Russia. Russia for her was her Mecca – Russia had achieved all the things she wanted to see in England to help the poor. There was such a lot of poverty. So when that pact was announced she was **shattered**. It was a Sunday, and her older son, Michael who was a don in Cambridge, was visiting her that day with his five children. So it was a very busy day for her when the news suddenly came out on the radio – it was unbelievable. And of course … within a few days there was a declaration of war.

Mrs Pease wasn't a bit surprised. She knew that what Chamberlain did the previous year was only a stopgap. He didn't understand and Hitler couldn't cope with him. So, (*clearing of throat here, and hesitation again*) in September '39, war was declared. Immediately blackouts came. They were on all the windows. Meanwhile, school had started early." (*His sudden shift to practical matters takes me unawares as I am neatly whisked away from the anguish this young lad must have been going through. We hear about Mrs Pease's problems – the astute and sympathetic boy has understood her dilemma and perhaps uses her conflicts to offset his own – the catharsis of drama – the blessing of a scapegoat. We don't hear about his terror that his beloved England is now at war with Germany – perhaps no longer consciously regarded as his mother-country as he had sworn to himself never to speak German again - but nevertheless the country where his parents are trapped. We can only speculate what terrors must have wracked his mind.)*

I include an article Gerard wrote about this period in his life. As soon as war is declared, he is classed as an enemy alien, which terrified him.

"You are permitted to have a bicycle in your possession"

On Tuesday, 5th September 1939, England was still basking in its Indian summer. The War was two days old, and, apart from one false air raid alert, nothing had so far happened. The school term had begun in August in Oxted County School as an emergency measure, because a London school was to be evacuated into our area and to share the school facilities with us.

I had arrived in England in May of that year as a child refugee from Nazi Germany. Most members of my family, including my parents, were left behind in Germany. I was one of the lucky few. A philanthropic elderly couple had guaranteed my stay in England and taken me into their home. What an act of courage on their part to take in an unknown sixteen-year old boy!

It was during the Physics lesson on that Tuesday when Molly, our School Secretary, came into the classroom and whispered something to the teacher. Callie was a brilliant teacher, but all his skill was wasted on me. The mysteries of Physics were beyond me so any interruption was welcome. Callie stopped the lesson, came to my desk and quietly said: 'Two policemen would like to see you for a moment. Nothing to worry about.' Police meant only one thing to me: Gestapo, arrest and never to be seen again.

Two men were waiting for me in the school corridor. I remember thinking that they couldn't possibly be policemen. They didn't wear a uniform and they were so polite. Henceforth, as an enemy alien, I would have to report regularly to the nearest Police station, I couldn't move outside a five mile radius, and I would be asked to attend a Tribunal which would decide my future status. Enemy alien ... me? I couldn't believe it. We were all victims of Nazi oppression. I loved England and all things English. This must be a horrible nightmare, and I would soon wake up.

The Tribunal was held on 18th October in Reigate. I was told that enemy aliens would be put into one of three different categories: immediate internment, or exemption from internment but with certain restrictions, or exemption from internment and from special restrictions. Before my turn came that morning, the Chairman had condemned several people to internment, and I did not expect any mercy. I desperately wanted to explain to him what England meant to me, but there was no chance. Just before giving the verdict he turned to the Police Clerk by his side; they whispered together; all I could hear was the name of Mrs Pease, the lady with whom I lived.

'Exempt until further order from internment.'

I was free for the time being, but certain restrictions remained in force. I had to give a full report about the tribunal to my Mrs Pease later that day.

'Who was the Chairman?' she asked.

I showed her my special Certificate of Registration. Her face turned purple with anger when she saw the signature, 'Oh, that wretch!'

She had never lost her Aberdeen accent, and the 'r' in 'wretch' received the full Scottish treatment. Mrs Pease was a County Councillor, a Magistrate, and a public figure of considerable influence and renown. I gathered that the Tribunal Chairman, also a County Councillor and Magistrate, but the bluest of blue Tories, was her arch enemy.

'And he is Scottish!' she added accusingly, almost ashamed that a fellow countryman should be so misguided. She was furious that the 'wretch' had not lifted all restrictions from my record, I now understood why Mrs Pease's name was mentioned in whispers at the Tribunal and why I had escaped internment.

I did not have to wait long for the sequel to this adventure. The following day I was asked to send my Registration Certificate to Reigate. When it was returned, I saw that the previous endorsement had been cancelled. I was the proud owner of a certificate that stated that I was exempted from internment and from special restrictions. There was an additional bonus: 'Notwithstanding the provisions of Article 2 of The Aliens Order, the holder of this Certificate is permitted to have a bicycle in his possession.'

Mrs Pease had won the day.

Gerard takes up his story again.

G "It was considered best to keep the children out of the way because of all this excitement, so we started school again in August (*These practical details are wrenching me away from the anguish I am feeling for the young Günter. I am finding it very hard to throw it off, and have to resist the strong temptation to stop him and ask my pertinent questions, but it isn't appropriate to push the water.*) Anyway, I went back to the school in the 5th form again, a whole year. I knew that Maths would not be any good – it wouldn't be any better at all! And of course, it was a *difficult* year. At first there was the quiet period. We weren't **aware** a war was on except that I couldn't write to my parents any longer, which made me a bit cross. (*I can hardly believe that I have heard this, said in such a bland way. For someone with such a fantastic command of our language this has to have been chosen deliberately – it acts as a signal to me that it is not an area to probe. I have to struggle with my own outrage and fury on his behalf whilst meekly writing notes – a good bit of feminine multi-tasking!*)

Meanwhile, I had **tried** to get them over. The **only** way, I thought, would be to get them a live-in position as a house cook and a butler, because there were plenty of big houses in the neighbourhood. I went round to various people I'd met through the Peases, but by that time it was all too late." (*This sad little phrase tears at my heart. I know we are about to gloss over the deep pain of all this. I know it will be in one of those apt little phrases that sums it all up and draws a line under it and I know that I will not have the heart to question him further.*) I couldn't do it. I was begging and re-begging, 'please, please, my

Mother's an excellent cook and my Father's an outgoing person who would make a very good butler.' (*He gives a very low key chuckle here, full of deep sadness at the absurdity of things. It neatly masks so many other less socially acceptable emotions.*) Pathetic isn't it. Oh dear! (*These last two little phrases are uttered very quickly and flatly, making comment inappropriate. He carries on speedily, in a monotone so unlike his usual animated speech.*) One had no idea what was going to happen – I had some kind of inkling, but err ..." (*He pauses here so I make a firm, encouraging comment.*)

M "**Yes,** I understand."

G "But I never thought of the extreme that would happen." (*There is a long pause here that I feel must be maintained as long as Gerard needs it – it is not uncomfortable. It seems as if we are both respecting the dead. When he is ready he moves on.*)
"Meanwhile, the air raids began in spring '40."

M "Yes."

G "Of course we were right over the airline to London."

M "Yes, I thought so." (*Our pace is slow and deliberate and grounding.*)

G "Very often, when they came back from their air raids, they still had some bombs and they scattered them freely, so we did get some bombing. And by the end of the school year I sat the School Certificate in a bunker! There were air raids - quite often - not always, but quite often. (*I wonder what terrors we are glossing over here.*) I got a distinction in Latin, French - and they encouraged me to take German - 'Take German! Take German!' I didn't want to. Hated it! I had three distinctions. I got a credit in English and History and I got a pass in Geography and Biology. Failed Mathematics."

M "So did I." (*Gerard chuckles sympathetically*)

G "So the Head **refused** point blank to let me go into the 6ᵗʰ form."

M "Stupid man."

G "I told him, 'I can never do Mathematics, you know. What do you want me to do? I want to get on'.
'Oh! (*Here Gerard makes the sound of a blustering English colonel, no doubt taking off the old Headmaster to a tee.*) Oh no, no. You'll never be able to do a degree if you don't have Mathematics.'
He didn't tell me, I had to find this out for myself later, at that time you **could** bypass Mathematics if you took the intermediate BA. You see, you had to take four subjects at what was the advanced level. If you took four academic subjects and did well at them it would exempt you from the School Certificate Mathematics. I found all that out for myself – he hadn't bothered to tell me. And there was a bit of pressure from Mrs Pease as well! Although, the real pressure came from my lovely Miss Morris!"

M "Yes. Good!" (*It assuages my righteous indignation a little to hear that somebody is fighting for this young lad!*)

G "She said, '**I want** Günter.' I was still known by my old name, you see. I was known as Günter. (*He spells it out not once but twice, slowly and deliberately, although we have had it many times before. At this point in his life, the early days in England, he has consciously dissociated from this part of his past in order to survive and that explains why he finds it so difficult to relate to the emotions associated with the Günter*

years. It is as though they are no longer part of him. But he realises that going back into his memories is helping him to make valuable connections with the seemingly buried part of his psyche, that has perhaps been influencing him unawares all the time.) **Good German Nordic** name!
And she said, '**I want Günter** in the French set in the 6th form!'
Like that – she faced him out, you see. I did English, Latin, French and History.

But by that time the air raids had increased. The Battle of Britain was fought overhead of us. We were not far from Biggin Hill, the famous airfield. And ...um... one morning, about four o'clock – August or September I think – as it was getting light, I was woken up by a crash of glass. This was followed by a very Edwardian **loud voice** shouting, '**damn!**' (*There is laughter on both sides. Gerard does it again! He leads me into a terrifying part of his life and through humour we slide out of it entirely unscathed by disturbing emotions. He later admits to a horror of planes that dogged him for decades.*) Mr Pease's bedroom was next to mine! Dear Mr Pease – he was very deaf and he'd no idea he could be heard. He'd been woken up and all his glass was broken – a bomb, you see."

M "Yes, you must have been terrified."

G "A lot of glass had been destroyed – it was all over the bed. Everything was just surrounded by glass. Mr and Mrs Pease had to move out – we all had to move out – friends down the lane took us in. And I realised that it was all getting too much for them having me to look after and so on. (*The 'and so on' illustrates what mastery of understatement Gerard has picked up from the English!*) In any case, by Christmas, 1940 I wanted to do some kind of war service. I had a choice of three things – either to go down the coal mines, or join R.E.M.E, the Royal Engineers, (but they wouldn't have had me because of my weak back,) or apply to the War Agricultural Committee to do farming. I chose the farming, which meant going on a training farm – I knew nothing about farming whatsoever – and then being sent on a farm, which I did throughout the whole war."

We leave Günter here, both of us knowing that we are nearing the time when we must talk face-to-face, tackling sensitive issues we left in Germany. But this of course is not mentioned. Instead we arrange dates, sleeping, meals and time of arrival. We settle on my arriving in time for afternoon tea in a very civilised manner and, in true English gentlemanly fashion, Gerard tells me how he will look forward to the pleasure of my and my husband's company in the evening.

Scene 4

The Land Boy

There is no longer a telephone between the travellers. They are face-to-face, so the journey can continue over rougher ground and in due course into the darkness. We are sitting in the front room in Gerard's home. He is ensconced on his throne, as I call it, whence he can give forth with presence – not that he needs this prop, as he could give forth with equal presence perched on a kitchen stool! The house is warm and welcoming and very supportive. Even if I had not been told, I would have known that such a lot of love has filled it over the years. It is just what we need – a solid base camp to give us succour.

The scene is rural England, 1940

M "Now, going back to wartime England, how long did you stay with Mrs Pease?"

G "I got there on the 3rd of May 1939 and the war broke out on the 3rd of September here ..." (*a long pause while he stops to think*)

M "Can I ask a question I've been holding in the back of my mind? Were there any conflicting religions? Here is this young, very Orthodox boy, suddenly immersed into a different culture altogether – you suddenly didn't have any Jewish people around you. You were stripped of your Jewishness, as well as your family, country and language. Didn't you miss it?"

G "Well, the Peases were profoundly agnostic so there was no conflict there. I tried – (*long silence*) I don't know what it's called – boys every morning after their Bar Mitzvah should say their prayers and put something on their heads."(*The fact that he has wiped all this from his very excellent memory shows just how much disassociation has taken place at a conscious level.*)

M "You mean the phylactery?"

G "And Mrs Pease found me doing it. (*wry laugh here*)
'It will be very difficult for you to continue,' she said.
So I – (*pause, three or four short panting breaths*) I wasn't strong enough, I think, so I dropped it off … There was so much else crowding in on me. (*nervous clearing of the throat and another very long pause*) You see, I was changing, and all my contacts were English. I was very profoundly thankful for it. You see, the refugees I knew about all had problems."
(*Dissociation is a very useful tool at times of great trauma. There is a very long pause, which is not uncomfortable, but it is heavy. I decide to break it.*)

M "So you were there about 18 months?"

G "Yes, yes." (*This is the first time we've worked together face-to-face. There is no longer the relative anonymity of the telephone between us. We know that we are going to be dealing with painful issues, but we both sense that we have to work our way up to that during the day, or the next day. I am concerned about remembering to show sensitivity over and above any desire to investigate and record. So, we ground ourselves by talking about farming.*)

M "Right, you were seventeen and a half when you went on the farm?"

G "No, I was turned eighteen. I had to repeat a year, you see."

M "Oh, yes, of course."

G "Then I had that very curious School Certificate result. That was in June 1940. The bombing had begun and we spent a lot of time in the bunkers. We even took exams in them. I told you about that didn't I?"

M "Oh, yes, I'm plugged in now – you failed the Maths so there was a problem and Miss Morris stuck up for you."

G "She went into the Head and was quite prepared to **resign**! (*Gerard gives a great guffaw here.*) She was a Yorkshire lady, you see – very tough, very tough lady – splendid teacher! (*We are quite relaxed now and have settled into the easy rhythm we adopt in phone calls.*) By 1940 the Battle of Britain had begun and we were called back early to school. We had morning school and the refugees from London had it in the afternoons. In October, November and December the teachers in turn were given two weeks because their holidays were cut short. Prefects were given the chance to do some teaching. Now again Miss Morris moved into action. I wasn't a prefect, needless to say – the Head would never have let me be one. She went to him again, I found out later.
She said to him, 'If Günter doesn't do some of my French lessons, I'm not going to have anyone else. He's by far the best person to do it.'
And so she got her way! He was frightened of her – I'm not surprised! (*There is laughter from me as I picture this feisty woman after my own heart. It is so obvious that he himself is rightly proud of Günter – i.e. proud of what he was.*)

So I got the classes – **I loved it!** Of course, that's what convinced me that's where I wanted to go eventually, you see. It was **marvellous** – teaching them French and so on. And then one day in November, I think it was - you see, we were underneath the German air force flight path to London and they didn't always drop all their bombs. Have I mentioned that?"

M "Yes, you said the Peases were hit."

G "It was all along the lane. We had to move out for quite some time. Mrs Pease found it all very, very difficult and I felt terribly sorry for her.
I said, 'Look, it's time I did some war service.'
I chose the farming and was sent to a Y.M.C.A training farm. And soon after Christmas I left Mrs Pease. The training farm was in Buckinghamshire and, my goodness, what an eye-opener it was! It wasn't just refugees – it was also for youngsters who were orphans, some from the East End of London – such a mishmash.

Gerard (far right) with trainees at the YMCA training farm at Hambledon, Bucks.

It was hard work – I wasn't used to it. Part of me quite enjoyed it in a way. But the son of this failing farmer ran the whole thing. He was a nasty bit of work, he really was. And I saw life as I'd never seen it before. (*Gerard gives a wry laugh here, which I suspect covers a lot. It must have been devastating for him to experience this, especially at a time when he was very vulnerable, having just left the relative security of the Pease's home.)*

Anyway, it was three months training, I think – three or four months – at the worst time of the year, winter.

Then we were sent on to farms. I was designated to a very small farm near Watlington - not very far from here near Henley – run by a Danish bachelor. Danes are of course excellent at farming. He was a man in his 50s. He had a **terrible** temper. I had to live in of course. There was a housekeeper there – she was terrified of him. She called him 'the master'. (*He gives another wry laugh here, which says a lot. I am sure she was not the only one who lived in fear. What this poor, sensitive young man was going through at this time we shall never know. I feel tremendous compassion for Günter that is painful. His next statement knocks me for six.*) I felt sorry for him because, of course, I was the only help that he had. He deserved better. I was totally unpractical, you can imagine. But somehow, the one thing I took to was milking."

M "I like milking too – very relaxing."

G "Yes – hand milking – no machinery."

M "Oh yes, hand milking. I couldn't cope with machines!"

G "There were about sixteen or seventeen mixed Jerseys and Guernseys. They were lovely cows, and they all had names ending in 'y' – Milly, Suzy, Lucy – anything with 'y'. And they got to know me. Well the farmer suffered from rheumatic hands and milking was an effort for him. He spotted that I was good at something. He decided that he would hand over the whole care of the cows to me. That was all right by me of course, except that I had to be there on duty seven days a week – early in the morning and in the evening. He insisted on my cleaning out the sheds twice a day, but it was interesting getting to know the beasts.

And what was also interesting was he had two working horses – mother and daughter. Now the mother he bought – Patsy – and he bred from her and he got a Topsy, which he had to train. And the difference – Patsy was calm, very well trained and obedient and Topsy was **wild.** It shows that man was too impatient. Interesting, isn't it? And she nearly caused me what could have been a very bad accident. I had to get them ready and saddle and harness them for work and I did something in the wrong order. She thought she was already ready and started to move off. My leg got caught in the chain. It could have been very nasty.

Anyway, I was there until the war ended, so it was four and a half years – long time really. However, in the summer we were working every daylight hour. There was double summer time so it was light till ten o'clock at night. But in the winter – he insisted on the cows sleeping in the sheds, you see – so once they were in I had free evenings to study." (*It is interesting that the man he lived with all this time is not named, but Gerard can remember the names of the animals. He has a fine eye and a fine memory for people normally and will struggle to name accurately those he has met in passing. It says a lot. At a later date he supplies the name 'Jorgesson'.*)

M "Can I stop you there for a bit? I need to ask a question. I've got a lot about what happened to you when you got to England and a lot of lovely stories, but not a lot about how this young lad felt."

G "How I felt?"

M "Yes, because you were only a young lad, especially when you first got here and were staying with the Peases." (*long pause here, whilst I look busy and rattle papers*)

G "Well, I think ... I think ... at this stage ... I think I should mention this ... a lot of my time on the farm ... was spent in ... um ... there was nobody else there, to work with, you see. I couldn't talk to anybody. I was alone in the field when I wasn't with the cows. And the farmer planted a lot of mangel-wurzels – food for the cattle and horses, chickens and whatever.

When the seeds came up they had to be singled out. I'd never done that and he said 'the span of a – what is it – instrument... (*We work our way through various planting tools and settle in the end on a dibber. I've given up hope of ever finding out how Günter felt at the Peases' and indeed what the young man felt, isolated on the farm for all those years. Perhaps feelings were a luxury in which he could not afford to indulge.*) ... yes, that's it – a dibber, and of course, me being totally impractical, I destroyed more than I'd done! (*He laughs here. He is on safe ground again.*) There were great bare patches and a very angry farmer! But anyway, when I got the hang of it – he wasn't good at explaining – he would never **explain** anything to me. Anyway, I eventually got the hang of it – it was hours and hours – up and down – up and down you see.
I said, 'This is so mechanical. I don't have to concentrate so long as I get the right distance.'

I gave myself thinking tasks and I got over that – got through that patch. It's been of great use to me over the years. My thinking tasks were mainly what would have happened if things had gone normally with us, and there wasn't an England to go to. I would have grown up in Germany. My Father would have wanted me to take over his business and I would have hated it. (*This is said very quietly and flatly. He continues in a flat monotone.*) I would have been no good at it. How pleased my

Mother would have been with my academic progress. So they were constantly in my mind. I was thinking of my parents mainly and my elder sister, because the other one was in New Zealand. I could correspond with her."

M "Yes." (*This is a firm, neutral affirmation on my part.*)

G "But you see we did not **hear** in the early years of what went on in Germany."

M "So you didn't get any letters at this time?"

G "I got two Red Cross letters a year from my Father. They couldn't tell me much."

M "Well, that's what I thought. So, my God, you know you must have been so lonely." (*He was ripped away from his country, family, culture, religion and friends and the farmer would not communicate with him.*)

G "Well, I learnt to live with myself which has been a very good lesson. You know what I did when I was out on the field with mechanical work - I gave myself those thinking tasks. It might have been a bit dangerous because it was all imaginative. (*wry chuckle here*) What would have happened if…."

M "It was like solitary confinement, wasn't it?" (*I remind myself there was no telephone or internet, only occasional letters that happened to get through.*)

G "Yes, yes."

M "You must have been a very strong person because you just didn't know what was happening to your family or anything. It would have driven most people round the bend, but you obviously came out of it very balanced."

G "There was my sister to write to, you see."

M "Yes, but how often?"

G "Quite frequently. But also I had the Thorne Family – I have mentioned them, haven't I?"

M "No, not yet."

G "Because they must feature. William Thorne, the father, he was a man Mrs Pease wanted to come to live in Oxted, because he was a strong Labour person. He lived on the other side of Surrey. He worked in the City and could easily go into the City from Oxted. His wife, a very vivacious woman, called 'Nan', and two girls, Gillian and Jennifer. I'm like a brother to them and they are like my sisters. Gillian became a biological scientist. She always wanted to retire to the Lake District and she lives in Keswick. She's a great walker. Jennifer, the younger one, wanted to be an actress."

M "Did she become an actress?"

G "Oh yes, she went to the Central School - much to the sorrow of her father – 'She's much too intelligent to become an actress!' Now, they came to one of Mrs Pease's tea parties very early on in my stay there and I found out later that, when they went home, they thought, 'Oh that poor boy with those elderly people. We must look after him a bit.' And of course I was actually blissfully happy! (*laughter here in his voice*) Anyway, they took me up from that day and I often went down to them. It was about a mile and a half – I had a bike. Fortunately, Mr Thorne was a great pal of Mrs Pease so it didn't look as if he was stealing me away from them. It became my home, in a way – I was treated so well."

90

*The two sisters now talk about the young Günter. First Gillian
Thorne remembers those early days.*

G.T. "I didn't see much of Gerard in school, because he was in a
higher year. We first met him at the Peases' house. They were a
very strange couple – very worthy, but definitely strange. He
seemed to get on with them though, especially with old Edward.
The trouble about communicating with old Edward Pease was
that he was terribly deaf, but Gerard seemed to manage all right
from what he's told me. I remember, when we went for tea up
there, old Edward would come out of his study, drink his tea and
go straight back! It couldn't have been easy for a young boy to
relate to him.

In those days we got quite involved with theatrical performances
given by the boys from Haberdashers, who had been evacuated
our way. Gerard was around at this time, because my parents
thought it would be good for him to get some younger company.

By the time he had to leave school to go to work on the farm, I
felt that I knew him well. I remember we got weekly letters from
Gerard, during this time. My Mother would reply, and I expect
my Father put in the odd bit now and again about current affairs
– it was an interest he and Gerard shared. Of course, whenever
he could get away, he would come back to us. He was always
very easy to be with. He seems to get on with everybody,
including youngsters. He was very much an elder brother to us
girls. It was so important for Gerard to be English and for a long
time only his closest friends knew otherwise. Our family helped
him change his name shortly after the war ended, before
applying for permanent teaching posts. When he eventually got
back to using the German language a bit, he had forgotten quite
a lot and had to relearn it. He had just had to block it all out in
order to survive." (*Gillian asked me to check this with Gerard
and he confirms that this is so at this point in time – he explains*

later in the section on Kristallnacht how the violent language used by the Nazis fills him with fear.)

Jennifer Thorne now talks about her memories of this time.

J.T "I don't remember meeting Gerard at the Peases' house, but I do remember going to tea there and that is where he was. I was very young then. I remember we had quite a lot of people coming and going at that time, because Haberdasher's School was evacuated to Oxted during the War and we always had a lot of sixth formers dropping in. Our house was opposite the secondary school, which they shared. Gerard just sort of gradually started to be around.

All I remember about his letters from the farm is that it sounded very cold, damp and muddy. It was absolutely horrible and I can't think of anybody less suited to working on a farm! He took his correspondence course degree at the same time and, looking back, I wonder just how he did it. It was amazing. I've never asked him why he chose to do part of his degree in French, but it might have been partly due to the influence of my Father, who spoke French very beautifully.

My awareness of Gerard just grew naturally as, over the years, he became part of the family. He was able to take little holidays from the farm and he came to us. A very early memory is of him teaching me to do a Viennese waltz! He was a very good dancer! We had a large living room that went right through the house. My Mother was considered slightly eccentric, because she had polished floors instead of fitted carpets! The Turkey runners could be whipped out of the way and then put back afterwards. When we had visitors, we danced to the gramophone. There was a record of 'The Blue Danube' that we had, and I liked to dance so Gerard taught me the old fashioned waltz very patiently. The next thing that stands out in my memories of him is his delight when he was naturalised – he was so thrilled to be English."

Gerard continues telling me about his life on the farm.

G "When the war broke out and I was on the farm, Nan wrote to me weekly - long letters - and I wrote back to her (*pause mid-sentence here while he reminisces and then his sentence continues quite naturally*) about books and literature. Oh it was manna, manna from Heaven. I love them dearly ... now why am I bringing them in at this time?"

M "Because they were a substitute family for you while you were on the farm and helped you by writing to you."

G "Yes. Now, there was the Youth Club in Watlington as well where I went sometimes. I just learnt to live with myself."

M "Yes, but amazingly so."

G "I don't think it was unhealthy."

M "You weren't depressed at all? You didn't have to fight depression?"

G "No, no."

M "That's strange, isn't it? You've lost your country, your family…"

G "My imagination was roving freely. And I was busy trying to pick up my education at every free moment I had."

M "That probably kept you sane."

G "That kept me sane - yes. Every free moment I was off. I was deeply steeped in French Literature, which was wonderful."

M "I bet you thanked God you could get the books."

G "Yes, yes – no there were some lonely moments." (*He does not expand on this comment and I feel I cannot ask without being invasive – a gentle balance must be maintained so we move on.*)

M "Did you find it hard when you came back into society – face to face - not just by letter. Did you find it hard to express emotions?"

G "No, because all those particular French Classical plays I had to study, and the English ones too, they gave me such joy and such depth of feeling."

M "But that's sort of second-hand - it's sublimated, it's controlled - I mean directly with people. Did you think, 'Oh, this is actually real'? I would imagine that you would have found it really hard to adjust to feeling your own emotions as opposed to feeling someone else's emotions."

G "Well, I suppose in a way, I was so thankful to be alive, you see. (*He might have felt gratitude, but there is a whole load of guilt in there as well, as we see from the quick succession of unfinished thoughts that are juxtaposed alongside this relief.*) What – why do I – why did … you know. Mind you, at that time I was still hoping against hope … I didn't know. You see, I did not know … no news came out. I was … one couldn't imagine what …what actually happened … it was unimaginable. (*There is a long silence, which I respect.*) When the news broke …" (*spoken in a whisper before he breaks off mid-sentence and lets out two gasps. I need to stop him.*)

M "We can talk about that tomorrow if you need to say more."

G "Another time, yes. Tomorrow, yes. Not now."

M "No, not now."

G "Not now, not in the evening. (*I am anxious to steer him onto unemotional ground, but before I can divert him he launches into something that he's made his mind up to get out.*) You see, most of my life, until I became a Catholic, I've had a feeling of guilt. But don't let's get on to it now." (*The last sentence is spoken very quickly.*)

M "No, of course not. Now, tell me about your studies."

G "My education was woefully disrupted. The first thing I had to do was to get my Higher School Certificate. But I thought that, because I didn't have Maths or a Science subject, I would never be admitted to a degree. But I found out that I could take the Intermediate BA from London University. That meant four major subjects - quite a tough course. Well, I took the London correspondence course and the four subjects were English, French, History and Latin - four very academic subjects. Obviously it took me much longer then because I didn't have a great deal of time.

Then somebody said to me, 'You're an idiot. Why don't you do German?'

I said, 'I don't want anything to do with **that** language!' It brought back too many memories.

And later I thought I was silly not to do it for Intermediate BA. Anyway, I did English, French and History first. English was difficult because I had no direct teaching you see. History, I'd already done a lot - and French, I loved it so much it was a pleasure."

At this point I would like to include an astute observation from Nick Rawlinson, a close friend of Gerard's.

N.R "I don't think I agree that he rejected his past. There are different shades to shutting off. I'm not sure that Gerard ever shut that off or put it to one side, because I think it has informed and coloured everything he's done. I think it's remarkable that somebody who is not sure that he is going to be accepted turns that into the ability to accept everybody as they are. That's the magic of Gerard. He is an alchemist. He is able to take base metal and change it into gold. I think it's a mark of his humanity that he has taken all the suffering and transformed it into something else. He may say that he's rejected it, but he's actually transformed it into something incredibly powerful that he's used to help other people.

Gerard's understanding of what it means to be the exile and the outsider has informed the ability to bring out the nervous, the oppressed, the afraid in every performing actor there is, and transform that into something incredibly powerful. He transforms what could potentially be very damaging into something positive. He has this powerful reserve within him that he's been tapping on all the time. He is not a repressive – I think his whole character has been with him all the time.

Rejecting is not a thing Gerard Gould does, until we get to bad theatre! Even then he wants to help change it to something better. It's not about rejecting his old identity – it's about finding a new identity from within himself. He's come away from what the world has layered on him – the identity of Günter Goldstein who was worth the gas chamber was placed on him by others. He's come out from underneath that description and he has become who he was always meant to be. It sounds strange in a way to say this, but Gerard has become the best person for the young Günter to have encountered."

The rest of this work hopes to prove the truth of this comment.
Gerard continues speaking about his studies.

"Well, I passed all three and then took Latin the following year.
I had to come to Oxford to take the exam. The farmer had to
give me a summer's day – he owed me lots of holidays I didn't
have. The exam building was in the High Street. I had to stay the
night and I went to a B&B place in Summertown. I went past
the Playhouse – you see Oxford in the war had a lot of civil
service evacuees. Half of the London offices evacuated here.
They thought Oxford was safe, which it was.

The Playhouse did weekly repertory and I saw 'Hamlet' – I'd
never seen 'Hamlet' and I loved it. I'd read it and read it and
read it. The theatre was very popular – there was very little else
to do – but I got a ticket. It started at eight. At twenty to twelve
the actor playing Claudius fainted on stage. The stage manager
came out and apologised and said they would continue as soon
as they could. The play eventually ended at twenty to one in the
morning. Of course there was no transport **whatsoever**. And I
had to walk – it was two miles and a bit. But I was in such a
whirl I couldn't have gone to bed immediately. The play made
such an impression - I mean I've seen umpteen 'Hamlet's since -
there are better ones - but that was my first 'Hamlet'.

I had completed my Intermediary BA. I passed my Latin and I
knew that would now give me exemption from wretched
Mathematics and Science. (*guffaw here*) I had a clear road to my
BA Honours. I'd chosen French as my main subject and English
as my subsidiary.
And somebody said again, 'You idiot! Why don't you do
German – it's only an exam. You'll probably get a first.'
'**No I'm not going to!**' Then I thought about it. 'Oh I am silly.'
I remembered what Fräulein Foerder said. Have I told you? I
don't think I have. I was the class spokesman – we were still in

that Jewish school – lots of my school mates – we all agreed that we did not want to do any more German."

M "No, you didn't tell me."

G "I said, 'Couldn't we spend the time we spend on German on more English?'
And Fraulein Foerder took it very well indeed – she was a brilliant judge of the situation. She taught us both German and English.
And she said – I can still hear her saying it – 'We must not blame what is happening in a country onto its language and onto its literature.'
(*There is a long pause here while Gerard is lost in thought.*)
I've never forgotten that, because she was right, you see. It was sort of schoolboys' anger. (*It was rather more than that, I feel, especially for Gerard with his very sensitive nature. The aversion he feels at this time in the Jewish School to the language that was used for such evil purposes by Hitler, and the newly instilled notion that he was not a true German, work together to make the young boy want to get rid of everything that causes him trouble. Being rejected, as they most certainly were as a race, brings about an urgent need for acceptance and respect. He realises that the only way he can find this is to become something else – i.e. English – his native tongue will not get him there, and neither will Judaism. Of course there is fury at this outrage, but it is probably never expressed in that way.*)
Anyway, I thought I'd take the German subsidiary. Of course I passed."

M "Really!" (*a little laugh here*)

G "French was a different matter. It was foolish of me. I'd have got a much better degree if I'd taken German as main. You see I'd never been to France – no chance of speaking French. I could just read, read, read, read, but that's not enough. One doesn't get the flow and the nuances of the language. I had to have several attempts at it. I took it too soon at first and didn't pass.

Well, the war in Europe ended in May 1945, but we had to wait to be demobilised. Then came the main peace in August after Hiroshima. There was one other boy in that area who was in the same situation as I was – he was a refugee. We met occasionally and had a drink in a pub somewhere. We met that evening when the war ended and we expressed our fears that we would be completely forgotten – nobody would ever bother about us – what should we do? So we both decided a plan of campaign. We would write to the chairman of the War Agricultural Committee - a very polite letter - and ask him to see us. **Meanwhile** (*a dramatic pause here*) meanwhile (*impish chuckle*) I had another stroke of luck. (*Time and time again Gerard has had this 'luck' for want of a better word and we both marvel at it. He seems to meet the right people at the right time without even trying.*)

Watlington had a youth club – quite a flourishing youth club – and I'd been asked to help there with it – do a bit of drama and so on, in the winter. And I met people through that. They were very nice people. And occasionally the club was visited by the Oxfordshire Youth Adviser, a man called Leslie Wood, with whom I got on very well.
He asked me, 'What will you do now?'
I said, 'Well, I want to teach, but I haven't got any money to set myself up.'
I'd saved a little bit from my farming. Most of it went to the degree work. I paid every penny of it myself. It was very difficult to do it externally. I wouldn't recommend it to anyone.
'I can't afford it. What do I live on?'
He said, 'Well, you've got some high qualifications. You could become a temporary teacher. You won't get much money, but it will allow you to start teaching. There are still lots of these new schools called Secondary Moderns and there aren't many young

men teachers.   They haven't been demobilised yet. I know all
the head teachers of Oxfordshire.'

```
            WATLINGTON YOUTH CENTRE

                   AMATEUR

               DRAMATIC SOCIETY

                   present

            THREE  ONE-ACT  PLAYS
            ──────────────────────


              And So It Goes On.
                    or
         What might have happened.
              An Extravaganza
                    by
               Violet Rutter.

              ─ ─ ─ ─ ─ ─ ─ ─


                 The Mask,
               A  Tragedy ,
                    by
              H.M. Harwood
                   and
             Tennyson Jesse.

               ─ ─ ─ ─ ─ ─


              Postal  Orders
                A  Farce
                    by
             Roland Pertwee.

               ─ ─ ─ ─ ─ ─
```

Programme of Watlington Youth Centre Amateur Dramatic Society
production with Gunter Goldstein producing 'The Mask' in 1945

100

```
                    THE MASK.
                    ----------

          Characters in order of appearance.


    James Glasson       ...   ...   ...     John Evans.
    Vashti Glasson (his wife)        ...    Ruth Rees.
    Willie Strick       ...   ...   ...     Ken Garland.

        TIME:  Present.

        PLACE: Kitchen in James Glasson's cottage in
               Cornwall.


        Produced by Gunter Goldstein.
```

He thought Rotherfield Peppard, just outside Rotherfield Greys,
would be ideal - a real country school - small school, single
form entry - eleven to fifteen. He sent me there to see the Head,
Freddy Anson - a very brave man he was! What appealed to him
was my **farming** experience (*great guffaws here at the irony of
this*) which I wanted to get rid of, of course!
And he said, 'Could you do rural Science?'"

M "Oh no, Gerard!"

G "And I said, 'Well, I'll have a go!'(*laughter from both of us*)
'Well', he said, 'I'd like to take you on. Your salary will be £12
a month.' He found me digs – a little chalet and an electric fire.
The place is still there. Do you remember, in Peppard there's a –
on the green – there's a pub called the Dog Inn?"

M "Yes, David pointed it out to me when we did our Grand
Tour."

Gerard aged 24 outside his lodgings at the Dog Inn at Rotherfield Peppard

I was all by myself and they would give me an evening meal. I would have a midday meal at the school. All that was two pounds ten a week. (*long happy laughter here*) I thought I wouldn't be there for long. It turned out to be four and a half years. Bill and Nan Thorne, who befriended me when I was at the Peases', put me on a very tough reading list, which I worked my way right through. They said I must read Jane Austen and I just devoured them – I simply loved them – my England as I had imagined it!"

Elizabeth Martin (née Ovey) was one of Gerard's pupils at Rotherfield Peppard Secondary School in 1948 and she has very fond memories of the young heart-throb teacher.

EM "Our English teacher was a dazzling creature, very exotic, and though I was too young to fancy him, I was aware that he was very handsome, with wavy dark-brown hair and brilliant dark eyes. He spoke English with a staccato accent, very easy to understand. I remember his clarity of expression, and his enthusiasm. One day a young woman from the village came into the classroom - it must have been Break - and sat on the edge of his desk. She spoke teasingly to him, giggled a lot and fluttered her eyelashes, and I remember thinking: 'so that's how you flirt!' I don't remember how long it lasted, but I was vaguely conscious that he wasn't comfortable with such a blatant display! We all really liked him, though we were slightly in awe of him, and nobody cheeked him - at least not in our year. I never forgot him, and in a way he became the model of what a teacher should be."

Gerard brings us back to the present.

G "I think we must take a break now – I need to put the oven on – will you let me go?" (*said quite mischievously*)

M "Yes, I'll let you go if you allow me come and help you."

We settle to getting a meal together in the kitchen. The conversation is compelling in between discussing pans and temperatures and I learn to have the recorder to hand. At table, Gerard is always ready to enjoy himself, whatever the subject of conversation, and again the little recorder is on stand-by in case he launches into a good story.

Scene 5

A Time of Becoming

The year is 1945. The setting is a tiny village just outside Oxford, where we meet a rather green new teacher called Mr Goldstein. The travellers are taking a meandering route in a lazy, leisurely way – the destination is Germany, but not yet.

G "Anyway, I was teaching. The day started - it was a Church of England School – the timetable started with morning assembly and prayers for twenty minutes. I then had to take a group of boys out in the yard for physical education for twenty minutes (*little chuckle here*) in the open air – gymnastic sort of thing. Then I had to take what they called the 'backward class' – about ten or twelve of them, mostly boys, on benches in the corridor – there was no other room – for simple Arithmetic and English."

M "It's a good job it was simple!"

G "That was the morning. There were four classes. For four afternoons I took each class of boys – half a class - for rural Science. In the winter it was cow keeping – well that was all right, I was knowledgeable – I had experience of cow keeping. I quite enjoyed that in a way. (*I start to chuckle as I feel Gerard building up to the crescendo – reductio ad absurdum!*) But the summer was **dreadful** - it was horticulture. I had to take the boys out gardening, and my gardening – oh – you know. Poor old Freddy Anson must have wondered what he'd taken on! He was very tolerant. Friday afternoon was hobbies and, of course, hobbies to me meant drama. Now a **miracle** happened! (*pause for dramatic effect*)

By the end of that first year I thought, 'This is **not** for me. If this is teaching this is **not** for me.' – because I still had to spend every evening working on my degree. By the end of that first year - one of the teachers in that school was a Mrs Crowther -

brilliant woman, **brilliant** teacher – I learnt everything from her. She was a graduate from London University and also she had a music degree. Her husband was a Flight Lieutenant – he was coming back from the war and he was badly wounded. He had to be taken care of, so she gave up three days of her teaching. I found out later that she went to Freddy Anson and said, 'I advise you to give my classes to Günter'. I was still Günter then – I hadn't changed my name. (*It is indeed wonderful that this happened at this particular point in Gerard's life when he was so down that he was about to give up on teaching. If he had, there would have been a sad knock-on effect. Would all those young people who were inspired by him to go into acting for a career have found inspiration elsewhere? Blessed Mrs Crowther.*)

It was very kind of her. So I took over her history classes, which I loved. (*The passing remark about her kindness is a typical understatement from Gerard. It must have meant so much to him, this token of acceptance and respect, echoing the earlier gestures from Miss Morris – so good for his self-esteem.*) So I got going, I got going on drama. The Headmaster had never seen anything like it – it was very new at that time, you see. It was classroom drama – there was no hall or anything. We shifted the desks and we presented things for morning assembly. I even did a little bit of Shakespeare and he was **thrilled to bits**. I became his sort of 'lucky draw', I think. The youngsters were marvellous – they took to drama like... (*Quite often Gerard does not bother to finish a sentence when his meaning is quite clear and the energy is gaining momentum.*)

I was **quite** ambitious – I entered them for a local drama festival – not just for youngsters. It meant that you would start in a local area. An adjudicator would come and give you a commentary in front of everybody. Then one team would go on to the next round here in Oxford. You just go on till the winner ends up in London. The first thing I did - talk about ambition - (*He* *chuckles here. Quite typically, Gerard aims high. He loves to make an impression.*) I chose the opening of Bernard Shaw's 'St. Joan'. There was a girl there and I thought she could do Joan – she could be a marvellous Joan. We had fifty minutes – that was the time allowed – so we did two and a half scenes. The needlework mistress, (*pause*) she helped with the costumes. (*I am quite sure that Gerard knows that you do not need the preposition here – 'she' is extraneous. I was about to correct it in the writing up, but realise it must be there for a reason – the reason is simple. He wants to present her, albeit very briefly, onto the stage – he is giving her recognition. Without the pause and the 'she' all we read or hear is that costumes were made. This is all quite natural on his part – he has no notes. He is producing his own play from the heart level.*) And the woodwork master, he knocked up a bit of a set and saw to the lighting. You see it was a complete school effort. I think Freddy thought I was mad. (*a joyful peel of laughter here*) It was a **huge** success. I don't think we won that round because we had a lot of very adult competition there, **but** what it meant was, I made the school famous, you see, in Rotherfield Greys, where your husband, David, grew up. It's very funny isn't it!"

M "Amazing links between us all."

G "You know Agnew, the famous family, auctioneers?"

M "No, I'm afraid not."

G "He lived there – very interested in drama. I mean it created a great deal of village excitement both in Greys and Peppard. (*There's a mischievous sound to his voice here. He just loves making a stir!*) And the youngsters, of course, they **loved** it, you see. It became cream for them.
And then I asked myself, 'What do we do now after having started like that?'

Do you remember a playwright who became famous around then, Christopher Fry?"

M "Yes, I've read him." (*The excitement in his voice is infectious.*)

G "I discovered that he'd written a lovely play early on ... ha, ha, ha! – well, I can find it out! Err ... (*long pause here which pays off as he remembers it*) ...'The Boy with a Cart', which he did in Sussex where he first lived. Any number could play in it. It was a boy with his mother - a boy with his daydreams - and they go from village to village. There was a chorus of umpteen speakers and all the locals. It was absolutely right for a country place. Perfect - difficult - because of Christopher Fry's difficult language.

The Rotherfield Secondary Modern School Dramatic Society production of 'The Boy with a cart' in 1950.

It was very demanding. Well, we did it as a whole play, to invite parents and so on, you see. Freddy gave me time – he was in seventh heaven! (*He gives a belly laugh here, as he is caught up again in the energy of the challenge and the sheer fun of it all and it is infectious.*)

THE ROTHERFIELD SECONDARY
MODERN SCHOOL DRAMATIC SOCIETY

PRESENTS

The Red Velvet Goat
by Josephina Niggli

and

The Boy with a Cart
by Christopher Fry.

Both Plays produced by
GERARD GOLDSTEIN.

Peppard Memorial Hall - 24th March, 1950.
Shiplake Memorial Hall - 27th March, 1950.

Price 3d.

Higgs & Co., Henley.

And I had a **wonderful** girl and boy as the mother and son – lovely. He was so right that boy. **You see, we saw aspects of those children that we had never seen before. It became a most wonderful educational vehicle.** (*The bold here is mine. I think this last remark of Gerard's sums up the whole of what teaching drama means for him. Being entirely suspicious of gadgets, I insist on taking copious notes as well in case the recording fails and I got a bit behind at this point. Gerard apologises profusely for going too quickly. He repeats the word 'sorry' about five times on a rising scale.*)
Am I giving you too much detail?"

M "No, not at all. It's good. I just want to make sure I get it! Ok. I've got there."

G "Well, anyway, I took an excerpt from it to enter next year's drama festival and again we got terrific praise from the adjudicator. So drama was beginning to play a very important part in my teaching life. I could see what it could do."

M "I suppose you hadn't had time to make any relationships."

G "Ah. Well, you see, in those years after I got my degree, through my school drama work I got an entrée into village drama. Rotherfield Greys had a family that David knows very well indeed – you know the Goyders?"

M "Yes, I do."

G "They were a lovely family. And Rosemary Goyder was a student at Oxford University and George was a bit older – very dapper man – very good business man - very cultured – well, he swept her off her feet. She left Oxford before taking her degree! **Yes!** (*His voice has risen in pitch.*) She was nineteen when she married him and he was twenty-nine. (*This little bit of village scandal is very interesting but I am wondering how it relates to* *the business in hand. As ever I should not have doubted!*) Anyway, Rosemary started up a drama group – very much village orientated, you see. **Lovely** house, near the church. And they were so good to me.

GREYS VILLAGE HALL,
DECEMBER 16th & 17th, 1949.

The Greys Players
PRESENT

ROBERT'S WIFE
A COMEDY IN THREE ACTS
By ST. JOHN ERVINE.

CHARACTERS (in order of appearance):

JUNE HARVEY	IRENE TURNER
ANNE	JULIET KEW
MISS ORLEY	WINIFRED BROWN
SANCHIA CARSON	EVA MELLOR
REV. ROBERT CARSON	HERBERT MORGAN
THE BISHOP OF WINTERBURY	GERALD AGNEW
MRS. JONES	MAVIS CLARK
BOB CARSON	GUNTER GOLDSTEIN
CHIEF INSPECTOR LINDSEY	WILLIAM BARRETT
MRS. ARMITAGE	MARY LOWTHER
REV. ARTHUR JEFFERSON	GUNTER GOLDSTEIN

Production ... Rosemary Goyder.

SCENE.—The living room of St. Michael and All Angels Vicarage, Combermere, an industrial town in the South of England.

THE FIRST ACT.

Scene I ... March, 1937.
Scene II ... A few hours later.

THE SECOND ACT.

Scene I ... September, 1937.
Scene II ... Two days later.

THE THIRD ACT.

Scene I ... October, 1937.
Scene II ... A fortnight later.

Higgs & Co., Henley-on-Thames.

Gunter acting with the Greys Players in 1949.
Rosemary Goyder directing.

We had a terrible winter '47 to '48 - **terrible** - and me in my little chalet. I caught pneumonia with pleurisy. I was very, very ill – couldn't be moved even. The district nurse came every day to look after me and she said that once I was recovered I had to leave the chalet as I couldn't go on like that. Anyway, as soon as I could, Mrs Goyder took me in and, to make it a bit easier for me, do you know what she did? The oldest boy – they sent them all to the village school to begin with, then at the age of nine they sent them to prep schools – they wanted him to go to Rugby, but to get to the prep school he needed Latin. He hadn't done any Latin so they wanted me to teach him and that would be a good excuse for me to be with them. Wasn't that lovely?"

M "It was very nice, wasn't it."

G "They gave me their best guest room – oh – I was in Seventh Heaven! I was so lucky."

M "But you have been, all the way through."

G "I **have** been lucky. The boy was delightful – very bright of course. They were thrilled to bits because he got a very good entry to this school. And I met so many interesting people. Then Mrs Goyder started to branch off into drama – she wasn't a director, I must admit that she wasn't. She did a Noel Coward, 'Hay Fever'. You see I wasn't an actor – of course I could act – but I didn't really like acting. I was a director, but she was directing so I had to act – but we had fun. And then **Rotherfield Peppard** wanted to start a drama society. (*There's amusement in his voice at the rivalry between the two villages.*) That's where the Agnews were and some other very well-heeled people – quite well known – (*belly laugh*) They came to **me**! Would I do a drama festival entry with them?
'Yes **of course**!' – as ever, I'm all ready for it! And do you know what I did? I chose 'The Browning Version'. It had only just become available, as it were – it had just been running in

London - Terence Rattigan - a beautiful play, a wonderful play set in a public school.

Well, it wasn't difficult to cast at Peppard (*his voice is sliding up the scale*) – just mention public school and there they all **were** you see! (*a good long laugh here*) I chose Agnew for the headmaster. I had to cut it a little bit, so I wrote to Rattigan and said, 'I want to present this at a drama festival, but we have to get it all into fifty minutes. I told him the bit I wanted to cut.
He wrote back saying, 'How interesting. I am just writing a film script for it and I've left it out too!' (*laughter again*) So he couldn't say 'No, you must keep it in!'

I did the usual school play as well, so I had two entries. Now the adjudicator was in raptures – that's the only way to describe it. Agnew was **marvellous**. He could remember his own school days – it was all so real to him – deeply moving. The wife was wonderful and the boy was very good. Of course we won that first round. And we won the next round (*belly laugh*) and we won **the third**."

M "Ah, lovely!" (*I am getting caught up in the excitement of it all – it must be like this when you back horses.*)

G "We were beaten at the one that would have got us into London, but of course they were thrilled to bits – their first attempt!
I said, 'Well, we must do this play and show our Peppard people. And we'll do it with 'Harlequinade''. I wanted to do the whole thing, so we did that.

We then got what I can only describe as a rave review in the Oxford Times signed by F.W.D. and that stood for Frank Dibb. He was the Oxford Times drama and art critic – very knowledgeable. He was in raptures over Agnew's Crocker Harris and it started a long friendship. He wanted to get to know me. He was very useful too – he came to every play at Lord Williams. I mean, they don't go to school plays."

M "No, of course they don't."

G "But he came and reviewed it – every school play. I was very lucky. See, I've gone into the theatre now, haven't I?"

M "It's ok. Let's face it, you're never far from it! In any case, we can go wherever we want to on our journey at our age, can't we! "

" The Browning Version,"

A PLAY IN ONE ACT.

Characters (*in order of appearance*) :

JOHN TAPLOW	MICHAEL WARREN
FRANK HUNTER	GRAHAM BROOKER
MILLIE CROCKER HARRIS	PEGGY PASFIELD
ANDREW CROCKER HARRIS	BARRY BOWYER
DR. FROBISHER	DONALD KNOWERS
PETER GILBERT	GERARD GOLDSTEIN
MRS. GILBERT	JOAN WALSHA

Scene.—The action of the play takes place in the sitting-room of the Crocker Harris's flat at a Public School in the South of England.

Time.—About 6.30 p.m. of a day in July.

PRODUCED BY GERARD GOLDSTEIN.

Programme of the 1950 Peppard Dramatic Society performance of 'The Browning Version' with Gerard acting and producing. Note that Gunter has now become Gerard.

Gerard acting in his 1950 production of 'Harlequinade' performed as a double-bill with 'The Browning Version'.

We have a long pause here whilst Gerard takes stock of things. It is a comfortable silence, like that between old friends. The clock ticks gently on the recording. When he is ready he moves into the next phase of his life.

G "Well, by 1949, Oxfordshire was just building its first purpose-built, post-war secondary school – not a grammar school, but a secondary modern school. It was at Wheatley, which is about five or six miles outside Oxford on the way to London. Freddy Anson was considered to be Oxfordshire's most progressive Headmaster so they offered him the headship. He was due to leave Rotherfield at Easter 1950 to start that new school in September.

He came to me and said, 'Look, I offer you the Head of English department – Head of English and Drama – there's going to be a terrific hall and stage.'

Oh dear! At that point I had my degree and I **did** want to go into a Grammar school. By that time I'd done nearly five years in a secondary modern school, you see, and I wanted to teach 6th form students.

'Oh, you're going to be bound up in exams.' (*Here Gerard takes off the Head's no nonsense manner.*) – 'You won't be able to do this, you won't be able to do that.' He painted me such a bleak picture!

I said, 'Well, look. I want to try.'

'Well, I can leave it open for a bit, but the time will come when you have to decide.'

Dear Freddy! (*It is obvious that Freddy recognises great potential in Gerard and wants to bag him. Again, this is a real boost for the fragile young man who needs to be respected and accepted more than anything else.*) Well, we got to March 1950. He was going to leave us at the end of March.

One day he came to me and said, 'Look, I can't keep it open much longer'. He'd kept it open until then. (*How much of Gerard's life, in retrospect, seems to have depended on meeting exactly the right people at the right time and those people making decisions that open up whole new realms of experience for Gerard.*)

He said, 'Look, I'm going out on Sunday to Wheatley. Would you like to come and look at the school?'

'Oh, you're tempting me, aren't you! All right!' (*here he laughs infectiously*)

I owed him so much, you know. So I went with him. As it happened, the hall and stage were finished. (*There is a mischievous twinkle in his eye here and then after a dramatic pause there is a long intake of breath followed by what I can only describe as a couple of orgasmic exclamations – such was the effect of this room on him.*)

'If only this were a grammar school.'

On the way back, neither of us spoke to the other. (*laughter*) He drove me.

Eventually Freddy said, 'Well?'

I said, 'All, right. You've convinced me. I'm coming.'

He was thrilled of course. (*This is said with a gentle quietness. If Gerard had made a different decision here, or if Freddy had not waited for him, or if he had not gone to Peppard, or not worked at the Youth Club and met Leslie Wood, who engineered his first teaching post, or if he had not been taken in by Mrs Pease, how very impoverished his life would have been. It is as though there is a mystical chain linking all these events*)

M "You made this decision quite impulsively! Now you're going to tell me it was absolutely the right decision, I'm sure!"

G "Now, I'm not making this up. This is absolutely the truth what I'm going to tell you now. (*He has me under his spell and on the edge of my seat!*) The next day, Monday morning, when I looked at my post at the school, I had a letter from Colchester Grammar School asking me to come for an interview – the first one I ever had. You see in those days, to move from a Secondary Modern School to a Grammar School was almost as difficult as crossing from the East of Germany to the West. I had to say, 'sorry, I'm already committed'. I couldn't - I couldn't do this to Freddy. I couldn't. (*Since he hadn't signed anything with Freddy he was not legally bound to bide by his decision, but he is a man of honour, who sticks by old-fashioned values. His word is his word. He might have gained in monetary terms and in prestige had he not been so honourable, but he would have lost so much more, and this loss can never be quantified in worldly terms. However, that is revealed in a moment – I must not anticipate the plot.*)

And so I went to Wheatley. Now we had to start early. The staff had to be there a week before term began – a new school, you see."

M "Yes, of course."

G "It was August still. I had a lovely classroom with big cupboards. Book parcels had come and I was opening them up. There were a few steps leading up to my little library. (*From the leisurely tone and gentle building up of the scene, I begin to suspect that he is leading up to something – just how momentous a something I could not have guessed*). It was midday. I couldn't drive. I'd gone out by bus. I'd found digs in Sandhills, which was on the road to Wheatley. (*Having set the scene he is now ready to introduce his character.*)

I suddenly heard a voice, female, 'Can I give you a lift into Oxford for lunch?'

I turned round and there was what looked like a little girl standing at the bottom of the steps. And the year was 1950. I still remember, she had a white shirt blouse and a sort of dirndl skirt and I looked down and thought, 'Oh, she's physical education'. (*raucous laughter here as Gerard makes a comment that I am not allowed to quote!*) Well, it turned out to be my future wife."

M "Oh lovely – oh bless her!"

G "That was Eileen – Eileen Bottrill. She was head of art and design. She lived in Oxford with her mother who had been recently widowed – her father had had a very sad death. Eileen had been teaching already in Northampton and she'd come out of teaching for a year to come back and help her mother. And I soon realised, what a jewel was there."

He gives a happy laugh here. Saying 'yes' to Wheatley leads him straight to the love of his life, who is waiting for him. As ever, the stage management is perfect. In five years he has become a very good teacher, an excellent producer and teacher of drama and, for the icing on the cake, he is about to become engaged! We agree to end here on this very happy note, with both of us knowing, of course, that tomorrow we get in touch with the shadow side.

The young Eileen

Scene 6

Margot's Story

We are travelling away from the safely of Wheatley, Oxfordshire. We return to the late Thirties in Germany, where there is fear and violence.

Margot – all I know about her so far is that she is Gerard's elder sister, beautiful and much loved. On the rare occasions he mentions her it is with deep affection, tenderness and a certain something else that I cannot quite trace – wistfulness is the wrong word. It is not until later that I realise it is profound anguish kept under wraps. Very untypically, Gerard has so far had great difficulty in introducing this character to us and allowing her to take centre stage. She has been kept in the wings where we get a very occasional brief and ghostly sighting. Even now, when the topic is scheduled and we have agreed it is the right time, there is a marked reluctance to begin. I remain quietly firm because I know it is something he wants and needs to do.

M "Right, I just feel that we have to focus now. So this morning I thought we would go back to things we've left because we wanted to do them face-to-face."

G "Yes."

M "You were going to tell me about Margot."

G "Margot?"

M "Yes, Margot. That's what you suggested last night as our topic for this morning." (*There is a pause and a clearing of the throat before he begins.*)

G "Yes. She was born in, excuse me, (*second clearing of the throat*) 1909 – the year after my parents got married. She was thirteen years older than I was. In a way I had a second mother! (*gentle laugh here, but his voice is not strong*) And ... umm ... I was very devoted to her. She was very serene (*long pause here*) and, according to my parents, my Mother in particular, very easy to bring up compared with Gerda, who was a tomboy – she should have been a boy! (*little chuckle here*) And ... umm ... (*very long pause here, then a clearing of the throat and another pause followed by a sigh*) Now where shall we ...."

M "You told me quite a bit about the school they went to and all that."

G "Yes, yes."

M "We actually got to the point where you told me what happened to Gerda – that she was able to get out and go to New Zealand. Then I asked you about Margot and you said it was a very sad story."

G "She was a very, very beautiful girl – very beautiful and she had lots of admirers. She was socially very attractive and I'm very glad to say that ... (*clearing of the throat*) umm ... you know she had been able to enjoy parties and dances and a group of friends. She had a good life - before it all changed. My Father took her into his business where she ... excuse me ... (*further clearing of the throat*) – I think she was working in the office as a sort of secretary. (*Gerard's usually fluent and word-perfect script is not working this morning. There is another hesitation, which signals to me that this is not easy and polished. It is the real thing – the nitty gritty of life that can never be rehearsed in our minds. It comes from the solar plexus.*) And at one of these parties she met a young man quite a bit older than she was – his name was Max and he was the only – well, let's call it 'sweetheart', that she had. Even though lots and lots of young men ..." (*coughing here in earnest*)

M "Shall I get you some water?"

G "No, it's all right. If it doesn't clear up... (*His sentence is never finished, we continue as if there was no interruption*) ... were after her, she was loyal to Max ... Do you want me to continue?"

M "Yes, if you can."

G "She married in '33. At first my parents were against the marriage because she never knew anybody else. She wouldn't look at anybody else. I remember, there were a few sort of scenes at home, which ended in tears. (*There is a little light chuckling here at this recollection of a normal family tiff.*) In the end my Father, ever generous, - he was the most generous person I think I've ever met - ever generous, decided to take Max into his business and offer him a proper salary on which to marry. (*Yes, there are three repetitions of the word generous in the one sentence. I decide not to edit it – words are never idle with Gerard – he has a feel for them and they work for him. Perhaps he needs this reassurance for himself that the lovely Father the little boy remembers was real and unblemished. Unfortunately, an adult must concede that even parents are flawed. The one time this lovely man failed to be generous was in respecting his wife's pleading to get them out of Germany – a sad truth.*)

That meant Margot would have to leave the business. In those days having husband and wife together just wasn't done. It wouldn't have looked good as far as our other employees were concerned. And Max, as far as I remember, proved himself to be very efficient. He was a very good-looking young fellow. He was ten years older than Margot. He was from a very Orthodox family. His mother had died giving birth to the youngest of five boys. He was number two. He had a lovely tenor voice and he trained to be a cantor in the synagogue ..."

M "Yes." (*I speak at this point to show that I understand what that entails and so avoid a deviation about the workings of Jewish ritual which Gerard would happily give at this point as he loves to inform, especially where deep emotion is lying just below the surface. It is safe to stick to facts. I realise that Margot has been upstaged again, and is lurking somewhere in the wings.*)

G "Of course, at that time, being a cantor was not a good financial prospect particularly. And in '35 they had a child, a little boy, and I was twelve at the time and so proud to be an uncle at twelve. And then ... (*there is a long pause followed by a hesitation and another long pause*) you see my Father's business was completely destroyed in Kristallnacht."

M "Yes." (*It is a very quiet 'yes', full of sadness*)

G "And ... err ... so they had to ... you know, they waited too long to ... to ... to emigrate. (*The stammer before the word 'emigrate' shows me how hard it is for Gerard to remain factual here. Emotions are pressing hard. His tone is level and controlled.*) By that time they were hoping that Gerda would help them."

M "Yes, yes, of course." (*I speak to reassure him that there is another human being here who can help to steer through the rapids.*)

G "Gerda did. And then came a bit of bad luck. It was very, very difficult for her. You see the capital of New Zealand is Wellington – they were living at the very bottom of the South Island, several hundred miles away. She had an interview with the equivalent of the Home Office in New Zealand ... err ... 4th September 1939, and she would have got the visa, but by that time, of course ... Sorry, I'm ... err ... err ... I'm jumping a bit. I've got to go back a little bit."

M "All right."

G "They had – they realised that they must get out."

M "Margot and Max realised?"

G "Yes. But by '39 it was very, very difficult. All sorts of rogues advertised something. One hoped it wouldn't be a trick or ... There was a ship going to Cuba taking refugees, providing that they would deposit a sum. I don't know what the sum was – something like the equivalent of a thousand pounds. At that time this was a lot of money. And they went on that ship. I had already come to England, of course, by then. My parents accompanied them to Hamburg – that was the port from which they sailed. They had a very pleasant journey to Cuba. When they got to Havana they were not allowed to land. The whole thing was a swindle. (*There is a pause here, but he has taken his own power now and can continue bravely on.*) Imagine sailing back to Germany. They would have been immediately arrested, imprisoned and Heaven knows what ... might have been better in the long run. I don't know. But four countries offered to take a quarter of the shipload."

M "I remember this, yes. I saw a very moving documentary about it."

G "The four countries were ours (England), France, Holland and Belgium. And they were selected to go to Holland. At that time, you know, Holland was safe ... quite ... and I could correspond with Margot. (*Here Gerard reverts to Gerda's bit of the story perhaps to give himself more emotional time.*) Then on the 4th of September, which was a Monday, – war broke out on the 3rd, which was a Sunday – on the 4th of September Gerda had an appointment in Wellington ... too late. And ... err ... she couldn't ... So, they were in Holland in a kind of camp – a refugee camp. It wasn't a prison camp - it was a free country.

Now, what was it called? (*There is a long pause while he tries to remember the name and apologises for not being able to do so. It is grounding to deal with facts and get things in order.*)

M "It doesn't matter."

G "We could correspond – write freely to each other you see." (*This is said in a strong voice as he remembers the good. He tells me later that he destroyed all letters from family because they were too painful to keep.*)

M "Yes, yes, I understand. The letters must have been a blessing."

G "But then a few months later, Holland was occupied. (*The last three words are spoken in hushed tones that sound like an urgent whisper. Gerard uses volume as well as tone to convey emotion.*) That camp became a – well you can imagine what it became. And with that little child, you see. (*This spoken in slow reverential tones. I did see, but I could not trust myself to speak. I expect I nodded, remaining the objective outsider and secretly brushing away tears when he wasn't looking. Gerard swiftly steers to safer waters.*) Some well-known people were there. You've heard of Edith Stein, have you?"

M "Yes, I have." (*I try to sound matter of fact but my voice is flat due to a massive lump in my throat.*)

G "Yes. She lived in Breslau and she had become a Catholic. She was a Carmelite nun and the German nuns had sent her to Holland to be safe in that camp. She was in Margot's camp. In a way, when I heard that years and years later, I imagine that she must have been a wonderful influence on people."

M "Yes, yes." (*This comes out firmly as an affirmation of hope – one positive contribution I can make.*)

G "She would have taken hold of that child, you see. I can imagine my sister would have been distraught – absolutely distraught. And from there, in '42, they were sent to a camp in Czechoslovakia, that also gained a great reputation, Theresienstadt (*spelt clearly and very distinctly for me*) which was open to inspection by the international Red Cross. So the Germans made jolly well sure when the inspection was on that this was a cultural place. There were a lot of famous musicians there, you see."

M "Yes, I saw a deeply moving film about it."

G "There were classical concerts etc. etc. And starving them. Starving them. From there it was Auschwitz. (*This simple statement is followed by a pause which we both respect. Our silence is a tribute to the dead.*) Now, my brother-in-law was, in a way, the most unfortunate of them all."

M "Max?"

G "Yes. He survived - can you imagine - having had his wife gassed - the child - and other members of his family? He survived. (*Again I can imagine only too well and I cannot speak nor is it necessary for me to do so. He knows I am with him all the way.*) And then the Russians liberated Auschwitz early '45. That's when we all began to hear what had gone on there. It was now open, and these **starving** skeletons, walking skeletons, they had taken them on a march to get them out of Auschwitz – not the Russians, the Germans. They marched them Westward, and of course they couldn't survive. And Max was in it. It's horrible, isn't it?"

M "Yes." (*My monosyllabic response in graveside flatness of tone is all that I can manage and thankfully it is all that is necessary.*)

G "The one thing that…you can't use the word 'consoled' but, well maybe, yes I will use it. By the Red Cross letter I received, I realised that my parents, because of their age – oh they were only 60 but it was an age – as soon as they arrived in that place – I don't want to mention it by name even…"

M "No. It's all right." (*I have to help him out here for my own sake. I cannot break down. I sound very matter of fact*) It would have happened immediately."

G "Immediately."

M "Yes, of course."

G "Immediately."

(*There is another silence. It is not uncomfortable, but I am desperate to say something helpful and positive.*)

M "And a consolation for your parents at that time would be knowing that their son, Günter, was out there living his life." (*He nods before continuing.*)

G "With characteristic German efficiency, I got – and so did Gerda – a Red Cross letter in late '45 giving us in more detail the date of - of - of my parents being killed. They kept what were complete records – millions of people … That's difficult to forgive, isn't it?"

M "Very."

G "Very difficult."

M "Yes, very difficult."

(Gerard has spoken all this slowly, with a lot of stuttering and in hushed tones. There is a lengthy pause here while we both keep respectful silence. All that is heard is the ticking of the clock. I want to take hold of his hand and tell him not to feel so guilty that it took him so long. It is amazing that it was accomplished at all. But I must not interrupt his flow or intrude upon his way of dealing with things.)

G "And, you see, the majority of the German nation would **deny** that they knew about it. Of **course** they knew about it. There was hardly a f - family that didn't have somebody in - working in - in - in - in … who was working in those circumstances. Of course they knew about it. *(The repetition here is recorded faithfully. Gerard is holding back so much anger, I think, possibly because he now sees it as fruitless and damaging to his own psyche.)* My Father went through the first war, of course, and he got an Iron Cross for some brave action – it was no use to him whatsoever – the work he did for the Fatherland. However, I mustn't dwell on that. It's a long time ago."

M "It's all right to do so." *(He doesn't hear me. He's moved on.)*

G "This is, in a way, what the Catholicism taught me, you see – reconciliation."

M "Yes."

G "And this was the main reason why I delayed converting. If I'd known reconciliation would come, I would have taken that step much earlier, but I thought it would betray my parents and it would - *(he breaks off mid-sentence and exclaims)* the guilt, oh the guilt, the guilt, the guilt!"

M "There must have been **a lot**." *(I want to assure him that I understand irrational guilt and that to some extent I have* *followed the somewhat obscure reasoning behind what he has just been saying. But I need to clarify things.*)

G "Yes ... umm ... yes. We'll come to that when we get to the Catholicism part. Umm ..."

M "Sorry, I'm a little unclear about your last few remarks. I've understood perfectly up till then. When you said it would betray your parents – in what way, exactly?" (*I am aware that I must tread carefully and my voice is hesitant.*)

G "By becoming a Catholic. I betrayed the Faith they died for." (*I think several things are going on here. He felt he could not convert to Catholicism whilst he had not taken the almost impossible step of forgiving the enemies' atrocities. In retrospect he sees that, if he had only realised, Catholicism would have helped him to do so at a much earlier stage. Alongside this is the guilt he feels that by making this act of forgiveness he is betraying those who died, particularly his family, plus the guilt of denying his Jewish faith. I can only begin to guess the years of agony of mind and spirit this must have caused in such a sensitive soul as Gerard.*)

M "Your parents were not strict Jews, as you said. I think they died **because** of their Faith, not for it. There's a big difference. And, because of all you have told me about her, I feel I've come to know your Mother a bit. I can't help thinking that she would have understood, and she would have encouraged you to proceed. She had a generous mind."

G "Yes. Yes."

M "So, the guilt that you and Gerda felt was that you got out and you hadn't got the others out?"

G "Yes."

M "Which of course is a natural feeling, but again, your Mother rejoiced that you two got out, I'm quite sure."

G "But it was even worse for my sister in New Zealand, for Gerda, you see. She was older and ... umm ... she had a number of ... umm ... umm ... oh what do you call it? ... when a pregnancy is ..."

M "Miscarriage."

G "Miscarriage, yes that's right – a number of miscarriages at that time. It was all because she took it very badly."(*There is a long silence here, which I decide to break.*)

M "You were able to write letters of support to each other at this time?"

G "With Gerda? Oh yes, yes."

M "Excuse me." (*Here it is my turn to have a fit of coughing. It eases the pain in my throat from holding back tears. I take an executive decision to continue on the same theme in order to be thorough for his sake*). "You said, 'it's hard to forgive. All that's so very hard to forgive.' "

G "It was hard. I - I've - I've - I've got over it now ... (*There's a slight pause before two words are quietly tacked on.*) ... I think."

M "It took many years, didn't it?"

G "Yes, I now know what reconciliation is and what it can do, you see." (*There is a long but not uncomfortable pause here. Gerard begins to say 'I can ...' but he breaks off and the silence continues until I ask another question.*)

M "So for many years of your life you've had this unforgiving state – this resentment?"

G "Yes, yes." (*spoken calmly and in a matter of fact tone*)

M "So ... (*It is my turn to speak with hesitation, being aware that I have the honour to be present when another human being is laying bare the innermost depths of his being. I am aware that anything I say at this point could have profound effect. There is no chartered route – intuition alone can serve as a guide here.*) I suppose, in a way, what Hitler **did**, he's still doing, while ever ..."

G "Well exactly. Yes, **exactly**. You see, some very dear friends of mine, older friends, talked to me about it. Of course, Eileen was the most wonderful person for that. I was lucky – very lucky." (*Here there is a long pause that is gentle and comfortable.*)

M "I am **amazed**, actually – the way you **have** coped, because it was quite obvious to me when I first met you that you're not holding any bitterness or resentment."

G "No, no." (*this is gentle agreement*)

M "You see people around you and you see the best in them, the good in them. It's not destroyed that for you."

G "Yes." (*By his body language he quietly lets me know that he is not only listening, but is also taking it in.*)

M "Because many in your circumstances would have just become anti people."

G "Well, yes. You see this is what I was very anxious to avoid when I came across this. There's one particular – is this the right time now to …?"

M "Yes, yes, of course."

G "Part of my job as a local authority advisory inspector was to go in and help if a headmaster or headmistress had trouble with a teacher. There was a school here – it doesn't exist any more – a Church of England school in the heart of North Oxford – you can imagine the catchment area."

M "Yes I can!"

G "A wonderful school. The Head had got some good staff there. He called me in one day – I don't know why he appointed this man.
He said, 'I've got trouble! – a middle-aged man – his father was a refugee from Germany.' Of course, he didn't know I was, you see! (*We share a much-needed laugh. We are almost at the stage where anything is funny.*) 'And he takes it out on these children.'
I questioned the Head. 'What do you mean, he takes it out on these children?'
'He's very embittered. He tells them they don't deserve to be here. If they'd known what it was like in …'"

M "Ah, ah."

G "I was appalled. I said to the Head, 'Oh, oh, oh, look, I shall have to go into his classes and get evidence.'
'Yes please. That's what you're here for.'
It wasn't just for one day. After one day I had enough evidence, but I had to go back several times and, what was so awful, was the little man trusted me." (*an ironical hint of a laugh here*)

M "Oh." (*as in a stab of pain - I realise how nasty this must have been for Gerard.*)

G "It was. I can't tell you how appalling it was, particularly with me in the class. Everything was emphasised."

M. "Did he know you were Jewish?" (*There is a pause and then a gasp of 'ah' followed by another long pause – I say nothing.*)

G "No, because nobody knew. Everybody thought I was French, you see. (*much coughing here and hesitation*) It was dreadful. I thought to myself, 'I am here. I've got to be careful here – very, very careful.' I had a long talk with him, (*pause*) and I was longing to tell him, 'Look. I can understand what you're feeling better than most, but you survived.' I didn't dare."

M "No."

G "I did actually say, 'But you survived. Why are you taking it out on these innocent children?'
He was quick to rejoinder, 'Oh, they don't know they're born, yush, yush, yush, yush – lucky middle-class children...' and all that. Oh, it was dreadful, dreadful. And of course, I had to report to the Head.
I said to the Head, 'Look. I don't think we can allow this man to go on teaching here. He's doing infinite damage.'
It was far worse than the Head had imagined, you see, because I saw it through a different eye, completely."

M "Yes, yes, of course."

G "I warned the Head that if this man went on like that it would lead to some kind of explosion. I was surprised the parents hadn't complained.
'Why aren't the children going home and telling?'
'Oh, they're terrified of him', the Head explained."

M "Yes, a great deal of psychological damage was being done. So in a way, Hitler's spirit was still alive and well through the

Jew himself. Ironic."

G "Yes." (*this affirmation is quiet and controlled*) I vowed I would never, never fall into that trap. And I avoided it.
I recall my first time back in Germany after the war. It was with the school tour of 'Twelfth Night'. (*He is referring to the school trip on which he took a party of young actors from Lord Williams's School on a working tour of Germany to perform Shakespeare.*) They had a wonderful time. They were all staying with German families, and they were treated as if they were professional English actors, and so on. They were thrilled to bits, and they'd been spoilt, really. They'd had a lovely time, as I hoped they would have."

M "But how did you feel? That was your first time back in Germany, wasn't it? Did you have to do a double take?"

G "Yes. I couldn't tell anybody." (*said in a very husky voice*)

M "No, you couldn't tell anybody, but I mean within you."

G "Oh yes."

M "When you met someone, were you thinking, 'I wonder if you were you part of the SS?'"

G "No, no. You see, I wanted to ..." (*He breaks off here with a gasp because he cannot put his intention into words for a minute.*)

M "It must have been an incredibly hard thing to do."

G "You see, one of my deep, deep thoughts was 'I want to ... (*He still cannot put it out to me, so he tells me what it wasn't.*) – not revenge. I didn't want to take revenge."

M "No, no. I can see that."

G "It was – 'these are English boys, you see.' I wanted to show what they could actually do. I was proud of them. Wherever we went, even the press came to review and said, 'This is something our German schools could never do.' And that thrilled me. Anyway, you've heard of Dachau, haven't you?"

M "Yes."

G "On the return journey there was a signpost leading to Dachau. And I asked the driver to just go along a little bit. 'I don't want you to go into Dachau. Just stop the coach wherever you can. (*a clearing of the throat here*) and I talked to them. I said, 'Now look, you've had a wonderful time and I'm very grateful to you and it was delightful. You read what the reviewers said, but there is another side. We are very close to Dachau, which was one of the three or four of the dreadful camps where people were gassed.' (*He is using sepulchral tones again and I am therefore surprised by a sudden brief laugh that seems totally out of place here. But of course laughter is just the flip side of tears and at the extremes one can easily blur into the other.*) And afterwards, in a way, I regretted having done that. They took it very well."

M "I think you were right." (*My voice is subdued, because I almost feel that it is not my place to speak, but the desire to ease his pain is pressing. Also it is the truth. I believe he was right.*)

G "Do you think I was right then?" (*He needs to hear it reiterated and expanded upon. There is guilt here.*)

M "I'm absolutely sure. (*Gerard indicates he has not heard me.*) **I'm sure.**"

G "I did it very carefully."

M "Yes, you would. You would. And you would be giving them less than your truth otherwise."

G "They'd been spoilt, you see. They'd been treated like royalty."

M "Yes, (*I can sense that the guilt and uncertainty is still there so I speak very firmly.*) **I would have done it.** I would have had to. You had to."

G "I **had** to. I had to. It wasn't a question of mission fulfilled or anything like that."

M "No, no. I realise that."

G "It was … I often think about it and was I right?"

M "Yes, **I'm sure.**" (*I chuckle a little here and it surprises me. But I think it is to imply that my assurance remains constant no matter how many times he asks me!*)

G "They were very quiet in the bus. They listened and err … you see, it wasn't so long after the war – '59. The wounds were still raw."

M "Yes." (*my turn to revert to hushed, sepulchral tones*)

G "Umm. Anyway …" (*Here Gerard gives a wry chuckle too. There is a silence so I ask a question to move us on.*)

M "I still want to know how you could manage this. Were you a Catholic at the time?"

G "No. No."

M "Oh, so you hadn't come across Catholicism yet?"

G "I was married to a Catholic, you see. I was married in 1952"

M "Ah, yes. But you hadn't become a Catholic yet, so you hadn't experienced that great reconciliation ..."

G "Oh well, you can't live with someone without it brushing off. What was funny - you see, because of my love of France, which I think I gave to Eileen as well - we went to France every summer. And I always went to church with her – abroad – somehow I couldn't bring myself to go with her in England." (*I pick up a sense of shame here perhaps, certainly of regret, so I try to ease it.*)

M "No, it's different here. Everybody **looks**." (*This pays off because he is tickled pink by the remark and dissolves into laughter.*)

G "Yes. Ha, ha! You're right, **you're right**! (*His voice is strained from laughing and he slaps his thigh to emphasise his amusement.*) Eileen, was very astute. She knew that it would come. Let it come. And I'm glad it came a long time before she died. (*He is speaking of his conversion here.*) And David, her brother, whom I'm devoted to, I must say, considering he was a priest, never put any pressure on me whatsoever of any kind."

M "That's the sign of a good Catholic, isn't it? - living it and not pushing it."

G "It couldn't have been easy for her mother either – having her only daughter marry a Jewish man."

M "So, you weren't a Catholic yet – so you hadn't got the strength of the Sacraments behind you. Here you were, going back on a trip to Germany. Let's face it, the ordinary people in the street could have been the very ones who were involved in Kristallnacht, for example."

G "Oh, yes. I stayed – you see I was put up – all the boys were in families wherever we went. We went round – we toured – and never stayed in one place more than two days – gave one performance in the middle and then moved on. I was always taken in by the head teachers, the directors, and one of them had a wife who was obviously utterly depressed. Medically depressed, I mean. And one night when there wasn't a play on he talked to me and he said, 'It's all to do with the war and the Nazi period. She hasn't got over it.' And I said, 'Oh, and what's the …' – it was exactly what I'd feared. Her father had been an active Nazi – well, they all had to be."

M "Yes. There wasn't exactly any choice."

G "And all the women had to be the, the, the – whatever it was – you see." (*long pause, which I decide to break*)

M "Were you able to help her – to speak to her about it?"

G "I couldn't. I didn't want to tell her I was…it's difficult. If I were to tell them, their attitude to me would be totally changed. (*long pause*) They would feel terribly guilty and, and, and … I didn't want that. (*There is an even longer pause before he continues in a stronger voice. He is ready to divert.*) You see, the Chief Education Officer for Oxfordshire – a brilliant man – brilliant man - difficult man but very brilliant - sent me on a missionary journey. He wanted every secondary school in his area in Oxfordshire, which was a big county, to be linked with a school in Germany in that little area called the Allgäu, which is in Southern Germany. (*We've moved away from the difficult area of his feelings at this time into the safer realms of Geography.*)"

M "Sorry, what was the area?"

G "Allgäu - beautiful area, mountainous, just the beginnings of the Alps."

M "Yes. Why did he pick that area?"

G "Why did he? Because it was so beautiful. He'd travelled round it, you see. Oxfordshire was very rural too. He didn't speak any German. He looked like Neville Chamberlain. Have I come to that yet?"

M "Not yet." (*I am frantically wondering how we can get back to the matter in hand.*)

G "Well, do you want it – should it be separate?"

M "I can move it – I can cut and paste!" (*I decide to go with the flow and give him the space he needs at this point and afterwards I decide to leave it exactly where it is because it shows the process of opening up painful areas and slowly assimilating them via quite a different route.*)

G "One German headmaster said, 'Well, I couldn't communicate with your Education Officer – he didn't speak a word of German and I didn't speak a word of English. (*laughter here*) All I knew was that he was somebody that looked like Neville Chamberlain with a rolled up brolly!'(*uproarious laughter from Gerard here as he pictures the scene again*) I could just **imagine** this non-communicado! Anyway, the Chief Education Officer's name was Chorlton, and he asked me to go on a missionary journey.
He said, 'You know all our schools. Find suitable link schools.' Well, my Head at Lord Williams's let me go – it was in term time – and he said, 'You find **us** a good school first!'
I said, 'Yes, **I will**!' He quite rightly thought he would make sure that Lord Williams did all right out of it if he had to lose a member of staff in term time!"

M "This was after your first trip with the boys – your Shakespeare trip?"

G "Yes."

M "So you'd already taken the leap."

G "Yes, I'd got over that. I came to a little place - Marktoberdorf - 'dorf' means village – lovely with the Alps in the background. It was a March day – sun was shining already. I got off the train and went to the local to have lunch – I was expected early afternoon at the school. (*The slow build up here and wealth of lingering detail makes me suspect a really good twist to the anecdote is in the offing.*) It was walking distance and I walked along the country road. In the distance I saw the school. (*Slow, long-drawn out words remind me of the leisurely pace of the old carthorses. I am seduced into leaving behind the conflict of mind and soul involved in Margot's story by listening to a good tale.*) I knew it had boarders – that was the attraction, you see, for us. (*At this point in time Lord Williams's School has a thriving system of boarders and day boys.*) I thought 'Oh, pray God it might be the right place!' As I got nearer and nearer I saw (*the tiniest of pauses here for dramatic effect – I am hanging on his every word*) a whole row of deckchairs with what looked to me obviously pupils lying in them sunbathing!"

M "Well!"

G "I thought, 'Oh, good Heavens! That's a school for us, obviously!'
Ha, Ha! (*There's a lot of jollification here as he hypes up the scene to create more fun.*) Ha, ha, ha. It was a wonderful sight, can you **imagine**! It was a mixed school and from the word 'go' it was a success story – the Head welcomed me because I could speak his language."

M "Rather fluently, yes!"

G "Well I had to put a few English accents in! (*I am laughing so much here.*) But by that time I had it quite naturally - my mouth had changed into the English intonation. (*There is a tacit understanding between us that does not need spelling out – he still does not want to admit to any German origins.*) I was treated as an honoured guest – they wanted the link with an English school. I thought 'this is it, this is it, this is it' and it became a very successful link."

M "Good." (*Gerard laughs here to congratulate himself! We don't give the idea of 'twinning' a second thought these days, decades after the event, but this innovative work of Gerard's relatively soon after the war is revolutionary. He is helping to bring about reconciliation in the minds and hearts of parents who had suffered in the war and he is educating the minds of youngsters, helping them to avoid inheriting prejudice and hatred. He is bridge building and acting out his forgiveness of the enemy. We see his nobility first hand, which is all the more charming hidden behind anecdotal humour. I include, at this point, an excerpt from a Lord Williams's School report*)

A look at the early years of the exchange between the Peter-Dorfler Gymnasium and Lord Williams's School.

Arrangements were first made to link schools in Oxfordshire to those in continental Europe in 1964. It was called the European Study and Travel Scheme. By arranging exchanges of pupils and staff, it sought to, in a small but fundamental way, establish common ground between traditionally suspicious neighbours not least because of the UK's exclusion from the Common Market. Initially, it only extended to schools in France and Germany.

In March 1964, Gerard Gould undertook an exploratory mission to the province of Schwaben in South Germany on behalf of the Oxfordshire Education Committee. He wanted to find out at first-hand the nature of the schools and their pupils and he did this by offering himself as a visiting lecturer to the senior forms and giving talks on modern literature, drama and education in Britain. By the end of his trip he had given sixteen lectures to about 2,000 pupils.

His first lecture was at Ulm and as he entered, he heard a pupil say 'Und nun fur den grossen Schlaf' (now for a good long sleep.) Fortunately, this proved to be untrue and all his talks proved lively affairs. Not least, he returned to the UK reporting how much the Nazi past was still a burning issue in the students' minds. But he was sad to find that old myths about the Jews still persisted with some. In one discussion a girl had remarked, 'After all the Jews used to hold all the key positions in Germany.'

In Lindau, he found the schools more relaxed, though most students because of the texts they were reading had an impression of the UK as it was in the late 1940s, and they were reading Oscar Wilde and Somerset Maughan as contemporary literature. But he also found that there was resentment of British attitudes towards Germany; they were concerned about the economic crisis that was gripping Britain; and hadn't the British invented the concentration camp during the Boer War? And why hadn't the Queen visited Germany earlier? On the other hand, he found that the students here were looking at very relevant issues in their own German literature lessons including one lesson where they were discussing Zuckmayer's controversial play

'The Devil's General' and the extent to which the German people themselves resisted Hitler.

However Gerard Gould noted that he was unhappy about the way that German pupils were didactically faced with their past. He was unhappy, for example, with the general policy of taking classes to see the Berlin Wall and being told that Berlin was still the real capital of Germany.

Overall, he was impressed by the way that the modified state education system had taken some of the best ideas from the public school system in Britain, without going overboard and taking all the bad features as well.

G "So I visited all the schools later on when we did some more tours. The next Shakespeare tour was in '66 – there was a big gap between '59 and '66. (*There is a long pause here, which took me by surprise.*) Did 'Hamlet'. (*Further even longer pause – there is something on his mind. He realises we left unfinished business behind us.*) I was billeted at a convent school – oh they were lovely nuns! They were delightful, delightful – they treated me like **royalty**! Ha, ha! I even had beer with my lunch you see! Ha, ha! Ah …" (*There is another silence in which he quietly lets the old memories through.*)

M "Did you tell them you were married to a Catholic lady?"

G "Yes. Yes."

M "Are you all right or would you like to stop?" (*We agree to go on for a while, as we are both aware that we have little time in which to accomplish much.*)

G "I only got to know what I'm about to tell you many years later when I went to visit my nephew in Israel. I've been twice – the first time which was about '98, I think. I met a cousin of mine – I may have referred to her already. She was the daughter of my Father's sister who had died in one of the flu' epidemics. My parents took her in. She was the same age as Gerda and they brought her up as a daughter."

M "What's her name?"

G "Ruth."

M "No, you haven't mentioned her by name."

G "No. My Father looked after her and she married a young man in '37. They wanted to go out to Palestine, which is now Israel. They certainly would be welcome as farm workers, but they had to do a bit of training, so they went to Denmark. And of course in Denmark they were caught in the German occupation. By that time they had a little child. You've heard of Count Bernadotte, have you? – Swedish."

M "No."

G "No, well he was a charitable Swede who set out to save as many people as he could. He had a fleet of ambulances that he took to Denmark, and he'd opened up the floorboards as a hidey-hole so he could put refugees in there and get them across the frontier. Now this is how my Cousin Ruth and her husband and the child escaped. He brought them to Sweden, which of course was neutral. From there he arranged for them to get a visa to Palestine. Cousin Ruth was still alive when I visited my nephew for the first time. It was an extraordinary reunion after 40 years. And she had three postcards written by my Father.
She said, 'They belong to you.'

And from those I could see that my Father used the – the – the … err … diminutive term 'Günterle' for my name – you know it was an affectionate term, 'little Günter'. He was thinking of me and …err … the love was there."

M "Did you keep the cards?"

G "No, I couldn't. I could not. It would be… It was too - too - too … deep. Yes, I've…well, look, I've tried to find them. I don't know what I've done with them. It may sound odd to you."

M "Not at all. Not at all."

G "Isn't it?"

M "I understand perfectly."

G "I have them somewhere in the house."

M "You didn't burn them or anything like that."

G "No, no, no."

M "You just 'disappeared' them."

G "I've put them somewhere so safe I don't know where they are. Now I can't … I've tried to find them, but I couldn't look at them anymore."

M "No, no. That's understandable."

G "It was so … I had – had – had …"

M "It's ok. I understand."

144

G "I read them and I absorbed them. (*There is a long pause, which we both decide to break at the same time. I yield at once.*) What was significant was that my Mother could not write to me. He, my Father, did." (*After another respectful silence I continue.*)

M "What was the last letter you got from your Mother? She wrote to you when you were at Mrs Pease, didn't she?"

G "Oh yes, at first, almost daily."

M "And then they stopped?"

G "Yes."

M "But your Father got some more through after that?"

G "Yes, but he wrote those to Ruth. He could get those through to Denmark because it was Germany, you see."

M "I think we'll give you a break now and resume later."

G "Yes."

Without further discussion, we both instinctively realise that it is not appropriate to speak of tea, or indeed to speak at all. What happens next is quite natural and totally without embarrassment or awkwardness – we hold each other, quietly. It is sustained. We are paying homage to the dead. When we part it is seamless and again beautifully natural. I leave the room, maintaining the silence. I will make tea slowly and we shall discuss the important issue of what we are going to create for the evening meal. Doing things properly and well is very important to Gerard. He is not happy to let things slide – there are standards and it is important to him to keep them up. There is a right way to do things and he does not intend cutting corners just because he is in his late eighties. Tea is to be served from a teapot on a nice tray with delicate cups and saucers. Lovely.

Scene 7

Kristallnacht

We both know that this is where we have been heading. It is something that could not be entered into at an earlier stage. We had to build up a sound working relationship first and give Gerard time to learn to trust me. I know how important it is that I should handle this session with great sensitivity. Gently, but firmly, we set out together, travelling back again to a troubled and anguished Germany. The year is 1938.

G "Well, it was…early November 1938. Now my sister Margot's birthday was on the 9th of November, which was a Wednesday that year. My Father was on a business journey, as he often was, in Upper Silesia, for most of that week. Now, on Monday the 7th, the news came through that the Number 3 in the German Embassy in Paris had been shot at by a Jewish Polish boy. I don't know what his title was – the German one. His name was Vom Rath – an aristocratic name. So we knew that we were going to be in for a big, big, big revenge. And it was top news. The boy had been arrested … . He'd been in the Embassy pleading for his parents. He wanted a visa for them to get them out of Poland. You see, what had happened was, there were quite a lot of Polish Jews living in Germany. They had all been de-nationalised and told to leave Germany - just **out** by a certain time - and he, the boy, was taken to France. He had an uncle living there who eventually asked for him to come and that was all right. He got out. He was already in France. It didn't all happen on that Monday."

M "Yes, I understand." (*Gerard's voice has been firm throughout this. He is on safe ground with history. We need this information for our understanding of the situation and he needs it to key into deeper things.*)

G "All we knew was that he'd gone into the Embassy and shot Vom Rath because they wouldn't allow his parents to come out. Unfortunately, Vom Rath died in hospital. The Germans were just waiting for something like that to happen – it was absolutely almost planned. On Wednesday, we were at a tea party at my sister's to celebrate her birthday. There were quite a number of friends there and umm... (*There is a long pause here in order for him to take himself back and open up very painful memories*) ...we listened to the six o'clock news on the radio. The death of Vom Rath was announced and already they threatened reprisals. We went home - it wasn't very far - walked of course. It was dark - a gloomy November night." (*Although nothing is said about this, and I dare not interrupt his flow, I cannot help but imagine these people, valiantly trying to carry on with their lives as normal by holding parties. But the fragile happiness of this is overcast by the looming shadow of reality – the 6 o'clock news cannot be missed. One can imagine only too well the damper that was put on the whole proceedings as fear rose in their hearts again.*)

Here I include an excerpt from Gerard's article, 'A Night to Remember'.

"My Mother and I walked home. Neither of us spoke. The streets seemed unusually empty, but memory may give me a false impression. We had only quite recently moved into a smaller apartment where we were still unknown. A few minutes after our return home the doorbell rang. It was Clara, my nanny for many years. She had married a widower and kept in touch with us at great risk to herself.

Clara came to warn us. Her stepson, who was a section leader in the Hitler Youth, had come home early under orders to prepare for an all-night operation. He had been bragging about the scale of this attack on Jewish people and property. It did not take Clara very long to wheedle more information out of her stepson even though he was under oath of secrecy. She discovered that our name featured on his list still under the old address. It would, therefore, be best for us to stay where we were but to make new plans the following day, because they would be bound to find out where we were living. She would try to get in touch with us, and we arranged a code.

Neither of us got much sleep that night. We were used to the marching and singing in streets, but these noises were different. Ours was a fairly quiet residential area. Sounds normally came from the main road a quarter of a mile away. We heard lorries racing past, screeching to sudden halts, doors banging, men jumping out and immediately launching themselves into a raucous chorus of 'Germany Awake! Jew Perish!' The more refined vocabulary of the English language cannot do full justice to the menace and grossness contained in the German words for 'awake' ('Erwache') and 'perish' ('verrecke'.) From time to time sounds of splintering glass could be heard from a distance. Too frightened to switch on lights we stood by a window. The north-western horizon, the direction of the town centre, was bathed in a red flickering glow. Two years later, when living near London, I was to see the same glow night after night - the unmistakable sign of burning.

That November night in 1938 seemed endless. Reflecting on it in later years I think that our feelings were beyond mere terror. We were stunned into a kind of dehumanised condition. None of it made any sense any more."

A picture of Gerard taken around this time, when he was 15

Gerard continues speaking to me about Kristallnacht.

G "The next morning, very early, we had a phone call from my sister crying on the phone. Now, as it happened, a friend of theirs had died that week and it was almost like the Irish wake. The Jews have a custom where they go and sit in the house of the dead and say prayers. My brother-in-law, Max, had gone to that friend's house to say prayers before going on to work. But in the middle of the night, lorries came and picked up Jewish men and took them to prison and from there to a camp."

M "So he was picked up when he was praying?"

G "Yes. My sister was notified and told to bring a little bag of clothes to the police station for him. So my Mother took me rapidly and we went back to my sister's. She wanted to be with her daughter, obviously, but she also knew that I was vulnerable. She'd worked out that if we went to Margot's house, because they'd already been there, they wouldn't come again. But meanwhile, my Father was expected back that day. It was a Thursday, you see. Now we had this very faithful Clara – she was my nanny and live-in domestic, but wasn't allowed to work with us anymore. She'd kept in touch with us and she came along before we left the house. She'd got a stepson – she married late in life – a widower – and the son was a storm-trouper. He told her to warn her Jewish family that there was going to be trouble and this, that and the other. (*Gerard's voice has been strong and unwavering, apart from a few hesitations, but here there is a long pause that I do not break – it would be intrusive. I leave him to ponder on the 'this, that and the other' until he is ready to continue in the same firm manner.*)

So she offered to stay in our house until my Father returned, because he wouldn't know anything about it, you see, and she would tell him to go quickly to his daughter's place – which

saved his life. He came – she did all that very quickly. She'd already packed his bag before he came home."

M "Yes." (*I cannot interrupt his narration at this point – he needs to let it flow, but secretly I note the bravery of this woman, who if discovered, would face certain death for aiding Jews.*)

G "She said, '**Go, go!**' And when he got to us... (*He cannot go on for a moment. No doubt vivid memories that have perhaps lain dormant for decades are floating back as he speaks.*) ... we spent the whole day lying on the floor in a room so the neighbours wouldn't see us. The neighbours were all non-Jews and they would have betrayed us immediately ... terrible isn't it?" (*The last three words are flat - and deadpan. It is as though there is no emotion strong enough to express the agony involved and we have come out the other side into non-feeling. My answer mirrors his tone.*)

M "Yes"

G "We lay together on the floor. It was a time to get to know my Dad and for Dad to get to know me. We talked a lot. And we were there for a fortnight until things had calmed down a bit. (*I was taken by surprise by his sudden use of the word 'Dad'. Before it has always been the formal 'Father' and 'Mother' and it sounds very weird coming from him. But, as always, words are not used lightly – it is precisely the word needed to reflect the new intimacy between the two of them. I gather there has not been much in the way of intimate talking going on before this. There is so much that is very moving in this session so far, but this, above all, makes it necessary for me to wipe away tears.*) Meanwhile, all Jewish businesses were destroyed and synagogues were burnt. My school was completely destroyed...complete destruction of what remained of the Jewish population there ... Now, after a fortnight, it was deemed safe to return."

M "Did you have to do it by night?"

G "I can't remember." (*It must have been a very fearful journey indeed if it is erased from conscious memory.*)

M "Did your Father come by night to Margot's?"

G "Well it was after his journey, you see."

M "So it was evening? The neighbours wouldn't have noticed too much?"

G "Yes, it was November so it was dark at five or so. And of course there was no school – not allowed to go out on the street."

M "How did you manage to support yourselves with no money?"

G "Well, my Father went back to his business. He opened up the premises. Meanwhile his very loyal staff had put a bit of order in there. It was wilful vandalism. (*Here his voice gets strong as he allows himself to express anger.*) They tore up yards and yards of precious cloth – all the glass – everything was completely destroyed. For my Father it was **shattering**, because he'd built up this business. It was his … (*The sentence is never completed. Words fail when we try to use them to tell what is untellable.*)

Now, years later, I came across a book written by a German and read something that we were never told. It sounds perfectly plausible – that Vom Rath was a homosexual – it sounds very plausible – and that he'd made a pass at the Jewish boy. Then, of course, the gang round him thought it must not be publicised because Hitler gave orders for the slaughter of his best friend for the same reason. And this was a Jewish boy and the German pleasure boys were blond. The story was that the lad accepted the pass because he thought it would get him what he wanted and he might have a bit of blackmail on Vom Rath to get a visa for his parents. It sounds very plausible, doesn't it?"

M "It does."

G "Extraordinary, completely extraordinary how nobody knew. It was completely hushed up. How they found this out, I don't know. I suppose it would be in the legal documents left after the war. Vom Rath was made a hero – killed by a Jewish boy, you see. 'This is what the Jews do.' I mean it was a **complete** waking up and it was too late."

M "When you and your Father were lying together on the floor did he express any regret about not having got you out earlier?"

G "No, he wouldn't admit that. You see, he wouldn't ... err ... Meanwhile ... err ... there was a boy in my school – he was a bit older than I was. His father was a great friend of my parents. There was no mother there – just a housekeeper and that boy had been taken to a camp and didn't come back ... he died. He was the most intelligent boy I've ever met. I think at that time I was doing a bit of hero worshipping – handsome, intelligent. We met the housekeeper in the street, my Mother and I. She told us – it was shattering – shattering ... (*This is quietly stated in a flat voice. There is not going to be any hysteria here. He knows I will accept that there is nothing more to be said. Words, even from such an orator as Gerard, are useless to portray such agony. The ensuing silence speaks volumes.*) My brother-in-law, Max, came back from camp. He was under oath not to reveal anything about what went on there."

M "Why did they let him out?"

G "I don't know. At that time they hadn't formulated a policy, I suppose. The war hadn't begun yet. I think they were still concerned about public opinion."

M "It must have been extremely difficult, to say the least, for your Mother at this point, because she'd been saying all along 'let's get out.'"

G "I know. They were putting all their hopes on their daughter. 'She'll get us out to New Zealand.' My brother-in-law, Margot's husband, was unfortunate – he'd already had experience of what was going to happen, you see. He was in Buchenwald – oh what is the name of the tree it comes from? Birch tree – the Forest of Birch trees – what a name for a concentration camp. It was in Saxony."

M "I haven't heard of that." (*There is a long pause during which I rattle papers a bit to give him space, but nothing comes.*) Is that complete now?"

G "I think about Kristallnacht. It's as much ... (*There is a pause after the incomplete sentence and more pops into his mind.*) You see, they pretended that the SA – the Brown Shirts – took it upon themselves to take that revenge. 'How dare a Jewish boy kill a German official?' It was all highly organised, of course, highly organised. And then from November to early May it was a grim time, in a way. There was nothing to do. I read a lot. The negotiations with Mrs Pease all took a long time, you see."

M "Your Mother must have been very anxious."

G "Very. Very, very ..."

M "She must have been an amazing woman."

G "Well, like so many. And you see meanwhile ... (*These four words are very useful for fielding and sometimes, as here, they*

have no other function, as they do not form part of a sentence.)
My Father was the oldest in his family. His mother was a widow
so he was the breadwinner. There were four boys and a
daughter, all younger. One brother had gone to Romania and he
died there, but the other two brothers had quite big families. I'm
sorry ... I'm sorry, but I thought they were exploiting my
Father."

M "Yes, I understand."

G "And he helped them all financially and personally. And the
youngest one, Georg, got help from my Father to get to Palestine
– paid for the whole journey for him and his wife and three
children. The other one, Leo, was helped to get to Shanghai."

M "I don't understand. If they could get out, why couldn't you
all get out? (*There is a long, painful silence and Gerard cannot
reply apart from sighing.*) Your Mother must have been going
demented with frustration."

G "By that time they were putting all their hopes in New
Zealand you see. But the business had to be tied up. He was told
to report to the Gestapo and hand in a certain sum of money – it
was quite considerable. And so did my Mother's youngest sister
– her husband had died a year before. He was very well off. She
had two little children. She had to go to the Gestapo and hand
over a lot of money."

M "How did you feel at this time? You were what, sixteen?"

G "I wanted to get to England."

M "Yes, of course. Did you in any way feel ... I don't want to
suggest what you might feel, but you must have summed up the
situation – seen your Mother's anguish about not getting out
earlier. Where were you in all this, because you were in the
middle between your parents?"

G "Err ... (*a little gasp followed by a little sigh*) ... confused."

M "Yes. (*My voice is soft to convey understanding. I continue when he cannot, not because I want to probe, but because I have a clear purpose in mind that might help him.*) Going back for a minute to what you were talking about in a previous session, you said that you felt very guilty some years later when you found out that they were dead. But I suppose, rationally, if the guilt has to be put **anywhere**, it lies with your Father for not seeing the signs and getting out earlier."

G "Umm ... umm ... No, I never blamed him."

M "I realise that."

G "Never, never, never. You see I knew what it meant to him to build up his business from nothing, you see, into a very flourishing concern. It was his - his ... pet object. And I think he was an optimist. 'They'll wake. The Germans will wake up one day. They'll wake up.' (*After a long silence he resumes.*) And again, I think I must make this quite clear, when you read about the German nation not knowing anything about this, it was **impossible** not to know. On the morning after Kristallnacht you couldn't walk along without seeing it. All the evidence was there - pavements full of glass and splinters, and broken bits of precious furniture thrown out of windows. It was **sheer** vandalism – sheer vandalism, **mass** vandalism."

M "I think mainly what they claimed they **didn't know** was what was going on in the camps. 'They were far away. We didn't know.'"

G "Umm. Yes, I suppose so. (*He sounds very weary here and flat.*) I don't think anyone could have been unaware of what was going on."

M "In other words, if they didn't know they could have made a good guess?"

G "Yes, yes."

M "Shall we draw a line?"

G "Mm."

M "Ok. So we jump back to England."

G "Yes." (*Immediately his voice is stronger and more animated as we flee back to the safe shores of England's green and pleasant land.*)

M "So, you told me how you met Eileen, but you've obviously skipped a little bit. (*I say this in a teasing tone to lighten us up.*) Let's hear about your other relationships!"

G "My girls."

M "Yes, your **girls**!"

G "There was a girl in my class first – Sonia Deadman. I asked her to marry me when I was on the farm. She was very touched by it and said, 'I am very honoured, but I am too young and so are you.' (*He roars with laughter.*)

M "She was probably right."

G "She was right. Lovely girl."

M "You couldn't see her, presumably, when you were on the farm?"

G "I got a little holiday once a year which I spent with the Thorne family and I saw Sonia then. And then in '47 - I was already teaching then - didn't have any money - spent all my summer holidays going on courses - nowhere else to go. I did a - typical of me - two weeks drama course."

M "Oh surprise, surprise!"

G "Yes, surprise! And then two weeks tennis coaching! Ha, ha, ha! In Loughborough of all places! (*His voice is full of mirth and has gone up several octaves!*) Well, you see, I thought I must do one sport as a teacher and tennis was the least objectionable! (*Here we both indulge in raucous guffaws. Any fly on the wall would be bemused by the strange creatures called humans, who can rise from extreme pain to party-mode gaiety in moments.*)

So I took tennis coaching and Mary was on that course – a very, very bright Norfolk girl and she was already a teacher. We had a lovely time and we were just beginning to become an item, but that didn't exist then. And then I blew it all!"

M "Oh yes."

G "My own fault, my own fault. I got my illness, the pneumonia and pleurisy and Mary – her mother was widowed – lived in North Walsham – very kindly invited me to come to them for recuperation. And after having been with the Goyder family at Rotherfield Greys, I went there. They were very, very kind to me, but I didn't have enough to do. Quite naturally, every afternoon I went to Mary's school to wait for her to come out and take her home. She was a bit embarrassed by that and asked me not to do it. (*Here he has a wry chuckle.*) She was a very sporty girl – quite the wrong girl for me. (*There is no humour in the last six words. The tone is surprisingly firm and on reflection I think that there is a little more than meets the eye to this seemingly throw-away line. Gerard has admitted to me a strong need to be accepted that is ongoing in his life. This is not surprising after all the contempt and rejection he experienced*

Gerard looking dapper. "Wimbledon here we come"

at a tender age. He must have felt rejected by this young lady when his natural eagerness to see her was not reciprocated, but quite typically, he blames himself for the problem.) It made me realise that I was not the right boy for her and she was not the right girl for me, you see. We got on very well together – had lots of things in common – she also was an amateur actress – I think she liked me. I don't think she loved me. She liked me."

M "And what about you?"

G "I'm not sure I knew what love was. Then I made a **big** mistake ... with the best intention. (*I laugh here because he sounds like a little boy.*) I went back into teaching at Easter for a year. I felt fine then – I'd recovered. I immediately got stuck into with the youngsters and drama festival time came and all that. Mary wanted me to come to her again, but I put the drama first!" (*guffaw here*)

M "You surprise me, Gerard!"

G "And that did it, you see! That did it. Now there was a sequel to all this. In 1950 when I came to Wheatley and I first met Eileen, at half term, Mary had invited herself to Oxford – she would stay in my digs etc. Well that was all right. But you see by that time I had met Eileen. What do I do? What ... ha, ha, ha! **Problem. Problem**! Well by that time – you see as soon as I came to live in Oxford I went to the local drama adviser. I said, 'Look, have you got any work for me – I'd like to have a group to direct?'
He looked at me and said, 'Well the only one that is looking for a director is Sandhills WI Would you mind?' (*Here it's my turn to laugh.*)
'No, I wouldn't mind in the least!' Of course, that's where I lived, Sandhills - convenient you see. They wanted me to do a festival play with them – have I told you all this?"

M "No! The mind boggles!" (*Gerard chuckles now.*)

G "I gave it a bit of thought. I knew that the WI would be very good at making costumes and all that sort of thing. Do you know what I chose? You'll never guess!"

M "I'm sure I won't!" (*I sense that it is going to be something obscure.*)

G "A play by Moliere – 'The Would-be Nobleman' – a full length play. I said, 'We'll do half of it.' They were all a bit flabbergasted, but they were willing to follow me as it were, ha, ha!"

```
1.   THE WOULD-BE NOBLEMAN (Molière)
                                 Sandhills Women's Institute

                          Characters:
           The Music Pupil      The Philosophy Master
           The Music Master     The Master Tailor
           The Dancing Master    Jane
           Mr. Jordan           Mrs. Jordan
           First Footman        Charles, Lucy's lover
           Second Footman       Judges, his valet
           The Fencing Master   Lucy, Mr. Jordan's daughter

              Scene: The Hall of Mr. Jordan's house.
                          Period: 1660.

                 PRODUCER: Mr. Gerard Gould

                 ————————

2.   TRIFLES (Susan Glaspell)        -        Greys Players

                    Characters:
                 Peters (Sheriff)
                 Henderson (Attorney)
                 Hale
                 Mrs. Peters
                 Mrs. Hale

              Scene: A gloomy farm kitchen.

                 PRODUCER: Miss Eva Mellor
```

Programme of 'The Would-be Nobleman'. Name **Gerard Gould** 1951

The chairwoman of the WI – I gave her the leading part. I thought for one thing, with seventeenth century costumes, women can play men. It's the best way of doing it. I didn't want to do one of these dreadful all-women plays that were about then. I didn't half put them through it. Her name was Mrs Reading – a very powerful lady. I confessed to her my half-term problem. She knew Eileen. She very kindly offered to have Mary. I didn't tell Eileen...Eileen knew though! Ha, ha! (*Gerard gives a tremendous guffaw here which starts me off. He often refers to the fact that time and time again Eileen seemed to know things without him telling her. Even now just how she did it remains a sweet mystery to him. I tell him it is a woman's sixth sense.*) Oh dear, it was **so** difficult!"

M "Were you and Eileen together at this point? Were you just friends or ...?"

G "Well, it was still early days, but she took me to school every day and we did things together. Oh yes, we were together, ha, ha! But those days you had to ... and a good Catholic girl, you see, ha, ha!"

M "No messing!"

G "No messing around, no, no, no. I distinguished myself when her mother invited me to tea the first time. They had a little dog and it kept on jumping up to me and because of that I upset all the tea over her lovely tablecloth and everything was ... (*He cannot finish the sentence for laughing long and loudly – it is such a joy to hear it.*) Not a good debut! Anyway, Mary must have guessed as well. I think Mrs Reading must have enlightened her a bit, and when I took her to the station to go home, I knew this would be the last time. It hadn't worked out. I was highly relieved, I can tell you. But it was difficult."

M "But how did you handle it while the two women were there on the same territory, as it were? Who did you spend your time with?"

G "Well, Mary wanted to do quite a bit of sightseeing in and around Oxford – I think I must have told Eileen."

M "I think you must."

G "I must say, Mrs Reading was a great help."

M "Well, Eileen was very noble!"

G "Very noble! I behaved shockingly! (*more laughter*) I wasn't proud of it, I can tell you. Well, Eileen had a boyfriend at that time."

M "Oh well!"

G "He was just a good Catholic and umm ... No, it was love with Eileen. I knew that."

M "Did she know? Early on, I mean."

G "I hope so. I hope so, yes. She had to be careful, you see, because of her mother."(*This is said in a quiet, grave tone. It makes me realise that I had to turn the volume down on the recording as soon as we made the journey back to England. Throughout Kristallnacht it was on full and even then I was straining to hear and had to play and replay some phrases over and over to tease them out even though it was all done in the same session. After being in touch with the shadows, Gerard can bounce back from the most extreme anguish by the use of humour. I suppose I instinctively pick up on this and ask the right question to get him on that bouncy track.*)

M "I did wonder whether the good Catholic boy was actually her mother's choice of boyfriend!"

G "Of **course**! Of course! But Eileen had a very, very strong will. She was remarkably restrained, but very strong-willed. We were already busy planning the opening of the hall - a tremendous spectacle for the youngsters to perform. Meanwhile, the WI was flourishing. We entered the drama festival – they won the first round. They won the second round. (*Gerard is gratified by my exclamations of surprise, and laughter enters his voice as he continues.*) They won the third round! (*explosive guffaws here*) I can't remember the first adjudicator's name – quite a well-known playwright – oh blow – anyway, he said, 'I've never seen anything like it!' (*Gerard can hardly articulate here for laughing. I get this idea that if we are ever short of the readies we could set up a flourishing laughter therapy clinic in a trendy part of Oxford together!*)

I was in my element – I love Moliere, you see. The choreography is so interesting to do. There was a huge cast, and all the husbands were roped in to make a set. Everybody was blissfully happy. They were a bit unsure at first – do you know the play at all?"

M "No, I don't know that one."

G "It's a delightful play, and there's a very difficult scene with the daughter, her young man and their servants – a quartet – and it had to be very, very strictly choreographed. They had to interplay the timing of that. It was so tricky – I spent hours and hours and hours on that. They responded wonderfully. It came as a great surprise to me that we got all those wonderful adjudications and really Sandhills WI had become ... (*Mid-sentence, we both laugh like sailors propping up the bar of some sleazy port-side pub, and it crosses my mind that the neighbours must wonder what on earth we are on! When we recover, he continues seamlessly.*) the thing of the year! Ha, ha, ha! Ah, dear, dear, dear! It was splendid.

We seemed to go from one festival to another, always in a coach. We were pipped at the end by a very polished group, who did a short Chekhov play. But Sandhills was thrilled to bits!"

M "On the map!"

G "Yes! (*There is a pause here while he reflects on happy times, then he impishly pipes up with a sudden quip.*) Much more interesting than Norfolk with Mary! Ha, ha!"

M "Absolutely, boy! Absolutely!" (*There is another comfortable silence and then quite naturally Gerard's thoughts turn to culinary matters.*)

G "We'll think of lunch, shall we?"

M "We shall."

G "We mustn't leave it too late – we need to work up a good appetite for this evening. The food's excellent at Pierre Victoire. Wonderful!"

M "Yes, let's just pull this little bit together and then we'll stop."

G "Yes, right."

M "So we've got you at Wheatley Secondary Modern where you met Eileen. I didn't want to interrupt you at the time, but it strikes me so forcibly it's amazing that your whole adult life centred on that decision – you could have gone to the grammar school, very, very easily. But you made the decision to stay with Freddy and all that love was opened up to you."

G "I know, I know."

M "Isn't it wonderful. You were blessed all the way through with right choices as though it was all set out. You must have thought, 'What would have happened if I'd made the other decision?'"

G "Oh, I did, frequently."

M "But to meet her then before school's even started – isn't that romantic! It's lovely! What would have happened if you had gone to the Grammar School?"

G "Oh, I think I'd have been bored!" (*again we dissolve into fits of laughter*) You see, teaching became a great joy because of the drama."

M "Were you happy at Wheatley?"

G "Oh blissfully."

M "And how long did you stay there?"

G "Six years."

M "Doing your drama."

G "Well, English - Head of English."

M "Oh yeah, yeah, yeah, but that was secondary ..." (*We both enjoy the joke.*)

G "That's what I earned my living at!"

M "You are certainly a man to 'follow your bliss'!"

And so this scene of our play closes on safe ground. We survive the shadow land of hellish memories and come out triumphantly into the light, by a deliberate turning to, and celebrating of, the good things in life, which includes dinner at the best French restaurant in Oxford.

I am reminded of Sir Michael Tippett's words.

'I would know my darkness and my light, so shall at last be whole.'

I think Gerard has always tried to do this, quite naturally, perhaps without being conscious of it. Now he is very aware of what he is doing. He is presenting the whole of himself to the world.

Scene 8

Eileen

Having recovered overnight from our rough journey into Germany and the horror of Kristallnacht, we are safely back on British soil. The scene is set in post-war Oxfordshire. Our journey through the years Gerard spent with the love of his life will not be entirely without suffering, but it is meaningful adversity, in that it is worked through in the context of a peaceful and rewarding relationship. Centre stage, in the spotlight, is a lovely lady called Eileen.

M "So, where were we? Do you want to go chronologically as we were – you are at Wheatley and you have just met Eileen – or do you want to do the session on drama that you had in mind? You take the lead now."

G "Oh, let's get to Eileen."

M "Let's get to Eileen! Ok! Now, tell me."

G "Well, you know how we met."

M "Yes, I do. It was lovely, yes."

G "It wasn't too easy, both of us being on the same staff and seeing each other every day. Before, she'd been at home for almost a year in order to help her mother when her father died. Once Eileen was appointed, Freddy, our Headmaster, used to visit her quite often. She would do practical things for him like making posters. He would refer to me by saying, 'You wait till you meet old Gould!' I was 'old Gould'."

M "Just a minute – so you'd changed your name by then?"

G "Yes".

M "I didn't take in when that happened."

G "Once I got my degree and I had fulfilled my years of residence, I could apply for naturalisation. I was longing for that, as you can imagine. I couldn't wait for it. And it was Bill Thorne and Nan who said, 'Well, it's a good time to change your name, particularly with the war only just ended. That name of yours is far too German.'"

M "It was, yes."

G "So I had the **joy** of choosing my own name! And I had all sorts of things – I was into Graham Green at that time – G.G."

M "Right!" (*We have a chuckle here.*)

G "And I thought, 'Oh Graham or something ... no ... oh, no, no, no. It mustn't be too English'. I felt there must be a slight sort of ... anyway, they came up with 'Gerard Gould', because there was a poet Gerald Gould. And now it's become second nature. So I applied for naturalisation under the new name in order to start fresh at Wheatley – they wouldn't have known my old name.
So, I was 'old Gould' and Eileen had a vision of a staid, middle-aged man, you know! Ha, ha, ha! She was very surprised when she saw me. (*There is a gentle pause here while he relives that precious moment again.*)

M "Did she guess you were 'old Gould' when she came to the steps?"

G "Oh she knew what room I was in, yes. She came to ... she made the first move! (*lovely belly laugh here*) I often went to tea with them. It wasn't easy to see her on her own, except that she was mobile – she had a car and could come to see me at my digs. It was very, very - how shall I put it? Once I got over the half-term hurdle, with Mary being around, it was a great relief when she disappeared. I was rehearsing the WI and Eileen was also involved with a drama company at her church. She played in a production of 'The Heiress' – do you know it – Henry James, Washington Square?"

M "Yes, I do."

G "Very good play."

M "Yes, it is."

G "Very good. Her mother was in that as well so ... (*The sentence is not completed. He gives a wry laugh instead.*) I realised that Eileen was very concerned about her mother. I must explain, you see, her brother was at that time on his six years' training as a priest in Spain. He wasn't even allowed to come home when his father died."

M "Goodness. That's a bit stiff."

G "You see they had a leave of absence in the middle of their course only. It was as rigid as that. He couldn't come out to his sister's wedding."

M "How awful. It's really to say 'The order is your first family now.'"

G "Exactly. Exactly. So her mother - of course as usual, the mother was devoted to her son - was very proud of him and her daughter came second. Yet her daughter did far more for her than her son could do. I realised there was no point in my questioning all this. I took her to the Thornes and introduced her. That first Christmas she and her mother went to an aunt's in Northampton and took me with them."

Eileen acting in 'Washington Square'

M "That was a good sign."

G "Yes. She was so astute - she knew exactly which of her relatives I would like and which I wouldn't! Ha, ha, ha, ha! And then after Christmas we were very busy with the show we were preparing for the opening of the hall and stage in the school. Eileen did all the design for it and I directed it. So that brought us into '51 and our Paris trip, which was not a total success. She loved Paris, but it was not a total success. You see, in the Paris hotel we had separate rooms."

M "Yes."

G "I wouldn't have wanted her to do something which was against her ... better judgement, her Faith. Difficult, wasn't it?"

M "Yes, very."

G "Very difficult. And the hotel we stayed at was pretty low. It didn't help – neither of us had much money. I took her to The Comédie Française to see 'Phèdre', Racine's classical tragedy, but her French was not good and she was really lost. But I also took her to a little musical with Edith Piaf performing in it – she **loved** that, loved that."

M "You saw Piaf live?"

G "**Yes**, oh yes. It was unforgettable. And then ... oh, I must bring her into it ... (*I realise at once that he is not referring to Eileen here and a new character is about to enter stage. His voice takes on a mischievous tone.*) A very, very dear friend of mine, **the older woman**, ha, ha, ha! – Olga Dommen who lived in a seventeenth century cottage in a village near Watlington – Britwell Salome."

M "Is that the name of the village?"

G "Yes. Now I met her through extraordinary circumstances. One winter's day I was hedging, if you please, along the farm."

M "It sounds a little technical for you!"

G "Terrible! My hands were like ... by the time I'd finished I'd hacked them around more than I had the hedge! (*He can hardly get the words out for laughing.*) Anyway, it was a bitterly cold day, and suddenly a little sports car drew up and a **very** handsome middle-aged woman stepped out and said in a very sort of English voice, (*which Gerard now takes off*) 'Are you the young man that takes 'The New Statesman and Nation?' Ha, ha, ha! You see, in the war you couldn't take out new subscriptions to newspapers if you hadn't had one."

M "Oh, I didn't know that."

G "There was such a shortage of paper – terrible shortage. You know the 'New Statesman'? – at that time it was the most intellectual and interesting weekly magazine. I had subscribed to it to attend to matters of the mind during the war."

M "Where are we now? What year is it?"

G "This was '41 or '42. She'd stopped at the farm to buy some cabbages or something or other and they were wrapped up in the 'New Statesman'! That was something amazing! She had been trying to get the paper and couldn't, and there we were wrapping cabbages in them! So she asked where the farmer got them.
'Oh, my young man.'
'Oh, do you think he would pass them on to me?'
'Well, ask him yourself. He's up the road.'
So that's how I got to know her, and we had a little chat.
'How did you get to work here and be reading the 'New Statesman'?'

I explained that I wanted to continue my education etc. She was very interested, very interested, and then before she left she said, 'Come and see me. Are you free in the evenings?'
'In the winter I am.'
'I've got a room with a fire in and you can sit there and do some work and then we can talk.'(*I fear my impartial observer's mask might have slipped a bit. I can feel my eyebrows lifting involuntarily. There is a distinct twinkle in his eye.*) You can have an hour's work and an hour's talk'.

So the following Monday – it was going to be Monday and Thursday I was going to go to her – and a sort of friendship developed. She was a self-educated woman – very intelligent. She was living on her own. She had her male escort who was intellectually very inferior, but nevertheless a good hunk of a man! (*He enjoys his own outrageous comments here very much.*) I wasn't allowed to meet him until much later. He came weekends only, so Mondays and Thursdays were quite safe. (*peals of laughter here*) She was a wonderful conversationalist – a great reader. She wasn't interested in money, really. She had a great family friend, an older woman, who lived in Sussex, to whom she had been a kind of companion and she went to see her from time to time.

That woman was a great traveller and wherever they went they took cargo boats – only 5 to 6 passengers. They'd been all over the world – the whole of South America, down one way and up the other way. They went to communist Russia twice in the Twenties. Before anybody else went to Russia, they went to Russia – not just to Petersburg and Moscow, but right into the heart of Russia. She'd read all the Russians and we talked books and theatre. She was passionately fond of theatre. She lived in London and was a great theatre goer, so we had lots of things in common." (*I am outwardly listening and taking notes, but inwardly I am putting all he is saying in context. He is on an*

*isolated farm in winter, with no mod cons and no one to talk to.
This woman coming into his life must have bowled him over.*)

M "Was she German, with a name like Olga?"

G "I'll come to that later."

M "Ok."

G "She asked me, once or twice to stay the night. (*I must look
very interested at this point, which gratifies him no end. He
keeps me hanging on a thread through a long pause.*) Nothing
happened."

M "Oh!"

G "I don't think she would have minded if it had! Ha, ha, ha!"

M "Would you?"

G "It never occurred to me."

M "What, that it could happen never occurred to you? Surely
you weren't **that** naive? Because you were what – 18 coming on
19? You'd read all your French plays! You must have known
what it was about!"

G "In a way I wish I had now. It would have helped." (*This is
said very quietly and wistfully.*)

M "Made love to her, you mean?"

G "Yes, it would have helped later."

M "Because she knew what she was doing, you mean?"

G "Because sexually I was totally ignorant. Anyway, it was a strange relationship. I think she was very fond of me, as I was of her. She came to every play I did. Of course, I told her about my various loves quite frankly. She never, never told me until much, much later. I discovered through Eileen that her father was German. She didn't want me to know that. Her mother had died before I knew her. By all accounts she was a social butterfly – wanted to remain young and beautiful. Well, I introduced Eileen to her and this is where Eileen was so astute. She soon got the hang of all that. She knew the role Olga played in my life. In a way, Eileen discovered Olga's strengths and her weaknesses. The result was the two women became great friends – both practical, you see. They got closer and closer and in the end Olga made Eileen her chief heir and executer. By then that travelling friend of hers had died and left quite a handsome fortune to Olga. Now it was very difficult for Eileen – I think I must mention all this – Olga decided to take her own life. She belonged to a society – what is it?"

M "Euthanasia Society."

G "Yes. She persuaded a doctor to give her a pill, which she finally used at the age of 84 in 1984. Olga had become very possessive. She expected Eileen to come out to her at once. She also expected her to assist with the euthanasia, but it was very difficult for Eileen to accept - being a Catholic, euthanasia, was of course ..."

M "A mortal sin, yes."

G "But Eileen had to agree to it, to the extent that she would clear up the house, and all those things. Very difficult."

M "But you were able to support Eileen."

G "Yes, yes."

M "You were Catholic yourself by then?"

G "No. Not quite. I don't think she felt a special guilt about it – she would have told me. It wasn't as though she'd given her the pill."

M "Oh no."

G "She simply agreed to do what an executor is expected to do. In a way she appreciated the long years of friendship – they were very valuable. Once or twice we saw her together, but on the whole she thought it would be better separate. Our interests were different. So Olga played a very important part in our lives. She told Eileen much more than she told me."

M "Women tend to."

G "Yes. And that's how I learnt that her father was a German."

M "Surely, by her name you must have guessed?"

G "Not necessarily. It could have been Scandinavian or Dutch or something. I got all her books, if I wanted them. A little bit of extra money was useful for Eileen – very useful."

M "It is absolutely amazing how many interesting people you met just by chance – she happened to buy some cabbages and all that came out of it."

G "Yes, all that came out of it."

M "Isn't that amazing! This is not through connections or working at it – you were just open to the meeting."

G "Yes, yes."

M "Sorry, I interrupted you. You were talking about Eileen."

G "Yes, back to 1951 and Paris."

M "Why did you talk about Olga in the middle of Paris – was she there?"

G "Well, Olga had French connections – as a girl she spent time there. Through her parents she knew two French ladies who had set up a pension for young girls in Paris and she was there helping with the teaching. She knew Paris well – she was there for over two years. I thought there was another reason why I mentioned her at that point ..."

M "We were talking about Piaf, and I just wondered why Olga suddenly fitted in."

G "Oh ... well, yes. She was the sort of person that Eileen had never met before. It was a new experience for her, you see, and she took it so well."

M "Well, amazingly she didn't feel threatened by this powerful woman that meant so much to you."

G "She wouldn't allow that. That would never have been an Eileen reaction. No, she would work her way through it. She was very, very perceptive."

M "Wonderful."

G "Very controlled and very calm."

M "It seems to me that you were very different people."

G "We were."

M "But doesn't it have its compensations because you can ..." (*I do not need to complete the sentence as he is there before me.*)

G "Exactly. Exactly. We became engaged soon after and decided that we would get married at the end of the summer term of '52. The whole of '52 was taken up with a lot of drama activity. By that time I had attached myself to the Oxford Theatre Players, which was the premier amateur theatre company in Oxford. There were nearly forty amateur theatre companies in Oxford at that time and they were the leading company. Eileen came in on it too. But I mustn't anticipate the theatre section – I will come to that."

M "You two were a good team! Now, all this was on top of school?"

G "Yes! And the WI! Eileen said, 'I would never see you if I didn't come and join the theatre players!' Ah dear! (*His voice is full of mirth. I cannot help wondering when they found time to be alone together for personal quality time. I can see that Eileen **had** to join him in his passion for theatre otherwise she would simply never have seen him. But this set-up obviously worked for them.*) Well, where were we going to live? I was afraid of what she might suggest.
 She might say, 'Oh, for goodness sake, there's plenty of room at my Mother's house and it would help me.'"

M "Yes, I bet that was a worry."

G "If she'd said that, I couldn't have said no. However she didn't say that and we moved into my digs. First of all the wedding – we were married in the Catholic Church and afterwards mother gave the reception in her house - very, very pleasant.

Gerard and Eileen on their wedding day.

I don't know - this has been worrying me for some time and I don't know - I never asked her. (*I am muddled here, but decide to wait as it may become clear.*) Nan Thorne had met Olga Domman. They didn't get on at all."

M "I can imagine!"

G "Two very dominant ladies having their paws on the same person. (*Loud laughter here, but I suspect that it is a bit forced in this case as he loved both of those women dearly and would have felt confusion over their discord, very similar to the confusion he felt as a child when his parents differed over the emigration question.*) Nan turned up ... and Olga. Throughout the whole of our wedding ceremony, Olga sat and shivered. I never really understood. I think I know what was behind all this, but I wish I hadn't known."

M "Do you want to elaborate on that?"

G "I don't know whether Olga thought 'this marriage won't work' or something or whether it was losing me ... I don't know. I didn't ask her. But it's been worrying me a bit. However, she took to Eileen, which was a great gift. I was delighted by that."

M "Perhaps it was something very simple, like she was unwell or very cold or something. She was quite well, was she?"

G "Oh yes, yes, yes. It was July. Olga could be very possessive."

M "Yes, I understand."

G "Now that was the year ... were you born then?"

M "It depends where we are."

G "'52."

M "Oh I was definitely born then!"

G "The allowance for travelling abroad was £25."

M "Really!" (*He has a good chuckle at my incredulity which is what I hoped would happen.*)

G "For a whole year!"

M "That's ridiculous! What!"

G "For **the whole year**! Well, by skilful wangling we managed to stay away on honeymoon for four weeks! I wanted to take Eileen to the Alps a bit – she'd never been there – never been abroad, apart from Paris the year before. Now, you could book that from England in pounds sterling. I booked a little inn in the Austrian Alps – a tiny little village – very peaceful. It was lovely – just what one wants after a hectic wedding and a hectic term. That was for ten days and we followed that with three days to Venice by coach, which we could also pay for from here. Oh, it was boiling hot – loved it, but Eileen suffered a bit – quite a bit. She loved Venice, of course. Then we went to Zurich where I had a friend. We could stay with her and her husband for four nights. After Zurich, we went by train during the night, third class, to Dijon where I had friends. They had us for four nights, so they got to know Eileen. And then, naturally, I wanted to end up in Paris. I'd saved enough money for that, and of course this time we shared a room." (*loud roar of laughter here*)

M "Cockroaches and all!"

G "And while we were in Dijon we went wine-tasting – Burgundy, you see. My French friend was a great local celebrity and he had entrée to all these wine-tasting places. Nobody had

told Eileen that you spit it out. She drank it and of course she was sick! Poor child – oh I felt so sorry for her.
She said, 'I'm drunk! I'm drunk!'
Ha, ha, ha! Oh dear. When we got to Paris she retired to bed and felt **awful** for a day. Otherwise, we had quite a good time. We were away for four weeks for £25! It was a lovely honeymoon **really**, a lovely honeymoon. (*The words 'quite' and 'really' indicate to me that there is more to come on this later when we go to a deeper level.*)

M "You did very well indeed on your allowance! Obviously some of your Father's business sense filtered through in the genes!"

G "And then, in my digs – I had a very nice landlady – she loved me dearly and I loved her too – she was elderly. She made us very welcome. We had a bedroom and sitting room and Eileen had use of the kitchen, but it wasn't what she wanted."

M "No."

G "After a few months she persuaded her mother to lend her some money to put down as a deposit for a mortgage on a little house. We found one on the Horsepath Road, which was on the way to Wheatley and Cowley. It was very pleasant, with a small garden – we were very happy there. And then, in '54, we went for another longish trip to France with some friends of ours. We went to Grenoble and stayed in student accommodation, which was very pleasant. Don, a friend of mine, took his car and we went everywhere in it and had a wonderful time. We ended up in Dijon again with my other friends. What it did was help Eileen to begin to appreciate France, which is what I wanted more than anything. She could begin to see what I had seen for a long time."

M "Which was?"

G "Well, style – a certain façon of living, beautiful countryside, lovely places to visit. She appreciated too the activity of the church, you see – being in a Catholic country."

M "Eileen being Catholic, of course, you were not allowed contraception."

G "Ah! Shall I mention that?"

M "If you like – we needn't write it down if you prefer – it just interests me." (*If it is here it has not been vetoed!*)

G "Nan, Nan Thorne, was quite adamant that I must help Eileen to use contraception. By that time I already knew enough about Catholicism to know that was not a wise move. I've regretted it ever since."

M "You broached the subject with Eileen and then regretted it, you mean?"

G "Yes. We were both young, although I was five years older than Eileen. It was very difficult, very difficult. She later regretted that we used it. Oh dear, it was so difficult."

M "But the contraception in those days was not too particularly difficult for the Catholic mind to accept – it was not abortive, only preventative."

G "Meanwhile, her mother had trouble. Once Eileen had left her she let two or three of her rooms. A very pleasant woman took these rooms, but my mother-in-law was the worst lodging-house keeper that you could ever meet. She didn't really like her lodger. There was trouble – continuous trouble. And what happened was, every day after school, Eileen dropped in to see her mother. It was too much for her – I was getting worried. You see at that time Freddy had to get rid of the former Senior

Mistress for being a troublemaker and he appointed Eileen in her place. This gave her a lot of extra work. So there she was above me! I didn't mind that, but I wasn't easy to control!"

M "Really!" (*We indulge yet again in hilarious laughter at this point.*)

G "She made a very good Senior Mistress – she was excellent. She enjoyed not so much the extra money it brought - money didn't interest her at all - but more the power. She quite enjoyed the powerful position - she'd never had it before. She didn't abuse it - on the contrary, she was very popular. She had marvellous control over every pupil, male and female.
'Yes,' she thought, 'it's high time he moves out of the school! (*of course, this is most highly amusing too*) She was pushing me to get into a Grammar school where I belonged. Well, I was lucky again ...!'"

M "Really, it goes without saying, Gerard!"

G "Betty Howland – I got to know her from drama – she was a very, very outgoing person and she discovered that Lord Williams's School in Thame was looking for a Head of English. I said I wouldn't stand an **earthly** chance. (*Lord Williams' School, founded in 1559, was at this time a small single form entry country grammar school situated about ten miles east of Oxford. It took day boys and boarders.*)
I remember Betty saying to her husband, who was a governor, 'Put in a word for Gerard! **You** put in a word for Gerard! Mullens will listen to you!' (*He says this in a high-pitched little voice!*)
Well, Harry Howland put in a word for me. He said to Mullens, the Head, 'At least you could see him'.
I did not hold out much hope. I knew that Mullens was very much a public school sort of Headmaster and he'd think of anybody from a secondary modern school as something the dog

had brought in! **Anyway**, Harry did. 'See him, see him' and Mullens did. Ha, ha!"

M and G in unison: "And thereby hangs a tale!" (*Gerard hoots with laughter.*)

G "Ah, how funny! Where was I? Oh yes, and I think I got off Eileen's back! She was thrilled to bits, not just because she'd be rid of me, but for my sake. And a new life began.

Oh yes, by that time too I was getting worried that every day she was seeing her mother.
So I said, 'Look, I can't drive. That school will be very demanding – much more demanding than this one. I think we ought to move to Thame.'
She was at Wheatley, which was halfway between Thame and Oxford so it didn't matter where she lived. So it was something else for her to plan. She loved planning – she should have been an architect, you see. It's what she wanted to be."

M "Really?"

G "She'd have made a perfect architect. She planned the new house and Harry Howland, who, as well as being a governor of the school, was also the local builder, built it for us. He found the site and he and Eileen were hobnobbing together like anything over that. I kept right out of it – I wouldn't know where to begin. I trusted Eileen to go ahead with everything. Ha, ha, ha!"

M "Not being of a practical turn of mind!"

G "No! No, no. I made the most of it! (*great belly laugh*) I just said, 'Whatever you do, just make sure your mother's rooms are separate from ours!' So Eileen designed a granny flat."

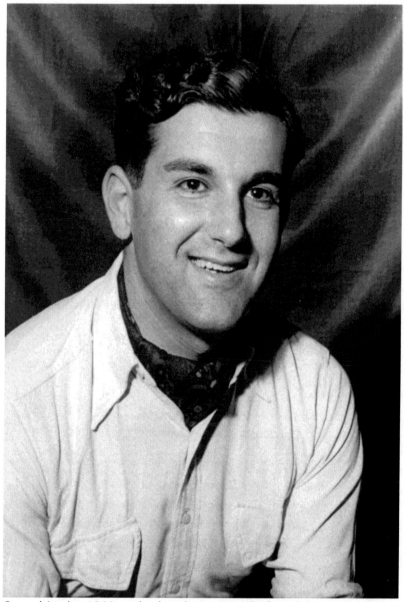

Gerard in the 1960s - the handsome Head of English and Drama at Lord Williams's Grammar School.

188

.M "You were taking mother with you? I know she ended up with you eventually, but I didn't realise it was this early."

G "Yes."

M "Oh."

G "She lived with us till she died ... well, I did it for Eileen's sake. I really did. Should I not have done it?"

M "What else could you do?"

G "What else could I do? It really made all the difference to Eileen, you see. Her mother – she lived entirely separate from us, except we had Sunday lunch together, and while Eileen was at school she made cakes – she was a wonderful cook. I praised her up. I was pleased for Eileen, but her living with us did cause tension. "

M "I wondered about that."

G "We tried. We tried and tried, but we couldn't have children ... and later I also got a hormone problem in my pituitary gland and had to have an operation on that. But I regret very much, for her sake – I had enough children in school. I didn't want any more! Ha, ha! But for her sake, for her sake, because we were ... (*The almost flippant bravado here does little to hide the pain he feels at the absence of children in their marriage.*) We talked about it later on. We couldn't have done half the things we did."

M "No."

G "We couldn't have had the French cottage, which she loved. (*Without being aware of it, he slips into direct speech here – he is talking directly to her again.*) 'You wouldn't have had all those high positions you've had'.

You see, when you're teaching, teachers make very bad parents."

M "I suppose that can be so, if they are very good teachers, because they're so dedicated."

G "Exactly. Exactly. (*This very thorough process of rationalization has done the trick. We are off on track again and the spirit of laughter will no doubt be summoned to lift us up.*) Anyway, I went to Thame and Eileen got rid of me! Ha, ha, ha! I was no longer a thorn in her flesh! (*guffaw here*) And then a few years later she and a fellow colleague and great friend, Pat Chantry, made a move. They thought they'd done long enough at Wheatley. There was a new school here in Oxford. Have you heard of Blackbird Leys?"

M "No, I haven't."

G "Blackbird Leys is a huge estate on the south east side of Oxford. It was the second biggest estate in England – over thirty thousand people living there and most of them were rehoused from London. (*I do not make any comment, but my eyebrows must have raised up at the thought of this immense challenge.*) Yes, quite. And it was the time the motor works were at their height in Oxford. If you lived there, you worked on the motors. A lot of the women had daytime jobs and the men had night jobs. The problem wasn't poverty, but poverty of spirit. Too little was expected of the youngsters. Anyway, Eileen was appointed as Deputy Head, and in fact she was a Head teacher, because the Head was a wonderful escapist. He spent all his time in his little room in front of a computer that just happened to come in! And she was extremely good with these very difficult children."

M "Very challenging."

Pat Chantry now speaks fondly of the years she spent knowing the Goulds.

P.C "I got to know Gerard through Eileen. We taught together at Wheatley for many years while Gerard was at Lord Williams's, and then we moved together to Redefield School, Blackbird Leys. We were both deputy heads alongside another colleague - it was a big school. Eileen was always very calm - nothing rattled her. She was very much a peacemaker. These qualities made her a brilliant deputy head. Staff and pupils alike would bring their problems to Mrs Gould and she would sort them out. Needless to say, she was also expert at keeping things calm when Gerard was heavily involved in directing!

We had some lovely times together. In the summer holidays we girls went straight off to the house they had bought in France, to get it ready for Gerard.

Vernodes – the holiday home in the Dordogne

They used to shut it up in the autumn, so we had to air it out and stock up on food. I stayed for three weeks and then Gerard came and I would go home. They were very happy times. They were both very good at making friends with the locals and that made all the difference.

Gerard and I both belonged to the City of Oxford Theatre Guild. Gerard used to do productions for them in the college gardens once a year. I used to have all the measurements of the cast with me and go up to Stratford for the costumes. My dining room would be full of stands for the costumes and people used to come to me for fittings. I wasn't allowed to cut, but I could take tucks! And then every night the costumes were taken to the gardens and I would be there with a needle and thread to see that everybody was all right. Gerard did all these wonderful outdoor productions for a two week run and somehow we always got good weather!"

Gerard continues speaking about Eileen.

G "And then gradually, over the years, the children from Blackbird Leys estate grew up and moved on and pupil numbers dropped in the school. The LEA had to close it. The teachers were given early retirement with quite good conditions and Eileen was retired before she could retire.

M "Did she like that?"

G "Yes."

M "Oh that's good. She could let go."

G "Oh yes. It was very hard work in that school. She enjoyed it – found it very rewarding, but she liked retirement too. Meanwhile we had acquired a cottage in the Dordogne, which became a sort of focus of attention for her. She had to have a project. She loved planning and running a new house.

Eileen being practical

I was delighted that she sometimes went three times a year to the Dordogne. I couldn't. I was still working. But we had twelve happy years going over to France."

There is a long, comfortable, pause while he remembers happy times.

Gerard being philosophical

I include here excerpts from Gerard's highly entertaining story, 'The Best of Times', which is a record of their wonderfully colourful experiences in France. The first snippet records the signing of the purchase agreement and sets the scene.

A few hours later we all sat in Pierre's kitchen celebrating the great event. As far as Pierre was concerned, we were already neighbours. Inevitably, the conversation turned to the war which, as I was to discover, still had a vivid reality in the minds of many people who had lived through that gruelling time. The demarcation line between occupied and Vichy France had run close to the Baranne valley that had proved to be an ideal hunting ground for the Resistance fighters. In the years to come we found that a sunny day, a good meal and a glass of wine would soon loosen the tongues of our neighbours for a rich fund of Resistance stories.

We now move to a section in which we are introduced to the larger than life character 'Eva'.

When we got to know our neighbours, Thomas was just recovering from the amputation of one leg, which meant the end of his farming life. Stubborn and obdurate by nature, he had neglected an ulcer on his foot, until an operation became inevitable. Ever resourceful, he took to driving a simple, automatic DAF car to St. Florentin on market days and to meet his mates in the bar. Thomas driving his DAF at full speed in the twisting and bending lanes became a distinct hazard, and it was prudent to swerve to a grass verge, slow down and let the whirlwind pass.

Eva was an admirable wife. Nothing ever ruffled Eva. Her serenity, outer poise and inner grace would have passed for aristocratic virtues in a pre-revolutionary age. She knew everybody, and everybody loved and respected her. Life had schooled her never to express surprise at anything that might happen.

Her immediate sphere of activity was the kitchen where she held court throughout the day and received an ever constant stream of visitors paying their homage. These would never depart without receiving some token of the respect they had paid, whether a tasty, home-made rabbit pâté, vegetables or, best of all, a glass of Eva's special brand of genièvre made from juniper berries and eau-de-vie.

Her realm extended to St. Florentin where, on market days, she exercised her own version of 'droit de seigneur' by wandering from stall to stall critically scrutinising the value of the goods and prices on offer, comparing, weighing, making judgments, recommending some, dismissing others. Her greatest delight was in trying on dresses. There seemed to be a token agreement between her and the stallholder that no purchase would be expected.

The piece that follows is a delightful anecdote, in which Gerard is involved in a little clandestine activity with the aforementioned lady!

The first time I received a telephone call late evening from Eva asking me to drive her to a man who lived near Chaptal, I naturally assumed that Thomas was in dire distress. I rushed to the car as if Thomas's life depended on every second gained, drove up the lane to the farm only to find Eva serenely smiling as usual, wrapped in a voluminous coat on a warm summer's evening and waiting for me. Mine not to reason why, we set off for Chaptal, a village on the other side of the valley. Dusk was falling rapidly; driving in ever twisting, narrow lanes at a time of day which the French so aptly call 'entre chien et loup' was not my idea of unalloyed pleasure, particularly as our journey seemed to be extending itself well beyond the confines of Chaptal.

Eva by my side was obviously enjoying herself commenting on the intimate lives of people whose farms we passed on the way, never with malice, always with good tact, as if it was the most natural thing in the world and spoken in a clear, well-modulated voice which revealed a rare sensitivity to the difficulties foreigners might have in French. I was too intent on driving within the flare of my own headlamps and observing the grass verges to contribute to the conversation anything other than occasional exclamations expressing amazement as another revelation of the home life of a respectable member of the community was disclosed.

Eva was an unfailing guide. We eventually arrived in what appeared to be a large farmyard with a big barn on one side in which a naked light bulb could just be seen. Inevitably, a cacophony of barking dogs immediately disturbed the peace of a starless summer night. Out of the shadows loomed the figure of a bulky man bearing a strong resemblance to Finlay Currie as the convict in that terrifying, never-to-be-forgotten opening sequence of Ronald Neame's 'Great Expectations.'

Eva had got out of the car looking almost as bulky and, without any explanation of the mystery, disappeared with the man in the barn. All was revealed later. When they emerged in torchlight holding five big jars I realised that I had unwittingly lent my car and myself to what could only be called a somewhat harmless smuggling operation. Local farmers were licensed to make their own alcohol for their purposes, the powerful potion known as 'eau-de-vie', which then would be added to fruit to make liqueurs and all sorts of other life-enhancing brews. But they were not supposed to sell the stuff.

This was harvest time, and Eva had no intention of allowing Thomas's debility to stand in her way of continuing, as usual, with her culinary activities, even though she could no longer make her own eau-de-vie. Hence this nocturnal visitation. For one brief moment I imagined a headline in an English newspaper: 'British Local Government official arrested in France for aiding and abetting the smuggling of eau-de-vie.' Meanwhile, an expedition like this could not be concluded without some celebration.

Boozing with the locals

On the way home I could not help asking Eva what would have happened if we had been stopped by gendarmes. Calmly, she replied that they knew and were also engaged in similar excursions.
'Why then do it all at night?'
For one brief moment she seemed taken aback by my question, but her ability to take everything in her stride soon returned: 'But that's how it's always done.'

Next Gerard describes preparations for a local wedding and we are allowed a superb little glimpse of the immense fun he and Eileen had in France.

Three days before the wedding, Lisette, Catherine and Stephanie called at our house to show us their new wardrobe. Among a great deal of hilarity we asked them to give us a fashion parade. They did not need much persuading. They vanished upstairs into one of the bedrooms from which much giggling was heard. To set the scene I put on a tape of an Offenbach can-can that I had with me, and three stunningly colourful ladies descended the staircase collapsing with laughter long before they reached the last step.

As an inveterate giggler myself, I enjoy inciting others to similar outbursts, and I had found my match in Lisette and her daughters. But they were a fine sight. They had saved up for years for this occasion, and there they were complete with new hats, gloves, and shoes.

We end our pleasant little detour to France with a story that Gerard is proud to tell, because it illustrates perfectly Eileen's tremendous ability to stay calm in a crisis which arises out of Gerard's valiant attempt to do something practical! He is putting the finishing touches to freshening up the landing with a coat of paint.

I fetched a small milking stool, which would be quite sufficient for me to stand on and finish the top piece. This old stool had served as a coffee table and occasional extra seating for a child. Final brush stroke in the top right hand corner, a little extra pressure on my right wrist, up on my toes and the stool wobbled, lost one of its legs and slid down the stairs.

For one brief moment I was suspended in mid-air clutching the wooden panel above the door with only the staircase beneath me. I called out for help, but at once lost balance and followed the stool down the stairs, head first. It seemed like a slow motion action. This was not happening to me; it was someone else rolling to a certain death. The stairs ended in a concrete floor. A natural instinct for survival made me reach out for the banister on the left. It broke the fall half way, but the forward impetus had been too great. A momentary respite before the fall continued. This second stage did all the damage.

Eileen and her brother, David, had arrived on the scene, caught me on the third step below, held me as tightly as they could and thus saved my life. The right side of my face had been badly bruised, fortunately far enough from the eyes not to do any permanent injury. A burning sensation on my forehead was caused by an enormous swelling which immediately erupted. I was lucky - I was alive. A full realisation that all that had happened to me came only when I became the object of Eileen's and David's solicitous attention. It was only later that it dawned on me how fearful their shock must have been when they arrived on the scene and saw a rather large bundle catapulting down the stairs.

Meanwhile, they turned themselves into a most capable on the spot accident unit. I was nursed back to life by words of calming assurance, and a series of ice-cold compresses was balm to the hurt head and mind. The swelling was not only arrested; it decreased. Like a film star, whose entire livelihood depended on his features, I wanted to know whether the face had received some frightful damage. This was a normal reaction and reassured my two nurses that I was beginning to regain control of my faculties. But it would be advisable to see a doctor. A young man, locum to our own doctor who was on holiday, arrived within twelve minutes. He gave me a thorough examination and then gave his verdict: 'It's nothing.' No fractures. I should rest a little, and all would be well. We talked about the house, the area, all in English in which he was quite fluent. His fee was fifty francs; it was all very simple and efficient.

After his departure calm and order returned. Eileen was worried about concussion, but I was already well on the road to recovery. Radio France Musique was a tonic at the best of times. I would just sit and listen. An hour later the telephone rang. Eileen answered. The conversation had a surreal quality:
'Ruth, what's happened? What did you do? Where are you? How did you do it? Is it very painful? I'll come straightaway. Gerard has had an accident but I can leave him with my brother David. I can't be away too long.'

Our dear friend Ruth, who had left us only that morning, had fallen on a flagstone step in her friend's house. Her left wrist was extremely painful. With no telephone in the house, she had dragged herself to the public phone in the village, and she obviously needed help. Eileen, calm and capable on normal occasions, surpasses herself in emergencies. Two people in distress - eighteen kilometres apart - she was needed. Fortunately, with David in the house, I could be left quite safely. I retired to bed, a relief to everybody, and Invalid Two could be attended to.

Ruth needed immediate attention. She had made a bandage for herself, but the wrist and arm were badly swollen and obviously causing a great deal of pain. We had already tested once before the efficiency of the local health centre after normal hours so Eileen knew what to do. She drove Ruth straight to Centre Medical. It was after nine in the evening, but a doctor was on duty. The Centre in the small town of Fleuviac had x-ray equipment. Within minutes a fracture of the wrist was diagnosed, but Ruth would have to be taken to the county town, forty-five kilometres away, for immediate treatment. The accident unit was alerted.

There were no long, unnecessary waits in the hospital. Ruth was seen as soon as she arrived. All this helped to restore her usually high morale and bouncing spirits. The full impact of the story of my fall had not at first sunk in, but now she began to see the funny side of the double tale of disaster. It was absurd drama that two such accidents should occur on the same day. Her spirits were slightly dashed when the doctor prescribed an overnight's stay in the hospital, an unnecessary precaution, she thought. Eileen returned home at three o'clock in the morning. She had telephoned from the hospital to keep us in touch with her movements and to reassure herself that all was well at our end. I had a restful sleep and wanted to know the full version of Ruth's story.

Next day Eileen returned to the hospital to collect Ruth and
to bring her back to our house. Eileen was going to have
both her invalid 'malheurs' under the same roof. Meanwhile,
at home, where I was still resting in bed but feeling much
refreshed, my sense of humour about the weird sequence of
events had got the better of me and I began to quote
Chaucer.
'And on a Friday fil al this meschaunce'." Never mind that it
had all happened on a Tuesday. Chaucer's Nuns' Priest would
not raise any objection to our transposing the day when all
the misfortunes befell poor Chantecler as long as we heeded
the warning. I continued to quote.
'Misfortunes never come singly. They usually come in threes.'
'If they do, I shall go back to England and leave you to cope
by yourselves.' That was Eileen!

*Gerard fondly continues speaking about Eileen for a moment,
before moving on to his later career.*

G "Oh we had such good fun together! Eileen and I had
developed our own lingo! We gave each other secret signals.
When one or the other needed quick reassurance we would say,
'Bustes en haut!' It meant 'chin up' only instead of chins it was
bosoms! I remember on one occasion we were staying in our
French apartment that we bought after selling the place in the
Dordogne. We were going down in the lift and for some reason
just before the doors opened I took it into my head to proclaim
to Eileen in my loudest tones, 'Bustes en haut!' I'd forgotten
that we were in France! As the doors opened we saw this
woman standing there. She'd heard the voice, but couldn't see
who it was! She was terrified! (*Gerard is weak with laughter
here, and he slaps his thigh a couple of times between guffaws!
He continues in strangled tones.*) I mean, imagine wanting to go

up in a lift and suddenly hearing a disembodied voice suddenly shouting, 'Breasts up!' Ha, ha! We could get away with it in England, you see. Nobody knew what it meant!"

M "What made you suddenly think of that? You just started chuckling to yourself and came out with it."

Happy days

G "I don't know – maybe because we were talking about our French project."

M "Well, I'm glad it popped up –it's lovely!"

G "By that time, of course, I had left Lord Williams's. Well, you see, the marking was hard, and so much time was taken up with drama and I'd enjoyed going into other schools. The time came I had to make a decision. I decided it couldn't go on – it wasn't fair on the Head, and it wasn't fair on the school. A vacancy occurred in the Authority for a general adviser in 1976. They had a senior adviser for central Oxfordshire and then two general advisers for the rest of the area. At that time, I was doing part-time advisory work in English and Drama. The lady who was retiring was a great friend of ours, Joan O'Donovan. She was a remarkable woman who was a novelist and also a teacher. She went to the Chief Education Officer on my behalf.
She said, 'There's only one person I would like to see take my post and that's Gerard.'
He said, 'Well, he's got to apply like everybody else. We can't have ... rah, rah, rah, rah.'

Well, there were two hundred and twenty-two applications. It took months. I had the main interview, and then it came to another interview before they decided between a headmistress and me. She went first, and I sat in my car waiting my turn. I saw her come storming out and I thought, 'Well, they won't see her again!' Ha, ha! It gave me confidence, you see! So I swept in and I got the job. Oh! I've remembered a funny story about Joan – shall I tell you?"

M "You know I can never say 'no' to a story!"

G "There's the French connection again – she had a property in the Dordogne too. We were all sitting outside one warm evening having drinks. We could see a hard-working farmer in his field down the end of Joan's property. She quite suddenly scooped up a drink from the table and waltzed to the fence in her long, flowing gown to offer this man refreshment. Feeling impish at that moment, as an accompaniment I quoted the famous line from Phèdre. 'The whole of Venus clinging on to her prey!' I quoted it in French, of course and in loud tones! And the farmer became quite terrified! (Gerard again dissolves into laughter!) It was so apt, you see. She was going to her prey! I used it in England too, but here no one understood what I was saying! Of course the farmer knew exactly what I meant! But it was what she was doing!"

M "You used it when she was vamping men!"

G "Exactly! You've got her – you've got her! Anyway, it's thanks to this lady that I got the position of General Adviser."

Here a colleague of his, Catherine Hartley, remembers the time she worked alongside Gerard in the '70s in the Education Department of Oxford County Council.

C.H. "I got to know Gerard properly when Oxford City Education and Oxon were amalgamated and we were given temporary office space in an old and decrepit vicarage near the station, the grounds of which were frequented by down-and-outs! It was a strange but jolly time, much enlivened when Gerard shared jokes and laughed very loudly in his infectious way.

He was a team leader and I was in his team. He was an inspiring 'captain', being well advanced in his thinking on education. He always expounded his thoughts clearly and succinctly – as they made sense, we all understood what he was telling us and felt motivated to act on it.

He continued to produce plays, especially outdoors in the college courtyards. Because of his endearing personality, he never had trouble in finding helpers. He also continued coaching and helping young people with their acting.

I count myself lucky to be a friend and to be able to keep in touch. It has been a great privilege and pleasure to have known him and to have had the benefit of his wisdom."

Gerard continues speaking about his work with the Local Authority.

G "I spent a lot of time in the weaker schools. The staff were just not together and working as a team. There were no heads of departments or coordinators. The trouble in the middle schools was there were no specialists. I had to do something to bind the staff together. It was a tremendous challenge. I had a brainwave. I chose a brilliant teacher from one of these middle schools and asked him to hold an in-service training session for all his colleagues in the Oxford City. It had to be after school. I had a bit of money, so I told him to lay on a good tea! Ha, ha!
I said, 'I want you to be the first – I want you to set an example.'

And he did. He was brilliant, absolutely brilliant at it. These meetings were held every two months and they became far more successful than I could ever have imagined. It meant that in turn, they all visited each other's schools and they saw what other people were doing. It's the best way of in service training. I was so touched when I retired. All of those groups gave me a special farewell concert – they had to compose something – they were working as a team! It was so funny and so witty – all beyond what I had ever dreamt."

M "Were your methods adopted in any other parts of the country?"

G "No, no. The District Inspector, Bruce Chalmers, and I became great friends. It was part of his job to work with local advisers. He saw my methods in action and was very impressed. It was a lovely job. One day, Bruce asked me to help Banbury School prepare for a forthcoming inspection. It was a big school and, rightly or wrongly, it had developed a bad reputation with the inspectors. It was not in my area, but our Chief Adviser was away ill so I agreed to do it. In a way I was persona grata, because I had been at the coal face for so many years – they respected me. It was fascinating. The Head at that time had a very weak team of seconds. It was a huge school, divided into four houses with heads for each. This is where the weakness lay, but he had some good heads of departments below them. So, I spent day after day after day in Banbury. I went to every staff meeting – very revealing – had sessions with the Head, Heads of Departments and saw probationers."

Here Gerard goes on to tell me a funny story about one young probationary teacher in the school who was very promising, but for one thing. She was having difficulty controlling the class. When he sat in on the class, he realized at once what was wrong!

G. "She wore a home-knit pullover, which, when she bent down, rolled up exposing a nice bare patch! And of course, boys of thirteen to fifteen felt embarrassed by that and they took advantage of her, even with me in the room. I spotted this immediately, and thought I had to do it through the Head of Department – I couldn't do it on my own." (*He goes on to describe the delicate exchange between the H.O.D and himself, each reluctant to tell the young lady!*)
'How did you find this out? I've sat in on her class and I didn't work it out', asked the very bemused H.O.D.

'Well', I said to him, 'it's so obvious to me with my sense of drama! They can't concentrate – they're much too interested in what's being revealed!'

Well, I was able to do a lot of preparatory work with them and at a meeting with the authority I praised the school and told them the potential was very, very high. I think they thought I was mad, but you can imagine what happened. The inspection report was good. I was called into the Chief's office, and there they all sat – all those who had appointed me, and had been pitching into Banbury School – it was lovely!
And they said, 'Oh, it was an excellent inspection report.'
'Oh, was it really. I'm very glad!'
They had no idea of the amount of work we'd done. Oh it was a lovely day – a glory day!"

M "Sweet power!"

G "Oh, yes, yes, yes. I didn't take advantage of it though. But the best thing was yet to come – we had a new Chief Education Officer, Brighouse, who, at my farewell tribute at the Playhouse, gave a speech. One line stands out in my memory. **'Gerard made me laugh. Gerard made me cry.'** I took this as a great tribute.
Once I retired from the Authority, Lord Williams's asked me to become a foundation governor of the school. It turned out to be for twelve years. It was hard work. I retired from this in '96."

Gerard was well respected by other colleagues in the education authority. Here I include excerpts from a speech Gerard gave at his friend Bruce's funeral, which illustrate beautifully the kind of working relationship he had with the District Inspector!

An unforgettable moment came when Bruce was guide to my wife and myself on a three weeks' tour of Classical and

Historical Greece. We wanted to see the Areopagus where St. Paul addressed the Athenians. The only way to the place was up a very steep and rocky path. Going up was possible but coming down was a different matter. So what did Bruce and Eileen do? They found a smoother stretch, which would have been even more slippery to attempt on foot, sat down and joyfully, like children let loose in a playground, slid down.

'We have heard the chimes at midnight' - Falstaff and Justice Shallow reminiscing in a Cotswold village - was one of Bruce's favourite quotations. There was one occasion, however, when we heard more chimes than we had bargained for. It was on New Year's Eve, a few years ago. Bruce had invited me to celebrate with him. We stayed in his Club, the comfortable RAF Club, at the top end of Piccadilly, and went to see a Sondheim musical at the Donmar Warehouse. We followed it with a late night supper at his favourite Italian restaurant in Windmill Street, in the heart of Soho, where he received a warm welcome. When we came out of there, it was well after midnight. Of course, not a sign of a taxi so we had to walk back to the Club across Soho, just as all the crowds were milling back from Trafalgar Square - not quite a scene for two elderly gents to be seen in. It was nearly two o'clock in the morning when we were safely in the shelter of the RAF Club, had a whisky in Bruce's room and shared a good laugh at that night's experience.

I can see that he needs a break, so I make a move to sum up this section.

M "So you and Eileen had remarkably full and satisfying careers. You both packed a lot in, but it was not all work was it? You had lovely fun together too."

G "Yes, we did. And we remained firmly in love through all the years. You know, I never so much as looked at another woman ..." (*I smile, and give him time to enjoy his memories of good times before suggesting a break.*)

M "Are you tired?"

G "A little."

M "Shall we stop?"

G "Yes, I think we should. What is it we have to deal with tomorrow?"

M "We thought Catholicism tomorrow."

G "Yes, Catholicism tomorrow."

There is no dramatic ending to this scene. There might have been had we both not had the wisdom to divert it. It will be dealt with in due course. We do not need to discuss it. We quite naturally sense that there is a right time for speaking about such things as death and it is not now.

Scene 9

Catholicism

We are now in Oxford, in the very pleasant sitting room with triple – glazing to keep out the noise of traffic on the main road. The man and woman are sitting comfortably opposite each other, speaking of serious matters. One might expect this particular interview session to be rather dull and erudite, but knowing him as she does, this thought never crosses her mind.

G "My first contact at all with anything remotely connected with Catholicism was as a child with my first Nanny, Hannah. She came from Silesian farming stock. She took me to her home one year. I couldn't have been very old – five or six I should think. We went by train and her father collected us in a wagon pulled by a horse. It was wintertime – a lovely spot and, what I remember is, that night was starlit – full of stars and silence. They were very devout Catholics and it left an impression – the peace, the silence and church bells ... .

A lot of my Father's customers were Catholic, but otherwise there wasn't any contact as far as I can remember. Then I came to England, and of course I realised very, very quickly that it was quite impossible to practice my Jewish faith in the Surrey countryside. And I was in a very strong agnostic setting. Even though Mrs Pease's father was rector of Aberdeen University, and you could not be rector without being a very good Presbyterian, she had rebelled against her family upbringing completely. It was the Darwin generation, you know."

M "Yes, I understand." (*He has spoken very factually about this loss of faith, but knowing him, I realise it cannot have been an altogether easy trip and I question whether he actually ever lost it as such. For one thing, he is a very spiritual person and he needs that dimension to his life. It is also different for a Jew to lose his faith, than, say, the average Anglican, because there is such a strong sense of national identity running through it. So much has been suffered for it and so many died because of it. Yet he is compelled to let it go along with all that goes with it. This is hard for an adult, so how much more must it have affected this sensitive boy who has been stripped of everything familiar. The only way to survive it would be to dissociate from it - at least for a time.)*

G "So the next real contact came through my studies. You can't study French Literature in depth without meeting Catholicism. I read François Mauriac - one novel after another. He also wrote a few plays. I came across one called 'Asmodée', which was based on Asmodeus. He was a legendary God who was supposed to lift the rooftops of people's houses to see what was going on. Mauriac's play was to have a profound effect on me and I did it – I directed it. Can we talk about that for a little bit because it's important?"

M "Yes, of course."

G "It's a profoundly Catholic play. Mauriac wrote his novels and plays in the Twenties and Thirties and they dealt with an aspect of Catholicism which I grasped very, very quickly. It was that sometimes you had to wade through mire in order to reach Grace. The only one in this country who dealt with this sort of thing was Graham Greene. I read him as well, of course, but it was Mauriac who left a profound impression because I wasn't ever quite certain that Graham Greene was a genuine Catholic."

M "No, no. I know what you mean."

G "He'd be horrified if he heard me say that, but particularly when my mother-in-law, who was a great reader – it was the one thing we had in common – didn't read Greene. She was a very, very traditional Catholic, you see. That opened my eyes a little bit. There was something there that wasn't percolating, but 'Asmodée', that play, it really captured me. Very briefly about the play – it's set on the estate of an aristocratic lady, who was left a widow at a permanent 39 or 40 – four children, and a tutor who was a failed seminarist – you know what I mean by that?"

M "Yes, I do."

G "Dangerous … very dangerous situation. What a collection! We never see the oldest boy - he is on an exchange with an English boy and Madame is expecting the English boy in return. He turns out to be 20! Ha, ha! He'd travelled through France with his ambassador father as a child and wondered why all the shutters were closed - and they are of course - wherever you go in France. He wondered what went on behind the shutters! This is where Asmodée comes in. He can lift the rooftops. Well, you can imagine what happens! Madame fell in love with the seminarist - the older woman, ha, ha! Another thing that captured me was the girl had just left convent school and she is full of compassion. That **compassion** turned to passion. You see that's very Catholic, isn't it, and I understood that completely."

M "Yes, it is."

G "She had a pash on the English boy. What a set up! In Act 4, it is the last day of the English boy's stay and he has been allowed out for a walk with the young girl for the first time. They have a wonderful scene together in the course of which the girl says 'I would have let you do anything'. Now, I did this play in '53 with the Oxford Theatre Players – very difficult thing to do for an English cast. I had two marvellous actors playing these two and I said to them, 'If you get the slightest giggle in this scene I shall never forgive you.' (*he means from the audience*) They didn't. They knew how to handle it - they were so convincing.

Then the last act – it was his last night and they were dressed up in evening wear. Madame has at last realised – she's giving the daughter to him as it were. She's stepping back, which is a deep, profound Catholic move. I loved the play, you can imagine. I began to get a profound insight into Catholicism through it, but perhaps it didn't help me in the long term. I discussed it fully with Eileen, of course, and she was a bit worried I was reading too much into it. Ha, ha! Why are you raising your eyes?"

M "I thought she might be!"

G "Yes! Ha, ha!"

M "Because I think that the day-to-day experience of Catholicism that one has isn't quite what you've got here."

G "No. I started with an ideal. Then you have to come down to your feet. You see, I came down with a wallop – that's why I'm mentioning all this. But I started off steeped in all the great French writers. The next one was Claudel – a profoundly Catholic writer. There's one play he wrote, 'La Partage de Midi', which is a personal statement and he forbade any public performance of it. It was his own life story – he came from a very profoundly Catholic family in the 1890s. After attending one of the big lycées in Paris he became an agnostic. There was such a division between church and state in France at that time, but at the age of 18 he had a miraculous conversion in Notre Dame Cathedral whilst hearing the choir sing on Christmas Day. Now I can understand that. Can you?"

M "Oh, yes."

G "I can **completely** understand it. When the Mass was over he went to confession. He came back to the faith and remained a devout Catholic for the rest of his life. Now, the play is very long, with only four characters - one woman and three men.

Jean-Louis Barrault, director of the Comédie-Française and also a very devout Catholic, wanted to do this play – he'd been begging Claudel to let him have it. There was no reason why he shouldn't have been given it, but old Claudel said, 'No, no, no.' In the end Barrault thought of a ploy.

He said, 'I'm going to choose the woman for this part and introduce her to Claudel, that'll do it!' (*a roar of laughter here at this very French manoeuvre*) And he **chose** ... (*He keeps me hanging on a thread with a long pause.*) now, I wonder if you've ever heard of her or seen her? She was Edwige Feuillère."

M "No, I'm sorry to disappoint, but I haven't."

G "Un moment ..." (*He gives a sultry chuckle and struggles to get up to find a book he wants to show me. At this point he is like a young man wanting to have his latest pin-up admired. He knows exactly where the book is and hands it to me triumphantly. There on the front cover is his idol.*)

M "Thank you. Oh, yes!"

G "She had **everything**! Beauty, grace – I should start with grace – la grâce, beauty, passion, the most wonderful voice – everything – but she was **Protestant**! (*His sudden use of bathos here makes us both helpless with laughter.*) Oh dear! You can look at her later on."

M "I will."

G "I had fallen hook, line and sinker! Eileen got so tired of hearing about her."

M "I bet she did." (*My tone is rather droll.*)

G "She wasn't the only one! My favourite actress in the Theatre Players said, 'If I hear that **bloody** woman's name again I'll ... (*He cannot finish for laughing. He slaps his thigh and simply roars till the tears start. He continues in a strained, high-pitched voice.*) I used to say, 'Now, Edwige would do this', 'Edwige would do that' and she'd say, 'If I hear that **bloody** woman's name again I'll resign!'"

M "I know the feeling!"

G "Well, Edwige, I simply adored. She was ideal for that part, you see – absolutely right. So Barrault took her with him and it worked. He agreed to bring the play up to date and it was a fantastic success in Paris in '48. Of course, I couldn't see it. So all this had a profound influence on me and I think it convinced Eileen that it would only be a matter of time before I converted, but that I must get over this idealism a bit first and get the reality. This was the preparatory stuff."

M "I understand. The seeds were sown back then."

G "Next thing was, many, many years later. We often talked about it. I had to explain to her.
'Now look, I still haven't eradicated my feeling of guilt. I can't do it yet – I'm not ready for it. I would take all that with me if I did it now.' (*thoughtful pause here*)
And in one of our many, many discussions about it she said, 'Don't wait too long. It might cause problems if you do.'
She meant, say, for a burial, if I died or something. It hadn't occurred to me – it was a very realistic viewpoint. I'd been up in the clouds a bit.

And whenever we were abroad, which was frequently, I always accompanied Eileen to Mass, but I couldn't do it in England. Well, the main reason was that Eileen and her mother went to their nearest church here where there was a very old priest.

Eileen did the flowers every week – she loved doing it. It emerged quite a bit later that what worried her, more than anything, was that, should I decide to convert, I would have to go to my local priest for instruction. She knew that it wouldn't work. He never had any converts – he was pre-Vatican II – he'd stood still – very stubborn."

M "I recognise the syndrome!"

G "Eileen was very, very concerned - how were we going to get over that one? That was going to be the stumbling block. I hadn't realised it till it happened. Well, after that kind of warning signal from Eileen about not leaving it too late, I thought I really must do something about it. We happened to be on holiday – a bachelor friend of mine – Bruce, the H.M.I Inspector – I told you about him earlier. He had taken a cottage in Cornwall and invited us to join him and his sister for a week. We were on Bodmin Moor, walking, and the two ladies went ahead of us. I cannot remember what made me do this, but I said to Bruce, 'What would you say if I decided to become a Catholic?' – just like that.
And he said, 'Eileen would be delighted and I would encourage you. I think you're ready.' That did it."

M "Was he Catholic too?"

G "No. He was a Presbyterian.
Then he said, 'Don't make a hasty decision. Now look, two years ago I made an inspection of Ampleforth School and I was most impressed with it. It's a great school. It's stood still a bit. Father Patrick wants to take it into the 21st century. They listened very carefully to my suggestions. Now, my advice would be to go on a retreat to Ampleforth.''
At that time Cardinal Hume was the abbot, and when he went to Westminster, Father Patrick, the Head, became the abbot. Bruce

said there was a meeting of minds that very rarely happens between the inspector and the school management

It was the best advice I could ever have. He arranged it for me – he still had quite a bit of influence there. I got a wonderful letter from Father Patrick and so I went to Ampleforth. I felt a lot of trepidation and excitement. They accommodated me in the monastery on the same floor as the abbot, Father Patrick.

Here I include passages from Gerard's article, 'In Praise of God'

The importance of the Psalms in the Jewish-Christian Tradition

King David, the 'Sweet Psalmist of Israel', was not to know that his praise songs would form the strongest bond between two apparently opposing beliefs: Judaism and Christianity. The fundamental theme of these lyrics - the love of God - succeeded in making a smooth passage from the oral tradition of ancient literature to our modern liturgy.

The Psalms were, however, far from my mind when, a few years ago, I arrived at Ampleforth Abbey for a retreat. So much depended on that visit. Was 'my wish' to be received into the Catholic Church, perhaps, 'father to the thought' of converting from Judaism to Christianity? Was I, emotionally and spiritually, ready to take such a step? Would I betray the memories of the many members of my family who had been forced to lay down lives for their faith in Auschwitz? All these questions created a turmoil in my mind as I approached Ampleforth from the narrow, winding Brandsby Road. And, suddenly, there lay the Abbey before me in all its formidable grandeur, reflected in a late summer afternoon sunlight.

Two hours later, after a warm and encouraging welcome, I attended Vespers with some awe and trepidation. This would be an unfamiliar part of liturgy. Imagine my surprise and delight when the words of the first Psalm brought instant recognition:
'Non nobis, Domine, non nobis, sed nomine tuo da gloriam'
(Not to us, O Lord, not to us, but to thy name give glory)
O, Israel, trust in the Lord - that is the message of this Psalm.

My mind went back to those turbulent years of a childhood spent in Nazi Germany preceding the destruction of the synagogues in 1938. Expelled from state schools we Jewish children were admitted to the rapidly diminishing number of orthodox Jewish schools. These 'safe havens' offered a rigorous, academic curriculum in the German classical mode alongside a strongly biased Jewish education in the Talmudic tradition. Latin and Hebrew were our staple diets.

And so it happened that a wise young Rabbi introduced us to the Psalms. As biblical instruction was considered to be an essential aid to faith, the simplicity of the Psalms made them particularly suitable for pupils in the middle range of their secondary education.

'O Lord, how many are my foes: many are rising against me.
Many are saying of me: there is no help for him in God.
But thou, O Lord, art a shield about me: my glory, and the lifter of my head.'

The message of the Psalms could have been a dangerous antidote to the poison that the Nazi propaganda machine poured into the minds and ears of all people living in Germany. But, as biblical instruction was banned from all German schools and the use of the Old Testament prohibited in the Christian churches, the Psalms ceased to have any influence except as a weapon with which to bait the Jews. On our way to and from school we could not help but be aware of the newspaper stands at every street corner displaying the obscene cartoons with which 'Der Sturmer' incited racial hatred. Misquoted captions from the Psalms mocked 'Yahweh saving his chosen people' and 'The apparent prosperity of the wicked in a world supposedly governed by an omnipotent and righteous God.'

Our own adolescent, developing scepticism did not altogether remain unaffected by these taunts. To see my Mother burst into tears almost daily at the wilful destruction of the family life she had so lovingly and painstakingly created forged an unforgettable image in my mind. We understood only too well what we read:

I have no food but tears: day and night and all day long men say to me, 'Where is your God?"

Where is our God indeed? Why do you forget us?

Our adolescent minds would have perfectly understood what it felt like to live in hope one moment and descend to the depths of despair the next. The calming voice of the Psalmist might have given us a timely lesson in true humility.

'But there is forgiveness with thee,
that thou mayest be feared.'

God is forgiving so we should look on others with forgiveness in our hearts.

'For with the Lord there is steadfast love
and with him is plenteous redemption.
And he will redeem Israel from all its iniquities.

How difficult it must have been for our parents and teachers to talk about 'God's grace' to us when it appeared as if that grace had been permanently withdrawn. It was only years later that I began to understand the meaning of these lines."

Gerard continues his account of his time at Ampleforth.

G "I was there for about four days and the Abbot saw me twice – wonderful. I can only describe it as 'wonderful'.
At one point he asked me, 'Have you ever experienced joy?'
When he asked that question I immediately thought of Wordsworth's poem about joy – there was a meeting of minds again. I told him about my fear, and all about my history. I had a wonderful reception there at Ampleforth and everything spoke to me. It was sheer bliss. I rang Eileen on the second night and I must have sounded full of enthusiasm and a little voice at the other end said, 'You are coming back, aren't you?' (*spontaneous mirth here*)
I said, 'Yes, darling, don't worry. I'll be back, but it might be a different Gerard returning.' (*His voice is still full of laughter.*)
I was."

M "Yes. I understand."

G "It's not easy to describe what had happened. I went to every function in those four days and it was so satisfying.
I came back and Eileen said, 'Well now you have to face the priest here.'
I've forgotten his name. He was over eighty already. It was very wrong of Birmingham diocese to leave him there all those years. There was no shaking of hands in the peace – Vatican II was completely ignored. The first Sunday after my Ampleforth, I went with Eileen to Mass. Afterwards, she went to the priest and told him what had happened. He said he would see me, but of course he hadn't had any converts for a long, long time and he didn't have any idea what to do. He was no teacher. He'd got hold of an American text book ..."

M "Ugh!"

G "Yes exactly."

M "They're awful. **Really awful!**"

G "Absolutely awful!"

M "If you can hold on to your desire to become a Catholic through one of those, it must be strong, because they are **so destructive** to one's sense of mystery."

G "So destructive. Well, he saw me every Tuesday, and assuming that I couldn't read for myself, he read every word of it – every chapter, week after week. He read it out to me, and he'd go 'woff, woff, woff, woff.' (*Here, Gerard takes off the Priest's reading voice – fast, squeaky and unintelligible!*)

M "I would have strangled him." (*From the wry look Gerard gives me I can only assume similar temptation crossed his mind too!*)

G "He had to use a microphone in Church and he made the mistake of hugging it – the worst mistake you can make of course – you pick up all the lisps and breaths and Eileen could never hear a word of what he was talking about. (*I am smiling here at the thought of Gerard itching to 'produce' the sermons and improve the priest's reading voice and whole teaching approach!*) Of course, that priest suited the older congregation who wanted to keep things as they were. I realised this was something I had to get through."

M "Yes. I can see that."

G "I remained very patient for six months and then Eileen asked me, 'Aren't you ready yet?'
'I don't know. He never says a word.'
So on a Sunday, Eileen dared to ask him if I was ready.
'Oh, no, no, no, no, no.'
The next session was about the Virgin Mary. He adored the V.M. which I've learned to be very suspicious of in some priests, who use it as a cover up for their lack of understanding of the female. I obviously did not exude enough enthusiasm. The next day I got a letter from him – I didn't keep it, but I can quote to you from it.
'You are as far from becoming a Catholic as you ever were. I cannot continue with the instruction.'
There never was any discussion of anything. There was no suggestion of where to go or what to do – just dismissed completely." (*His voice is stern here and I am pleased that he is able to express anger. Gerard needs handling with the utmost care and tact at this very difficult point in his spiritual life. This priest has no conception of Gerard's position and his outright rejection of him would have made a lesser soul say, 'a plague on*

both your houses!' and consign the two great faiths in his life to the bin.)

M "Oh, Gerard, I just don't know what to say. It's so disturbing."

G "I was very upset, of course. (*understatement of the millennium here*) It was such a rejection – a sheer rejection. Do you know what Eileen did? I found out sometime later.
She wrote to that priest and said, 'I shall in future continue to pray alongside my husband and I shall continue to support my church here financially, but I will not attend'.
Now that was a strength of mind, wasn't it?"

M "Yes, it was."

G "Wonderful. Absolutely wonderful. Now what happened on the day I got that letter was an absolute miracle. It was a bleak mid-March day – wet, half frosty – a terrible day – and that week I was looking after two lovely Labrador dogs for a very dear friend of mine who had a leg injury, so I took them out. You don't know Port Meadow, do you?"

M "No."

G "It's about a mile or two from here – it's a big open field going down to the river. On that day it was totally empty, of course. It was late afternoon and getting misty. I was a bit worried about the dogs. Suddenly, I saw a shape on the horizon... (*I am ready to hear anything at this point – the way things happen in Gerard's life, I would not be surprised to hear that it is God!*) I realised it was another dog, so I called the two dogs back. They were very good and they came straight back to me. But the other dog came bounding towards us! (*Could this be 'the hound of heaven'?*) It was another Labrador – a black one. I thought, 'I know that dog. Who's with him?'

With him was his master – a man called Alex Eaglestone. I knew him slightly. One of his great friends lived in the Banbury Road. We'd met once or twice. I knew he was a Catholic and he asked me how I was getting on – he knew I was under instruction.

I said, 'I'm not getting on,' and I told him.

Oh he was angry. Oh ...

He said, 'It's my birthday tonight and all the family are coming, so I can't do much tonight, but tomorrow evening I'd like you and Eileen to come to supper with us. By that time I will have rung the university chaplain, Father Roderick Strange.'

He was true to his word. The following morning I got a phone call from him – Father Rod was very interested and he wanted to see me. That night we went to supper and a very, very firm friendship started. Alas, he's no longer with us – he died over two years ago. I do miss him. I can't tell you how much I miss him. We became part of their family, you see."

M "Yes. Lovely the way that happened."

G "We had weekly meetings every Tuesday for a pub lunch. Lovely people, wonderful children. I do miss Alex so much. I miss Bruce too – entirely different – two entirely different men, but great friends. Anyway, I rang Father Rod. Just my luck – he was in his last term at Oxford. He saw me and gave me a very long and searching interview in the chaplaincy.

At the end of it he said, 'When do you want to be received? You're ready.'

I nearly collapsed! Ha, ha, ha! I couldn't answer him. He thought I could do with a little more instruction to undo some of the mess."

M "Yes, I'm sure."

G "He had, as an assistant, a very interesting man called Father Peter Cornwall, who was one of the first Anglican converts. Of course, it was like an Oxford tutorial – it was wonderful, absolutely wonderful."

M "This is one of those chances again, isn't it? You happen to be taking some dogs for a walk ..."

G "Exactly. Exactly."

M "And in comes the very person you need on the very day – not a week later, but in the very day just when you most needed it. Link, link, link."

G "Yes. And Alex was wonderful and Father Rod was wonderful too. I ended up having about six sessions with Father Peter, or more. I rang Eileen as soon as I got out of the chaplaincy and of course she was thrilled to bits. She got going **immediately** by booking a room at the Randolph Hotel for luncheon, following my reception. Alex became my sponsor and I was received in the chaplaincy. We'd been going there to Mass for some time and we went for several years. I'm glad she had a few years of me being a Catholic. And then Father Peter left Oxford and became the chaplain of Prior Park School. There's a sequel to that. When he went to Prior Park, his daughter, Liz, was just about to go into her last year in the 6th form at Oxford High School and, quite understandably, she didn't want to transfer her schooling at that juncture. At his farewell party in the chaplaincy, Father Peter said he was a bit worried because she still had not found anywhere to stay. Eileen and I looked at each other - didn't have to say anything.
Immediately Eileen said, 'Would she like to come to us?'
We had her for a year – lovely girl. Eileen and Liz were close – she's never forgotten Eileen, lovely girl. It was like having a daughter in the house, you see."

M "Yes, it must have been lovely."

G "It was a good ending. He lives in Bath now and we still write to each other."

I now include a tribute from Father Peter.

F.P "It was after I had become a Catholic and had been, in 1988, recycled as a priest in that Church, that I first met Gerard. A Church, that did not quite know what to do with a married priest, found me a niche, which involved being chaplain of Oxford Prison and an assistant at the University Catholic Chaplaincy where our good friend Fr. Rod Strange presided. One day he asked me to see if I could help Gerard on his journey towards the Catholic Church. It was clear that this was not an easy journey.

Gerard took seriously his Jewish roots. How could he fail to when so many of those closest to him had died in the Holocaust and when his own memories of them and of his own escape with his sister, were so vivid and painful? But he had married Eileen, a deeply committed and thoughtful Catholic, who had the greatest respect for his position. There was no conflict between them, nor eager jostling. Gerard had simply found his own way of becoming a Catholic fellow traveller. If he were to go further and become a Catholic he had to be able to be a Jewish Catholic. The question was, could he take that decisive step of being baptised when baptism had become such an emblem of disloyalty to that past? Gerard had had happy encounters with Catholic priests, especially Eileen's brother David, but also some unhappy ones. It seemed there were still those who were infected with the poison of anti-Semitism. In any case Gerard and I met and had long and relaxed conversations, which I certainly greatly valued. In the course of this we were able to explore how the Second Vatican Council had begun to open up ways in which Christians could reclaim their Jewish heritage and affirm their brothers and sisters who share these Abrahamic roots. So the time came when Gerard could make the move.

He was baptized in the Catholic Chaplaincy where he was to become a regular worshipper and a great supporter of its work. Despite moments of irritation with students who seemed ill prepared to read scripture in public, Gerard found this a good place to dig in and grow in a faith, which was always properly questioning and critical. It seemed to me that, as time went on, Gerard found both a new freedom to affirm his Jewish roots and the courage to face up to and talk about those painful memories. That does not mean that he always had a smooth ride. The embrace by the Vatican of a notorious Holocaust-denying bishop and the welcome back of the Tridentine rite for Good Friday with its offensive prayer for the conversion of the Jewish people, caused Gerard not only deep pain but also justified anger.

But all this, for me and for the family, was far more than following a personal spiritual journey. In Eileen and Gerard we had won new friends. Together we could share their passion for literature and the theatre. Hilary and I have particularly happy memories of attending one of Gerard's Shakespeare productions in Merton College gardens. It was I recall 'As You Like It' with another old friend Freddie Madden as Jacques. Such was the friendship that, when we had to move to Bath and our daughter Liz chose to stay behind in Oxford to complete her final year at the High School, we were delighted when Eileen and Gerard welcomed her to stay with them for that year and a very happy year it turned out to be. It was during Liz's time at Leeds University in 1996 that Eileen suddenly died. That was, of course, a devastating blow to Gerard, a wound which remains with him, but is lived with through faith. But it shocked us all – especially Liz who had found in Eileen both a gentle listener and a firm support."

Gerard takes up his own story again.

G. "I found my Catholicism in the end."

M "You had to fight for it."

G "Yes, I had to fight for it. It went right down to the depths, you see. I think I had to go through that. And I know that Eileen knows that I am still faithful. (*We both maintain a long, respectful silence, which Gerard breaks in the end quite abruptly.*)

Well, I made myself useful in the chaplaincy. The administrator there was a wonderful man called Vaughn Fowler, and he was one of our ex-R.A.F. heroes of the war. He flew a plane behind the enemy lines in Paris to rescue French Resistance people and bring them over here – a very brave man. He got cancer, poor man, and he came to me. I don't know why he came to me – I'm not an administrator. He needed someone to stand in for him – he thought he would come back after his operation. I had to say 'yes' – I couldn't leave him in the lurch. So I took over the administration of the chaplaincy though it was difficult – old building, students living there. – every day something happened that needed attention, but I did it for a long time until a new chaplain came. By that time Vaughn Fowler had died."

M "Is your prayer life important to you?"

G "Yes."

M. "I don't mean just once a week at Mass. Do you spend time in prayer at home?"

G "Oh yes, yes."

M "It seems to me all along you've had a very deep spiritual side to you, even if it was not always being expressed in terms of formal religion."

G "Yes, exactly. You're right. I think the idealism I went through in terms of French literature didn't hinder me at all."

M "No, not at all. Because surely, religion is about something 'other' that we link into and then it can come into our everyday life and affect it, obviously, but in its essence it has to be 'other'."

G "Yes. Exactly. And I began to read. As you go up the stairs here, all those books you see, they are all theology - spirituality. I read and read and read. And for Eileen it was a new Catholic life."

M "Yes, it would be a breath of fresh air."

G "She realised, once she started going to the Chaplaincy, what she had missed. And it also formed a new link with my brother-in-law. He's a wonderful priest."

We now hear from that 'wonderful priest', Msgr. David Bottrill.

M.D.B "I began my studies to become a priest very early on in my life, but I took four years off to be in the R.A.F in the middle of it. Immediately after the war I went back to it and the Bishop sent me out to a college in Spain. Travel was very difficult at that time and also the regime at the college was very monastic. We were only allowed to come home once in the six years of our course. My Father died while I was out there, but I did not get home.

Gerard and Father David picking grapes "fruit of the vine and work of human hands .."

I came home for a summer break in 1951 and I think by that time Eileen and Gerard were engaged. I met Gerard then, but I was not able to be with them when they married. So it wasn't until I came back in 1954 that I really got to know him. They came to my ordination in June of that year, and then I was sent to a lovely little town on the River Severn, Newtown, Montgomeryshire. This is where I got to know my brother-in-law in a much deeper way. As the community grew, the Parish Priest realised he needed a bigger church and he bought one of the mills and converted it. It seems incredible in this little town, but he founded a choir school. It was quite feasible because some of the exiled Polish families were resident in the area. The local people wanted their children to be educated as well at this wonderful new school, so he opened it up and it was an all-age school. To make ends meet, he ran a summer school for paying foreign pupils. Gerard and Eileen came to visit me there, and Gerard got on very well with the Parish Priest. It turned out that Gerard volunteered to help out with the teaching in the summer.

He was delighted to do it and came two or three years running. Of course he had a wonderful time with the students – he took them to Stratford among other places. They got on famously together and I got a chance to get to know Gerard well. Later on, when they bought the house in the Dordogne, I had some lovely summer breaks with them there."

M "I think you need to take a break now, Gerard. I am going to put the kettle on."

G "Yes, good." (*He closes his eyes and I make a very slow cup of tea whilst he is hopefully dreaming of his lovely wife and their time together as Catholics.*)

Scene 10

Enduring Love

Gerard indicates to me that he has more to say about Eileen, the love of his life. Knowing him, as I have come to do, it will not be a sentimental journey. There is a sense of urgency in his manner - there is something difficult about to come that he needs to get out. We are plunged at once into her sudden death.

G "Eileen's death was the first one I'd experienced first-hand ... it was unexpected. She had an operation for a heart bypass and the operation was technically successful, but she just wasn't strong enough to survive the dangerous moments that follow that sort of procedure. (*His voice is level and measured and has the weary tone that was there when speaking of the anguish of the past in Germany.*) And ... my brother-in-law, David, was here, fortunately. Eileen had arranged all that – I think she knew. (*long pause*) We got a call from the hospital, late, in the middle of the night ... David went in to see her. I couldn't. I wanted to remember her as I wanted to ... you know ... and I had some wonderful tributes, letters – very, very helpful to me. I gave vent to my grief. I was told not to harbour it, as it were."

M "Absolutely."

G "I just let it out, which was very, very good – very helpful. And in a way, that is part of a strength I've got, I think. I just remembered all the lovely times we had together, and there were so many. And I still do."

At this point we hear from Father David Bottrill again.

M.D.B "Gerard loved France. They always loved to go over there, and he always went to Mass with Eileen when they were there. Just before his conversion, he said nothing to Eileen and nothing to me, but he mentioned it to his friend Bruce, who very wisely sent him up to Ampleforth. He didn't say anything to us, except that he was going up there. When he came back he told us the joyful news that he wanted to be received. When the time came, we had a wonderful ceremony in the chaplaincy, in Oxford – I baptised him. We had a beautiful Mass and a little celebration in the hotel afterwards. From that day to this, he has practised his Faith and I think I can say quite categorically, that if it hadn't been for his Catholic Faith, I don't think he could have coped with Eileen's death.

Eileen and Gerard used to come down to the Presbytery to stay with me at Christmas and Easter. It's very peaceful here. We had some lovely times. When Eileen heard that she had to go into hospital, she asked me to come and stay with Gerard, so that's why I was up when she died. We had a call from the hospital to say that she was all right after the operation, followed by a second one to say that things were very serious. We were called to the hospital. Pat Chantry, a dear friend of Eileen's, came in with me to see her. Gerard came with us to the hospital, but he couldn't come in. It was just too much for him. He and Eileen were so close – they were an ideal couple."

Gerard is pleased for me to include here part of a tribute made to Eileen at her funeral by a curate friend.

Eileen Gould - In Memoriam 6th March 1997

Her language betrayed her heart - sensitive, attentive and present to others.
She spoke little, but said much by her being.
She possessed the sincerity of one who witnessed to the Truth.
With her, you never felt inadequate or worthless,
For she had no unrealistic expectations of you.

She never made demands.
Best of all, she was simple and transparent.
Single-minded, her choice was made.
The joy of her self-giving was radiated in peace.
And so her life has passed.
Like spring touching mysteriously its first rose,
She has touched our hearts with her giftedness.
Who was Eileen Gould?
Just one you have been privileged to know.

When he is ready, Gerard continues speaking about the time after his loss of his beloved wife.

G "One of her friends said so often that Eileen would have been thrilled if she knew how well I'd been coping."

M "Yes, yes. I'm sure."

G "Just take the cuisine, as an example. She was a splendid cook. It wasn't a question of not being allowed to do any cooking, but it didn't occur, you see. The cuisine, because of our French connections, meant a lot to both of us. And so I slotted in quite easily. I watched her and it was very, very important to both of us. And then, looking after the house – I see it as her house – and everything I do, I do for her still. With David as my brother-in-law too – he is always convinced that Eileen knows just what we're doing."

M "As does your Mother, I'm sure."

G "Yes, yes ... yes. (*This appears to be a new consideration for Gerard, and he ponders on it for quite some time.*)

M "When you were talking about Eileen's death, you said that you were able to express grief at this point. I was wondering, when you eventually got to hear about what happened to your family, were you able to grieve then?"

G "Um ... Um ... (*he nods his head*) But not fully."

M "And, of course, you did it totally unsupported, apart from the letters."

G "Yes, yes, yes, yes. And a bit of me from time to time asks whether I should go to Auschwitz. Eileen was always quite adamant, 'No!' In fact, she would not allow me to have anything to do with concentration camps, not any films or documentaries or anything like that. And she was right – absolutely right.
She said, 'Do you believe that there's still something of them there in Auschwitz?'"

M "Yes, precisely. I was going to say that too. They're not there."

G "No, they're not. And you don't want to admit that they're there."

M "No. And they were probably **never** there." (*I don't know now what makes me say this, but he likes it and echoes it.*)

G "Never there."

M "No, because they would have lifted themselves above it all."

G "Yes, yes."

M "I think Eileen was wise, wasn't she?"

G "Yes, very wise. Very wise indeed. Now occasionally, once or twice, I've seen the beginning of something on the television that Eileen would not have let me watch and I've switched it off."

M "Yes. She was wise, because it isn't a question of not wanting to know – you know all right."

G "Yes, I know everything that needs to be known. That's why I didn't even go back to Breslau, you see. I mean, what is the point? What is the point of that?"

M "But you did go back to Germany, of course, and that was good."

G "Yes, but not to Breslau."

M "You mentioned earlier that you went to Israel – that was a brave thing to do."

G "Yes. For years I just couldn't go. I have this terrible fear of flying. A dear friend of mine pointed out that we all have to die – but it's not that. I'm not really afraid of dying. I don't know what it is – it's irrational."

M "Perhaps it was because of the bombers coming over in the war. That seems a very rational response to me. It must have been absolutely terrifying for a young boy, especially one in your situation." (*Gerard is determined to be ruthlessly honest with himself here.*)

G "I suppose it was. I'd never thought of that. But I kept putting it off anyway, because I didn't want all my lovely English friends to know about my past. I was embarrassed about all the miseries. **I wanted to be accepted**. People would have turned on a pitiful expression. I want to be accepted! (*This is spoken in* *the present tense. He thumps his hand on the chair arm as he speaks.*) England made me, for which I am extremely grateful."

M "Gerard, I think **you** made you. Perhaps we just helped a bit along the way."

G "What I mean is, that without England, I would not have been able to follow my ... Anyway, I did it in the end about 1998. I travelled to Israel with Bruce Chalmers, my H.M.I friend – a charming, very sensitive person. We visited Yad Vashem – the Holocaust Museum. I had to, because I did not express my grief in any other way before. I could go as a Catholic. I left details of the family there. The last place we went to was the Children's Museum, which is a most extraordinary place. We went in – there was nobody else there – pitch dark in there – they put on, continuously, the voices of some of the children. (*I hear on the recording that I gasp here.*) And you know I lost a little nephew. It could have just happened – I'd be there and I would hear little Joachim, you see. There are unfinished pillars, left deliberately to show unfinished lives. Bruce burst into tears." (*After a long silence I decide to ask a question that is in keeping with the solemnity of the moment and which I know will not cause Gerard any problems in answering.*)

M "How do you feel about your own death, which for all of us is approaching, obviously?"

G "Ah, ah."

M "As we become older, we are more aware that it is closer."

G "Oh yes. I'm not afraid. I'm very thankful I've lived as long as I have. (*His voice is strong and clear and purposeful. There is a pause while he gathers his thoughts.*)

Margot and little Joachim

I think I'm ready." (*He says this in a very firm and matter of fact manner. I leave a tiny pause too to let him know that I took his remark seriously and understood it, before making my quip.*)

M "Not yet, you're not! You're finishing this first!" (*This gets the lovely laugh I wanted.*) Are you pleased with your life? Are you satisfied with what you've done?"

G "I've never ... that has never occurred to me."

M "I think you've been too busy living it!" (*He gives another little laugh here.*)

G "Yes, yes. I've just been very lucky. I'd never admit to being satisfied – that would be a bit smug."

M "Ok. Can I rephrase it. Do you feel complete – satisfied with your achievements?" (*After some consideration he replies.*)

G "No ... no, because there is always room for further development – there's always room for it."

M "You're not too old to learn?"

G "No, no, no, no."

M "That's good."

G "I mean things that upset me a bit now are very much to do with the use of the English language – the muttering that goes on in church, on television and even on stage. You see, English is such a rich language and it's being ruined." (*Although he speaks in deadly earnest here he laughs at this point, because he realizes that perhaps he sounds a little pompous. But he has no need to worry – I'm a kindred spirit!*)

M "I'm sorry! I've been smirking! I have exactly the same feelings and people get tired of me going on about it."

G "Yes, yes, I know." (*This is heartfelt on his part!*) You see I compare it with – if you were singing all this it would be very clear – singers haven't got this muttering problem. Dancers – I know they're not speaking, but they exercise a great skill and if they do a false move then it will soon be corrected – or if a singer sings a false note … Why is it that people speaking the language fall into this trap of ruining it?"

M "If we're shaving off the language all the time we are also, in a way, curtailing the richness of our emotions and our relationships. We're not expressing nuances."

G "Yes, yes, exactly. And I don't really know what 'blog' means and some of the new language and I'm not really interested in it. I like to know just some of the basic stuff a bit, because it's used daily, just in the way that I learnt the internet and using the computer. I'm not enthralled by the computer."

M "It's useful."

G "It's just useful, yes." (*There is a pause here, until we are inspired to go on in a new direction*)

M "Do you have any regrets?"

G "Yes, I regret very much that I wasn't able to give children to Eileen. She would have made a wonderful mother."

M "Um. (*There is a pause, as I wish to respect the seriousness of this last statement before we move on.*) Do you have any active regret? Is there anything you regret doing? In a way that was passive, because you couldn't help it."

G "Well, I wish I'd become a Catholic earlier. It would have helped Eileen particularly … (*There is a long pause here while he considers and this time I do not interrupt with another question. After a while he continues.*) And, of course, I regretted Eileen and I couldn't have had a little bit longer together."

M "Yes, of course, but that, again, is a passive regret."

G "Passive regret, yes, yes, yes."

M "A little while ago, in the kitchen, I popped a question for you to be thinking about. Do you remember I asked you if, having all this wealth of experience in your life, there were any pearls of wisdom or advice you might like to pass on to anyone who is younger than you."

G. "R.E.F. Do you know what that stands for? Respect, Enthusiasm and Fun! Do you want me to explain that? I don't think it needs it."

M "No, they can work it out for themselves! I remember reading that article in the New Statesman when the new editor, Jon Barton, was appointed in 1996. When asked which figures had an influence on him in his early years, do you remember his answer? – his father and you! He remembers you as Head of English when he was teaching in his first comprehensive school. You impressed him with the 'importance of whoopsiness at work'! Now, can you define this 'whoopsiness' for me?"

G "Well, you know – staff mustn't take themselves too seriously! Remember to have fun in life and when there are problems don't make them bigger than they are."

M "What do you think got you through the painful and difficult periods in your life? What actually got you through that time on the farm, because it was almost beyond human endurance? One would expect you to have come out of that extremely scarred and weird, and you didn't."

G "Well, oddly enough a sense of achievement. I was doing something totally alien to me, working on that farm with no idea what the future would bring."

M "But by then you had no input into your spirituality – it had been capped, so you couldn't draw on that for sustenance."

G "You remember all the mangel-wurzels I had to plant – endless rows of them. It didn't require any kind of intelligence so I set myself thinking tasks, which was a very good lesson. I lapsed into imaginary thinking and it sustained me -'reverie'. It's a skill I've never forgotten. On the operating table I redirect a play in detail and it's very soothing – very useful. Theatre stopped me being bitter – it refreshes me and absorbs me. Take 'Hamlet' for example – there are so many different layers ...

M "You are a very humble man, in a way, about your achievements which are amazing. The way you've affected positively so many people – you've stimulated so many people. You must know that and allow yourself to feel proud."

G "No, I honestly didn't realize the effect, say, my own love of theatre, for example, had. I mean like that ex-pupil that came up to me at the New College dinner. He was a scientist – he came on every school theatre outing I arranged and said it made all the difference to his life! Now that thrilled me enormously. Now that was a wonderful reward."

We now hear from the very prestigious actress, Margaret Tyzack, who confirms that Gerard's informed enthusiasm for drama is stimulating and inspiring not only to the young, but to those well experienced in the field.

M.T "My acquaintance with Gerard has only been brief, but I've had the pleasure of discussing Racine and Phèdre with him. I found his knowledge of the subject all encompassing, and was overwhelmed by his scholarship and by his passion for all aspects of the Theatre."

We now return to my interview with Gerard.

M "Well, Gerard, we have spoken very openly about 'the last things,' as it were. Is there anything you would like to add before we finish this section?"

At this point Gerard hands over something he has kept by him for me to read. It is in the form of a letter to Eileen, written on the first wedding anniversary after her death. It is a very intimate and deeply moving piece of writing. I query with him, not once but twice, as to whether he feels it should be included. The fact that it is here means that he is very sure about this.

Beyond the Final Silence

Today is our wedding anniversary. Today, forty-four years ago, we vowed that we would no longer be two but one flesh. You asked God's blessing to give you the grace of love and peace, a blessing that was amply fulfilled. I promised to put my trust in you and recognise that you were my equal and heir with me to the life of grace - except that in the pre-Vatican II year of 1952 those were not the exact words the Priest used. But we both perfectly well understood the meaning of the nuptial blessing that was given to us in the language of that period. In the spirit of the sacrament we joyfully gave ourselves to one another 'till death us do part.' Now death has parted us, and this is the first wedding anniversary without you. I wanted to place a bunch of sweet peas on the grave today, but the dry summer has not been kind to this delicate flower. You chose sweet peas for your wedding bouquet. They were your favourites. The mixture of pastel colours was very much to your taste. And how adorable you looked in that satin dress you designed yourself and that funny little cap perched jauntily on your head.

The morning post brought a card from our young friends, Ben and Harriet, who are spending an idyllic honeymoon in Umbria. The card shows part of Piero della Francesca's 'Polittico di Sant Antonio', from the panel in the church of the nuns of St. Anthony of Padua in Perugia. The angel making the annunciation against a background of white columns in ever diminishing perspective looks a real angel come straight from heaven. Seeing the name of Sant' Antonio reminds me of Fr. David, the kind young priest of the local church of St. Anthony of Padua, who gave you the sacrament of the sick.

Another kind young priest will be celebrating a private Mass for you and me this evening in the Chapel of St. Benet's. For our readings we have chosen Isaiah on 'the messianic banquet', Psalm 27 'In God's company there is no fear' and St. Paul to the Corinthians on 'The Resurrection:'

On this mountain he will remove the mourning veil covering all peoples, and the shroud enwrapping all nations, he will destroy death for ever.'

This mixture of prophecy and prayer about the divine banquet on Mount Zion to celebrate all the nations' final victory over death is so evocative.

'The Lord is my light and my salvation: whom need I fear?'

Oxford University's inscription is a reminder of the important role that education played in our lives.

'Death came through one man and in the same way the resurrection of the dead has come through one man.'

Paul's letters had a special meaning for you, didn't they? I shall never forget how you scrambled up the steep and rocky path on the Areopagus by the Acropolis to stand on the very spot where Paul preached to the Athenians. The descent from that barren rock could have been even more perilous so you simply sat on your bottom and slid down like a child tobogganing on a hill.

Was it Paul's unquestionable authority as both a pastor and a theologian, a wise man and a gifted teacher that meant so much to you? Did you feel that Paul, more than anyone else after Jesus Christ, set Christianity on its arduous but so very distinguished journey? Or was it, perhaps, Paul's Jewishness that attracted you? After all, you showed great courage in marrying a Jewish man. I cannot bring myself to write a 'Jew.' That word has set up so many ugly resonances in my mind and ear.

Deeply steeped in the Catholic faith as you were from birth, with a priest as your brother, you set your face against prejudice at a time when an unbridgeable gap separated Christianity from Judaism. In following your heart you remained true to yourself and unshaken in your faith. And we were overwhelmingly in love, weren't we? We still are. Nothing can destroy that great love we have for one another. There is not a single part of you that I do not know, remember and deeply cherish. You knew that, and you gave me ample evidence of your great love for me.

A few days ago I saw a wonderful production of Ibsen's late drama 'John Gabriel Borkman' at the National Theatre. In the middle act Ella Rentheim, played by Vanessa Redgrave, reminded her brother-in-law Borkman (Paul Scofield) of the great love that he aroused in her. '*You entered into my heart ... you kindled my love for you ... and then you killed it.*' She refers to a 'mysterious sin' mentioned in the Bible for which there is no forgiveness, 'the great unpardonable sin – it's the sin of killing love in a human creature.'

How such lines claw at one's heartstrings! One thinks with sorrow of all the couples in whose hearts love has been destroyed, just as one thanks God for the love that has remained steadfast and loyal.

Our friends understood the special love that bound us one to another, 'potent and enabling' as Robert put it. But it was Joanie who put it best of all to me:
'You were her husband and her child, her father and all her joy; and when you freely joined her in the faith which she had so long and so faithfully held, the circle, for her, was completed.'

I am sorry that my decision to follow you in your faith was not taken sooner, that we had only seven years in which to share this particular grace. It took me so long to be ready for such a momentous step. You knew how I shouldered a burden of guilt about the fate that befell so many members of my family, including my parents and a much loved sister.

They died for their faith in the cruellest of circumstances at Auschwitz. Why did I escape when nothing could be done to save them? Would it not be an act of betrayal on my part to deny my Jewish roots and become a Christian? These questions haunted me for decades.

Deep inside me I had been longing for some time to be received into the Catholic Church. I wanted to pray with you, to take Communion by your side, but how could I be assured that all this guilt would be exorcised and would not return to haunt me in fresh measure and drive a wedge between us? The New Testament had been a closed book to me. As a child I never had an opportunity to read it just as the Old Testament did not come into your spiritual orbit till much later in life. When I began to understand the continuity that existed between Judaism and Christianity, the scales fell from my eyes.

You knew, in your wisdom, that it would be only a matter of time before I would take the vital step and ask to be received into your Church. How delighted you were when Ampleforth Abbey offered me a retreat to discover whether I would be suited for the preparation that would lead to admission to the Catholic Church. My enthusiastic phone call after a few days at Ampleforth took you by surprise, and I remember the mock-anxious tone in your voice when you enquired: 'You are coming back, aren't you?'

Our disappointment at the unnecessary delay in the time schedule of my instruction period was, therefore, so much the greater. You feared that the parish priest would not be the best person to undertake this task. A pious man and popular with the elderly parishioners, who shared with him a nostalgia for the pre-Vatican II era of certainty, he was not at all happy with the new rite. When, after six months, nemesis struck and the priest did not feel able to complete the instruction, you showed tremendous courage.

Thanks to the timely intervention of a dear friend, I was warmly welcomed to another community. It was then that you decided to continue supporting your parish financially but to worship with me where I was to be received. You took such pleasure in sharing in the delights of my newly discovered faith and in the unexpected renewal of yours. Now this faith is gently teaching me how to cope with grief, when to yield and not resist it, when to recognise it as a creative force and give it free rein. I am much comforted by T.S.Eliot's lines from 'Four Quartets':

We die with the dying:
See, they depart, and we go with them.
We are born with the dead:
See, they return, and bring us back with them.

Fr. Don, in his homily to-night, will refer to the last lines in Graham Greene's novel 'Monsignor Quixote':

'My love continues to grow and develop ... in spite of the final separation and the final silence ... '

It's true. My love for you grows and develops just as I feel your loving presence within.

Gerard

Only silence can follow this deeply moving writing, but in true Gerard fashion, tomorrow we shall soar from this into the busy world of theatre.

Scene 11

A Passionate Affair

In this scene Gerard unashamedly reveals an affair of unbridled passion that overtook him very early on in his life. It is still driving him to this day. I think it was Augustine who pronounced that a man's self love dies one hour after his death. I think this will also prove true of Gerard's love affair with the theatre!

M "Now, you are going to talk about the theatre. Fire ahead!"

G "**Theatre and drama!** Ha, ha! Let's begin with my parents and German theatre between the wars. My parents took out an annual subscription to the city theatres. There were four of them in that league. The opera house was one – very old, very grand - **real** opera house. Then there was the Playhouse, built round the turn of the century. Now it was very, very German in a way. It was for musical comedies – what rubbish! It was very much a German/Viennese concoction and they had a permanent company specialising in it, believe it or not. They changed their programme every fortnight. And then there were two other playhouses for straight drama. By taking out a subscription, it meant that they went very frequently and it was considerably cheaper too.

Then my Mother had a wonderful idea. My nanny, Clara, decided she would like to stay on with us, even when her nanny functions were not needed so much. My Mother had this **brilliant** idea. Every Tuesday afternoon there was a matinee and she asked Clara if she would like to go and see one of these operettas. And 'Oh yes, yes!' – eyes glowed.
'Well, you may go, provided you take Günter with you!'
Ha, ha! So my Mother gave her this treat – and it was a treat."

M "Yes, you'd hardly be any trouble!"

G "We went every second Tuesday. (*And now Gerard places on stage the whole of the pre-war German theatre company performing a lively operetta.*) They were colourful and I saw a **huge** number of these operettas. Their chief quality was the music. The libretto was trite and rubbish – well, at the time I didn't think it was trite and rubbish. I was five or six years old. There was no afternoon school at that age. So we went, Clara and I, and she was thrilled to bits. I think whatever one can say about these operettas, they have a certain magic. And my goodness, they were well sung. They had an orchestra and a very glamorous array of permanent singers. You see, they had a company. I still remember some of their names, would you believe it?"

M "Yes, you have the ability to remember people way back in your past, who hardly can be said to have had a major effect on your life."

G "Yes. The leading soprano, Margit Suchy – glamorous! Ha, ha! And the leading tenor, Waldemar Frahm. I think he was a good deal older than he was intended to be! The leader of the company was a middle-aged man called Adolph Wiesner. He directed and played the father role in all the operettas. It was very light, but it was great for me and I'm sure that the seeds were sown. The next thing was I started to copy them, and, on days that we didn't go, I ran the company and did the whole lot! (*The thought of this gives us both a great deal of amusement.*)

M "Now, tell me how you went about that."

G "Oh, I just occupied a room and I wrote my own script."

M "But how was it performed? Did you play everybody?"

G "Yes, I played all the roles! (*We both indulge in raucous laughter here and we like it, so we go on a bit longer.*) And then, you see, I started going to school at five and a half, but that didn't spell an end to the Playhouse – there was no afternoon school. So I could **go** and continue going. One of my Mother's greatest friends – oh the maddening thing is I've forgotten her name ..."

M "I'm going to stop you just a minute, because I haven't quite finished with these plays you wrote at the tender age of five. What were they about?"

G "Oh, I followed very closely the script of the operettas – I **loved** 'The White Horse Inn' and there was one number in it called ... (*Here he breaks into a lovely 'la la' of the tune he remembers from so long ago.*) and I would interrupt myself and say, 'Come on! Come on! More voice!' (*Again, we laugh like sailors on pay night.*) Now my Mother's friend – oh what was her Christian name? Her surname was Baron. They had a girl called Lia."

M "Oh, your first girlfriend."

G "Yes. She was a girlfriend too. (*He says this in such a coy way it makes me smile. He sounds six again.*) My Mother was a great walker for exercise and every afternoon on a fine day we walked to the South Park, which was – oh I don't know how far it was – about one, two, three, four, five, six tram stops from our house. (*I can see him counting them in his mind's eye as he visualizes the streets of Breslau again all these decades later. He is reclaiming it and embracing it, as not only being part of his past, but also recognising that it was instrumental in shaping what he is today.*) So, quite a distance and the South Park was lovely – it had refreshments there and a pond. Lia's father was the resident director at the opera house, who takes over when the visiting director has departed.

Now, The Opera House had famous singers – mention Erna Sack to any opera lover. Lea's mother was in the chorus, so of course we got all the back-stage gossip – not just on stage, but offstage too. I was **lapping** it up! Opera was open on Sunday evening and very often that was when my Father's Lodge had a ladies' night with dinner and dance etc. So my Mother went to The Opera House to have a hairdo with the resident hairdresser there! Ha, ha! Yes, ha, ha, ha! She did curl her hair wonderfully, and of course I got free tickets for the opera now on Sunday afternoon."

Breslau Opera House in the early 20th Century

M "So how old were you then?"

G "Six or seven. You see, it was all professional theatre that I was involved in. And then the next stage was in '33, when everything came to a stop. For a short time the Jewish community was allowed, graciously, to have their own theatre. It didn't last long, I can assure you. One play I remember seeing has just been shown in London and it was a huge success – a Spanish play by Calderon called 'Life is a Dream'. Oh, one thing we could do was go into the gods at 'The Opera House' and Gerda was going out with Kurt at that time – he was a great music fan. They were told that they must take me. My Mother was very insistent, because she could see that I was showing more than just interest. By that time there'd been years of regular theatre going. So they had to take me and I saw 'Tosca' and 'Madame Butterfly.'"

M "How old were you at this time?"

G "I'd be about eleven."

M "And you were presumably interested in them?"

G "Oh fascinated! Then the next thing was that I formed my own company again. There was a boy, a bit younger than I was, who was **highly** talented – he was already doing professional work. He was Jewish, so it must have stopped.
My Mother said, 'Now if you are going to employ him, you must pay him. He's used to being paid!' Ha, ha!
'Oh, Mummy, Mummy, Mummy, what do I **dooooo**!'"(*The 'do' is drawn out and high-pitched. His voice is that of the young lad as he replays and reclaims this lovely bit of his life.*)

M "What did Mummy say?"

G "She said, 'You must give performances. We'll all pay.'
We had two rooms that were separated by velvet curtains - all done at home. It didn't last long."

M "So, you wrote your own thing?"

G "Yes, but I don't remember what – honestly – nothing very original."

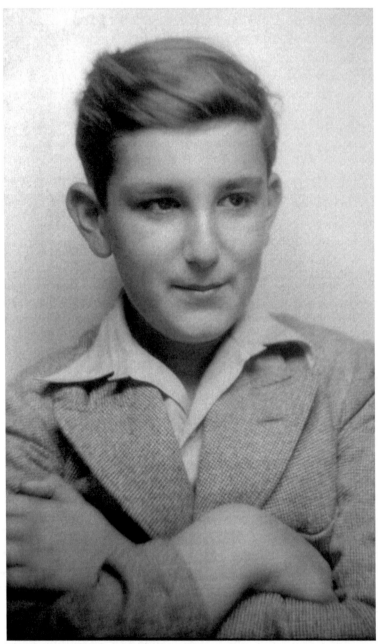

The Young Director aged 11 or 12

M "And who did you have playing alongside this boy?"

G "Anyone who wanted to come."

M "I see, you accepted anyone and then trained them up, as it were!" (*All these vivid thumb-nail sketches of people long-since dead seem to bring them back to life for a brief and beautiful moment as they appear on stage to charm us, before passing into the shadows again.*)

G "And then gradually school took over. Once I'd left that gymnasium it got much more interesting. There wasn't much theatre to enjoy. I didn't want to accuse my parents, but I wanted to keep reminding them.
'I haven't been to Berlin! I haven't been to Berlin! And now it's too late, I've never been to Berlin.' (*This is said in a very whiney voice.*) Berlin was a real theatre place, but of course as soon as the Jewish actors were stopped it became terribly dull. So that was the beginnings of my passion.

Now, there was a revival for me, that last year when I couldn't go out anywhere. I just read book after book after book. I read Shaw and Ibsen, and Strindberg – there they all were. That was the beginning of the second section. It proved very useful when I got to England of course, with Mr Pease who had Shaw as a regular friend."

M "It's such a shame you never met him, isn't it? It must have been tantalising."

G "I was a bit too late. If I'd been several years earlier I would have been all right, but by 39 he was in his eighties. Of course, there was no theatre-going at the Peases'. It started up again in '43 – right in the middle of the war. I had a week's holiday a year." (*he chuckles here*)

M "Wonderful! That's stretching it a bit!"

G "I spent it with my lovely Thorne family in Surrey. By that time, Mrs Pease had died. The holiday was always between hay-making and harvesting. There was always a gap of a week and ... hee! ... the farmer had to milk his own cows! Now, they were great theatre goers and we all went. I saw 'Watch on the Rhine'. I can't tell you who wrote it, but I can tell you who was in it. Do you remember Valerie Hobson? And there was a German Jewish actor who had fled to England, Anton Walbrook, and that was West End quality. It was a real eye-opener.

The Thorne's were very theatre orientated. Jennifer, the second daughter, had already had private drama lessons with the sister of Dame Sybil Thorndike. And I told you when we were talking about my farm years that I got involved with a youth club in Watlington."

M "Yes, I remember."

G "In the winter months I was finished with my duties by seven o'clock so I started a youth drama club. I started to direct. By that time I'd seen enough to have picked up some of the important things I needed to know about directing and I had an instinct – an **absolute** instinct for it. I didn't like acting, but of course young men, at that time, were very precious and they wanted me in the adult company.

There was an ex-actress – oh what was her name – a double-barrelled name, Archer, something Archer - who had evacuated to Watlington and her daughter was an actress. Mama wrote for daughter and I played a series of very, very inviting parts. I still had a very broad Germanic accent. Fortunately there had arrived in Watlington a woman called Elizabeth Jupp – all this was as if

it had just been made for me – ex-R.A.D.A, divorced, actress and now earning money as a youth club leader.
She took me on and said, 'I will eliminate your accent as far as we can.'
And I owe that to her. She directed! Ha, ha!
She said, 'We can't both direct. We need you as an actor.'
I thought, 'Oh blow! I want to direct, I want to direct!'(*I hear again the voice of the young boy who wanted to go to Berlin! We both laugh.*)
Isn't it extraordinary how the drama always sort of ..."

M "But your life always has been extraordinary hasn't it? One door after another opens without you doing anything at all."

G "Oh yes, quite extraordinary. And she really was an amazing woman. So the rest of the war was made tolerable by this job. She did sort of West End comedies written by Ivor Novello – rubbish, but it was fun! Meanwhile, Mrs ... oh, I nearly had it."

M "The other one - Mrs Something - Archer."

G "Yes. She was jealous that I'd gone off and done something else! Her theatre was a very different kind – it was very artistic, you see. Elizabeth Jupp's was West End – it was gayer! Ha, ha! Anyway, I tasted both. Then, of course, I went into my first school to teach – you already know that."

M "Yes."

G "Well, it didn't take me long to pick up the drama threads. I think my Head, Freddy, was beginning to despair of me – he thought I was a tip-top farm teacher! (*raucous laughter here at the absurdity of this*) I just got hold of pupils and we rehearsed in the lunch-hour. We did a concert sort of thing – various poems and little sketches and so on. (*There is a distinct feeling of déjà vu. We are back in pre-war Germany with the Goldstein*

household and there are the velvet curtains opening on a cast of
young people, directed by Mr Goldstein junior.) Freddy was in
seventh heaven.

'It's just what the school needed. It's exactly what we needed!'
It had quality, you see. (*There is no false modesty in Gerard. He*
*has not become **that** English! He would not have let it be*
performed if it did not reach his high standards and therefore it
was good, so he might as well say so.) I was thrilled to bits,
because I was beginning to despair – would my real talents ever
come out? With my £12 a month salary, things were not good.
But once I had unveiled my drama skills things changed for me.
And of course, the pupils were thrilled to bits. Then, as I told
you earlier, I entered them for a drama festival."

M "Yes, you mentioned that before and you didn't win, but you
kept moving up the pecking order!"

G "Yes. And the second year I was a bit more ambitious. We
were allowed fifty minutes and I took Shaw's 'St. Joan' just as
far as the fifty minutes would stretch, you see! I thought we'd
got enough to show their parents – they deserved to see it. You
must remember these were secondary modern pupils – some of
them just could not learn - so for them I did dance mimes with
music to a story that I invented so they didn't have to speak. It
was a family story of a Victorian father who was very stern with
his children. Marvellous! They just loved it!
Then I got more ambitious. I produced 'A boy with a Cart' and
any amount could play in the village chorus. You remember, I
mentioned it before."

M "Yes, and again you did amazingly well!"

G "Nobody does it now. At the same time the two villages
wanted me. Rotherfield Greys wanted me to act – oh dear, I
wanted to **direct**. Then Peppard got jealous and wanted me.
'We've got a lot of talent here. Will you come and direct?'"

Dance Mine at Rotherfield Peppard Secondary Modern School

M "And you said, 'Possibly! I might!'"

G "Ha, ha! No, no! I said '**Yes**!'

M "What a surprise! You jumped at it!" (*We grin at each other.*)

G "I chose 'The Browning Version'. I told you all about that before."

M "Yes, you did."

G "And we went from festival to festival to festival! Ha, ha!"

M "Yes, I remember, and you were beaten just at the end."

G "Oh, it was such fun! Then we did that with the second play 'Harlequinade'. This was not for a festival – this was how Rattigan presented it in the West End – the two plays together. After that, I left the area, because I went to teach at Wheatley."

M "Yes, I remember."

G "Now at the same time there was another piece of luck. At these festivals I met a brilliant director, a woman named Margarethe Bayliss. She was directing for Oxford's number one amateur company, The Oxford Theatre Players, where nearly always over half the members took professional training before going on into professional theatre. Among them was Ronnie Barker and Maggie Smith. The director himself was a young man who had deliberately chosen the coal mines for active service, so he could come back weekends and get them all rehearsing madly day and night. He went into training eventually, and Mrs Bayliss took over. She was a **superb** director and she had all the human skills as well. Her choice of plays was not all that ambitious, but her productions got these **glowing** reviews in the Oxford Times. She won the drama festivals and then, poor woman, she fell ill. She insisted that the committee would ask me.

Now this is interesting, I think. (*Gerard is aware at this point that he has been speaking without any interaction with me for a while and he wants to ensure that I am alert still!*) The moment I came to Oxford I joined the Theatre Players and they knew all about me. Do you know what the first thing was they made me do? (*I shake my head, not wanting to interrupt his flow.*) **Assistant stage management.** I had to learn from the bottom up!"

M "Oh! You must have been frustrated!"

G "That's professionalism! That's professionalism! Well then they were left in the lurch by poor Mrs Bayliss.
'You must ask Gerard Gould. There's nobody else,' she said.
They asked me what I wanted to do and I chose a Spanish comedy, 'The Romantic Young Lady'– good title.

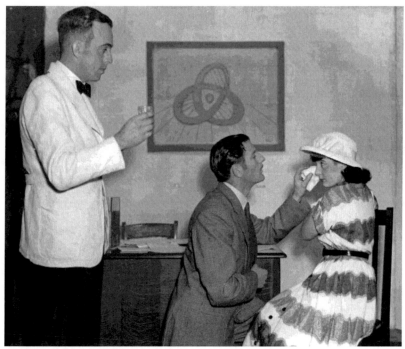

The Romantic Young Lady (1951)

And Eileen asked me to let her design the setting. They'd had a wonderful designer, Maggie Smith's brother, but he'd left. So they had Eileen and me!" (*He roars with laughter here.*)

M "What a combination!"

G "Yes! Oh it was a joy to do that! There was a girl in that company, Pauline Kershaw, who had done professional training at the Old Vic, but hadn't had enough confidence to dip her feet a bit further than the toes. She wouldn't come with me into 'The Romantic Young Lady'. Actually, there wasn't a part for her in that one – 'Watch out, watch out for that part to turn up!' I thought. We played in October, January, the drama festival early March and then another full production in April/May. It was a busy schedule. So the next production I wanted to make sure that Pauline could not resist taking the role I offered. She came in on 'Harlequinade'. They were all superb in that. Oh yes, Pauline came in on that and became a great friend. I didn't do the festival that year, because I was too busy."

M "I should think you were! It all sounds pretty manic to me!"

G "Yes, it was too much. I mean, I was teaching as well. The school hall wasn't completely finished, and I was planning an opening for the school.
Eileen was beginning to nudge me a little bit, and say, 'Look, all your time goes to the theatre players and you're here for the school!'
Ha, ha! So I had to do something really tip-top for the opening of the school hall! So we did!"

M "Of course! It goes without saying! When was the opening of the school hall?"

G "That was 1951. Well, then I did Shaw's 'You Never can Tell' for the spring production.

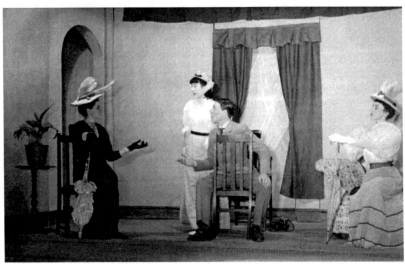

You Never Can Tell (1953)

I continued with The Theatre Players – I couldn't leave them. Once I got to Thame, I couldn't have done it, but Wheatley wasn't all that demanding."

M "Just going back to this 'tip-top opening' for the school hall – what did you do?"

G "It was a whole evening's programme, consisting of the dance mimes again for 4B, who couldn't learn lines. 4A did a short Shaw play. Then there was some dancing and a short play I'd written myself. The whole evening was a composition – a complete variety, which is the right thing to do to show off the big stage and lighting. (*I love the way he makes sure everyone is catered for – there is a great deal of compassion and loving care in his teaching. He is a teacher and pastor in one.*)

It's hard work doing this kind of thing – every item must be polished. Eileen designed the setting again – it was a complete cooperative, and, by doing it by class, it meant that I could use school time. And so I began to get more ambitious and finally, my farewell show to Wheatley – **wow**! Ha, ha! I did a Victorian melodrama and a short Molière, 'The Ridiculous Young Lady'. And I ended with a music hall! (*tremendous laughter here*) All in one evening!"

M "I bet it was tremendous!"

G "It was. Oh, yes, yes, yes, yes, yes. (*There is a pregnant pause here before he comes up with a droll, prize remark guaranteed to make me laugh.*) Not good for my successor."

M "We agreed that as theatre was going to be a big section we would do it in two parts? Shall we break here, as it seems a natural place to pause?"

G "Yes, and we shall begin again after lunch with my new post at Lord Williams's."

So we happily take our break and have a leisurely lunch together. Gerard chose to leave the section on drama until the end, so he could enjoy it, knowing that the rest of his journey was complete. I also suspect that quite early on he realised we would be able to get a good ending out of it!

Scene 12

Passion Abounding

The scene is Lord Williams's School, 1957. Gerard is eager to reveal more about his passionate affair with drama. The stage is set for a grand pageant.

M "Now, you are starting up drama at LWS."

G "Yes. When I left Wheatley, I had to start all over again at Thame! There wasn't an indoor stage, only the open-air stage the boys had built themselves. Oh dear, dear, dear. Now you remember at my interview, we talked all about drama and in the course of that the Head said, 'I love the 'Merry Wives of Windsor'.' So I made a mental note – he was already talking about, 'when you're here'. I knew he was going to take me. Ha, ha!

Then he came out with a real cri de coeur, 'I've always wanted to play Mistress Quickly!'
But by the time I came to do it, he was leaving to take up another post. Nick Woolfrey was the star at that time – tall, very handsome, lovely voice, slim.
People were asking, 'How's he going to play Falstaff?'
'Oh, you wait and see – he's got a voice for it, he's got the Falstaffian voice.'
He was **superb**. He was **absolutely superb**. I got the costumes from the Old Vic." (*This is thrown out in a dead pan sort of way as if it was nothing in particular.*)

M "Oh sure, so you just rang them up and they said 'yes'."

G "Ha, ha! I went up to see them!"

M "Did they know you?"

G "No."

M "Gerard, you've got audacity!"

G "They'd done the play, you see. As soon as I saw those costumes I knew they were right – they were superb. I mean if you're going to do an open-air thing, you need something for the audience to look at." (*I've been chuckling throughout this last bit.*)

M "How did you have the gall just to walk in there and say, 'I want some costumes for a school play,' and expect them to hand them over just like that? They don't do that sort of thing!"

G "They did with me!" (*And of course we both enjoy the joke tremendously and at length!*) Ah! Dear, dear, dear! Oh, it was fun! They all wanted to be in it. It was a great success. My only quarrel with the boys at Thame was that they were beggars at learning lines. I'd never known anything like that. I was used to people learning lines, and when I said, '**scripts away**', scripts were away! But not at Thame – so I read the riot act.
I said, 'Look, I shall stop directing until you've learnt your lines. I'm not going to waste my time here.'
Now, Nick Woolfrey, who saw himself as a bit of a leader of the company, piped up, 'Oh we still hold the scripts on the dress rehearsal, Sir!'
'**Not with me you won't!**'
'And we still get a lot of prompts on the first night – nobody comes to the first night!'
'**With me they will.**'
Anyway, I saw to it, we had an absolutely full house. I had a following in Oxford and they all came."

Here the man Nick Woolfrey is, as ever, unable to resist answering 'Sir' back! He takes his place centre stage for a moment.

N.W "Here are my thoughts on a teacher extraordinaire!
Gerard joined LWS in September 1956, when I was just beginning my second year in the Sixth Form. I was a fairly relaxed boy at this stage in my development. I rarely felt 'under pressure' – never from my parents, and rarely from any master in the school. My reports clearly indicated that I was a very 'average' student. I still had no idea what I wanted to do with my life. I knew that National Service was on the horizon, so I reckoned that I had two years then, in which to find a solution to the problem of a life's career. There was no pressure.

But Gerard's arrival changed all that! From my point of view, he was the 'original' Mr Motivator! His approach to teaching was different from anything that I'd come into contact with before. He talked to me face-to-face. He seemed genuinely interested in knowing about me, what interested me, what made me tick, and he fed me with a wide range of 'modern' books – they were certainly modern books that hadn't hit our library as yet! - books by Françoise Sagan, Iris Murdoch and Wilson's 'The Outsider'. Their characters exposed their innermost thoughts, their fantasies – they even talked about sex – and that was all unheard of in those days! What happened to our customary diet of 'Richard III' and 'Ivanhoe', Biggles and Gunga Din? In the years BG (before Gerard), young men's behaviour in the big wide world had been largely governed by Rudyard Kipling's poem 'If', and, possibly, your father's younger, ne'er-do-well brother, while you both lounged in deck chairs in the garden on a hot summer's afternoon. These new writers gave me, if not all of us, a different perception of what went on beyond the confines of a boarding school.

I don't want to simplify what Gerard did for me and the other boys he taught. In fact, I could not do that if I tried. Gerard had an enormous natural skill as a teacher. In 1956, he was in his early thirties, but, even to me, it was clear that he had knowledge, experience and a maturity that belied his years, and I was impressed. I wanted to learn from him, and that really wasn't difficult - even for a clot like me who had a natural in-built truculence, which, because of my immaturity, always had a habit of surfacing at the wrong time. But nothing fazed Gerard; he just momentarily adjusted his approach, and carried on teaching me as if nothing had happened. He was a wonderful communicator. As time went on, I quickly learnt that the problems were never his. They were mine. I just had to grow up – and, of course, I did – eventually.

Gerard's style was deceptively soft and accommodating, but those who were taught by him soon came to learn that this man invariably won in the end! If he didn't, it was your loss. He was just as tough as the next man, and probably more so, but he was clever enough to hide it. If he wanted me to complete a book before tomorrow, and be prepared to discuss it at length the next morning, then I soon got to know that that deadline was not negotiable. Many a time I sat up in the library late into the night, and I quickly came to realise that that, too, was a privilege, and not an imposition.

The one subject that really whetted my appetite was Drama. I had acted in two or three school plays over the years, and although I enjoyed the experience, I never felt that I ever got involved with the character that I was supposed to be playing. I am sure that there was not that much difference between my Edgar in 'King Lear' and my King Claudius from 'Hamlet'. I was never led to think seriously about the character I was playing, until Gerard appeared on the scene that is. He got me to read a range of plays that went way beyond just Shakespeare and Moliere. He made me think about the way the author had constructed the play, the messages he had wanted to get across, and the part the characters played in making the work come to life. The following morning we would be talking about style, motives, relevance to the real world today (this is in the second half of the fifties, just ten years or so after WWII), the characters, their personalities, their motivations, their hidden agendas, and, of course, all about the author. For me, it was exciting.

Gerard had no time for superficiality, and banality and amateurism were never in **his** vocabulary. He was on a mission, and he had no time to waste. He always came to our lessons well prepared, and although he seemed to get through a fairly big agenda, he deliberately varied the speed at which we moved. One minute he would discuss something at considerable depth, probably to make sure that I had thoroughly understood the issues, and then the next moment he'd moved on with several asides: 'You should look at that relationship again', or 'I don't think that you fully understood what was happening in that section. Try and find time to read it again.' He constantly pushed the responsibility for my learning on to me, and I enjoyed that. That's probably one of the marks of a gifted teacher: motivate, delegate and move on.

So, in a matter of a few weeks, Gerard had given me a metaphorical kick up the pants, but without any trace of violence! I was suddenly coming alive. There was much more colour, more dimensions, more passion in my world, and I was enjoying the process of learning. My horizons were widening by the moment. That year – 1957 – he gave me the part of John Falstaff in 'The Merry Wives of Windsor', and, this time, I really enjoyed the whole experience – and I think that the rest of the cast did too.

Gerard raised our standards to a much higher level than anything we had experienced hitherto. He made us work harder, work

272

longer, and with much more professionalism than ever before. Learning with Gerard was hard work but it was also fun, and everyone involved seemed happy to run that extra mile. This occasion was also our first real opportunity to meet Gerard's wife – Eileen – who, as far as the partnership was concerned, was the practical force in the relationship. Eileen worked hard behind the scenes, and there was nothing she couldn't do with a screwdriver, or a pair of scissors. She could just as easily run up a costume for one of the cast, or if necessary, build the whole set, and, to my knowledge, she never once lost her cool, or her lovely elegance. Eileen was the perfect partner for Gerard. What he couldn't do, Eileen could; their skills were complementary.

Nick Woolfrey – a splendid Falstaff (1957)

In 1959, nearly two years after I'd left LWS, Gerard offered me the part of the Earl of Essex in 'The Lion and the Unicorn', which was planned as part of the school's Quatercentenary celebrations. I jumped at the part despite the fact that both Gerard and I could see some real logistical problems ahead by accepting the role. At the time, I was a second lieutenant in the Royal Artillery, miles away in Shropshire. In those days there were no motorways to speak of, my transport consisted of a 1932 Singer, whose lights had a tendency to suddenly give up on very dark nights, and whose brakes were notoriously unreliable - so rehearsals promised to be a bit of a nightmare. When I explained all that to Gerard, he just smiled benevolently, and said something to the effect that 'it doesn't matter, Nick, as long as you get to rehearsals on time!'

Gerard always had everything planned, and he forged ahead as expected, but, one day, he invited me to see a play at the New Theatre in Oxford called 'Eighty in the Shade'. The two stars of the play were Dame Sybil Thorndike and Sir Hugh Casson, and both of them were remarkable. It was a performance to remember, especially since at the time, they both appeared to be in their eighties! The power in Dame Sybil's voice was astonishing. But the point of the story was that it was a matinee performance, and, after the play had ended, Gerard and I went around to the back of the theatre to meet the great lady, and Sir Hugh Casson, who was her husband in real life. They welcomed us with great informality and infectious enthusiasm. Gerard then had the dubious pleasure of asking Dame Sybil whether she would consent to the school putting on 'The Lion and the Unicorn' for our Quatercentenary. Apparently, she was contracted to play the Queen. Needless to say, Gerard's good looks, and his Gallic charm (which he can put on at the drop of a hat) won the day, and we left the theatre with their very best wishes. At the time I wondered what Gerard would have done if she had denied permission; camped out in the foyer until they gave way? No! There was no Plan B. He knew that, on this occasion, at this time in Dame Sybil's life, she was never going to say 'No'."

274

As Nick Woolfrey leaves, another former pupil, Philip Quartermain, takes his turn to pay tribute to this much admired teacher.

P.Q "Gerard is one of those people that made a huge difference in my life and I owe a great deal to him. He was a very inspirational teacher. The school tradition tended to emphasize college entrance, particularly Oxford, and took great pride in the number of students that it had that went to Oxford. That was one of the things that Gerard did, and he must have identified me at some point as somebody who had that potential, although I didn't have much inkling of it.

One of the high points of the year for me was being in the school play, because it was an opportunity to do something together. The esprit de corps of being in a group of players was tremendous, and, in addition, we got to mix with the girls which was wonderful for us because I came from an all male family and I went to an all-male school. I felt terribly deprived, so the opportunity to meet girls was extremely valuable. I loved the plays. I think Gerard realised that I wasn't much of an actor so I got very small parts. Since I was a student of literature, he would give me parts like Hamlet's ghost, which consisted of declaiming fifty lines of Shakespearian couplets, not grand couplets, but Shakespearian verse that I could manage. I really appreciated being included.

We were always curious about Gerard's past. There were rumours. There was a little bit of information but not very much. We never really touched on this subject, but I understood that he was an immigrant and that he had grown up in Germany.

After leaving school in 1965 I went on a two month exchange to a German High school. I had no idea at the time that Gerard actually had been the one who had set up the exchange - I learnt this much later. So I owe that to him as well because going to Germany for a couple of months and mixing with German students was a tremendous cultural opportunity – very eye opening. Gerard shared this with me on my last visit to him. He was filling in some of the pieces about the past. He tells me that Brian Williams, who had been in the year ahead, had gone to Keble College to read English, and his tutor there was Dr. John Carey who was at that time a very young, up and coming don. He wrote to Gerard and said, "I'm going to St. John's now to take up a new post. Please send me some more of your students as I really enjoyed Brian". Gerard wrote back and arranged for me to go and meet Dr. Carey. This was in 1965 before I took my Oxford Entrance Exam. This introduction was extremely key in my history because Dr. Carey then knew about me, and, as a result I got admission to St. John's and got an exhibition. I owe so much to Gerard because that was my start in life. That gave me the sense that I had unlimited potential and I could do whatever I wanted to do.

Later, I lost touch with him. After my degree, I went off into my own world and didn't really think much about Gerard. My Mother, however, stayed in contact with him. I moved to the States in 1974, but came back periodically.

On one visit my Mother said, 'You know you really should go and see Mr Gould. Here is his address and phone number. He's living in exactly the same place in Banbury road in north Oxford'.

So I eventually did go back to see Gerard a few years ago, and now I've been back to see him two or three more times. I assure him that I am doing well and let him know that I am grateful for everything he has done for me – at least belatedly – and he seems not to mind."

Gerard now continues to speak about his early days at Thame and his 'taming of the crew'!

G "I thought I had to do something about this lack of application in the boys – I could not work in those circumstances. (*We see first-hand in this note how naughty some of the boys were! They were preparing for the 1959 tour of Germany with 'Twelfth Night' and did not want to go back to school for rehearsals in the holiday. It reads 'We the undersigned utterly and absolutely find it impossible to come to LWGS on Tuesday for a play rehearsal which Mr. Gould has ordered us to do.'*)

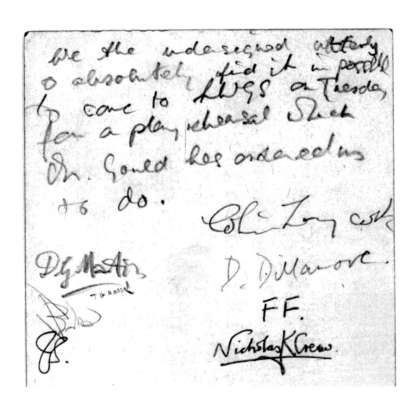

I hit on the idea of taking them away from home territory. At school, they were used to playing to domestic staff and parents and friends, who all loved them. They had to face an audience who didn't know them – the only thing to do. This is how the 'Twelfth Night' tour to Germany came about. It was a difficult thing to organise. The school year in those days did not begin in Thame until after Thame Fair, which was the third week in September. The tour had to be at least three weeks to make it worthwhile, so the first three weeks in September were excellent. It did what I wanted it to do – you see they had to face an audience who didn't know them – no fond grannies. I warned them we would get a new review everywhere we went – we did, and of course they couldn't read them! Ha, ha! **I could**! They were excellent, of course and it was wonderful publicity for the school. It didn't impress the new Head very much, though." (*There is bitter disappointment in his tone that he did not get the positive feedback he expected and needed.*)

Here I include an article Gerard wrote for the local paper.

900 TURN UP FOR 1st PERFORMANCE

Twelfth Night Tour

LORD WILLIAMS'S GRAMMAR SCHOOL

When the group consisting of 24 boys, the school matron, her niece and myself left Thame on the afternoon of September 1st on a pioneering Drama Tour of West German schools, no one realised how adventurous this journey would prove.

Our arrival in Bad Homburg on the second day was delayed by four hours as a result of unfortunate breakdowns on Belgian and German roads. Our hosts had meanwhile taken turns in awaiting the arrival of our coach. A rousing welcome greeted us at 10.30 p.m. and, with characteristic efficiency, the task of allotting our people to their respective hosts was quickly accomplished. To our great surprise most of us found ourselves accommodated in what can only be described as luxurious villas. Hospitality was on a truly, lavish scale. Our performance of Twelfth Night' was the main attraction of the annual School Fete. As this was the first occasion on which an English group had performed in the town, a great deal of publicity previous to our arrival resulted in an audience of about 900 people, including the Mayor and Councillors, parents, former members of the school and senior pupils.

The actors rose splendidly to this exacting occasion slowing down their tempo of speaking. Next day "Rave" notice appeared in the 'Frankfurter Neue Presse' praising particularly the clear diction of the principals. Two performances on one day were given to a large school in Frankfurt - again in a new assembly hall to large audiences. Terence Connor's interpretation of the Countess Olivia began to create a sensation with audiences unused to seeing - boy actors in female parts. In fact, queues outside dressing rooms became somewhat of a nuisance. As in, England, Nicholas Crew was highly praised for his excellently timed and controlled fooling as Sir Andrew Aguecheek.

Five Days in Munich

The group then spent 5 enjoyable days in Munich. Two performances were given to senior classes of Girls' High Schools - an experience very much enjoyed by both parties, especially as the girls had made a special study of the play and were most appreciative. A never-to-be-forgotten visit was paid to the famous Munich Hofbräuhaus with no dire consequences. (*This is a huge beer drinking hall where brass bands play traditional Bavarian music.*)

Countess Olivia caused a sensation with German audiences unused o seeing boy actors in female parts. 1959

The City Education Authority, whose guests we were in Munich, treated us to a luncheon party in a restaurant overlooking the Tegernsee and to a conducted sight-seeing tour of the city.

On to Frankfurt

Another day's journey along the endless autobahn brought us back to Frankfurt - this time to a mixed High School of 1400 pupils. The school authorities did not think their assembly hall good enough for our performance and had hired a large, brand-new theatre with electrically controlled curtain and every other up-to-date equipment. Unspoilt by success and by no means stale after so many performances, the boys gave a fine account of themselves that day. An invitation to return next year was extended, and even the choice of play was discussed. In the afternoon the school treated us to a coffee party in a shooting-lodge outside Frankfurt, and their hosts provided for our boys an entertaining Saturday evening at various house parties or jazz clubs.

Mayor Gives a Present

Two more performances were given before our return: one at Neuwied where the Mayor presented us with a beautifully bound and inscribed set of Shakespeare's plays in German and the other at Ahrweiler, a small town set in a large wine-growing area.

The tour was a tremendous success. Our boys gained an interesting insight into the school and family life of another nation, while once again the music of Shakespeare's verse and the skill of his comic inventions brought pleasure to thousands of people, this time not native to the Master's craft. In the 400th year of its existence, Lord Williams's School has worthily upheld its Elizabethan tradition.

G. Gould.
Extract from a review in one of the Oxford papers.

SCHOOL TAKING FINE "TWELFTH NIGHT" ABROAD
The production of Twelfth night by Lord Williams's Grammar School will be seen once more in Thame this evening before the school party leaves tomorrow to perform the play in Germany. Already the production has been tried out before the public at Rotherfield Greys on Friday and in the Unicorn Theatre at Abingdon on Saturday. The director, Gerard Gould, has demanded a high standard of his young players, and only in a few cases do they fall short of it.

Sir Toby Belch, Feste and Sir Andrew Aguecheek in 'Twelfth Night' (1959)

Mr Gould's company deserves, and I am confident will have, a successful and enjoyable tour.

282

M.P.H.

Positive feedback may have been lacking from the then Head, but there is an abundance of it from others. We hear from Liz Whitaker who worked alongside Gerard in his years at Thame.

L.W. "Gerard was the inspirational, visionary Head of English and Drama at Lord Williams's School when I was appointed under him as Head of English, Lower School, in 1972. He was an interesting and intriguing Head because he wasn't 'mainstream'. He didn't tread the known path but was innovative in his approach to teaching. We, his team of staff, learnt to follow his example in using drama to engage the minds and the feelings of the students.

Gerard's approach was to strive always for perfection; but his philosophy was, and is still, that whatever you do, do it with aplomb - even when it comes to milking cows! He expected high standards from staff and pupils alike. He said that teachers should know where they are going with their work and should aim to take their pupils with them, and to develop their creativity. He understood well that you get creativity and invention only if you open people's minds to possibilities, and then give them the knowledge and the skills to develop their talents. This was his consideration also when leading his English team.

When Gerard became an adviser for Oxfordshire, he set up annually an English Day for English teachers working in the Authority. Well known, lively authors, academics, and members of Her Majesty's Inspectorate responsible for English and the creative arts were invited to enthuse us with new ideas, recharging our educational batteries. Teachers can find themselves in a rut, but these days created so much energy that we were jolted out of it.

Pastorally, Gerard was excellent. He was neither judgmental nor sentimental, but had the ability to be dispassionate. Like a good stage director, he could stand back from a situation, assess its possibilities; and then guide staff and students in a new and enlightened scene. One would wish such skills to be evident in government educational departments."

It was not only teaching staff and pupils who felt such warmth and admiration for Gerard. We now hear from a parent and friend, Anne Vessey.

A.V "It is extremely difficult for me to convey what Gerard has meant to me and my family over the years. There is a chemistry, an affinity, that defies the spoken word.

It is around thirty-five years since I first heard that famous laugh. Our older son, Rupert, was attending the new pupils' evening at Lord Williams's School. I spun round and saw him flapping his arms up and down and thrusting his head forward and backward. When I had retrieved him, and asked what his conversation and gesticulation had been about, he explained that this master had asked him whether he liked drama. Rupert had replied that in his experience it was rubbish because all he had been asked to do was be a chicken, which involved a lot of flapping and nodding! Subsequently, Rupert won a prize for drama donated to the school for the most promising student in drama by no one other than Gerard himself. I would add that at that time, Gerard did not know that Rupert was our son! In time, that developed into a close relationship and Rupert became one of the many of the young people who became special to Gerard. Ben, our second son and Alice, our daughter, were also among the fortunate ones who had access to Gerard's special qualities and, dare I say, magic.

A little later I became the lucky person to take on some administrative work for Gerard. Every Monday morning from 9 until lunchtime, I typed out varying pieces of work on drama and the arts for him when he held the post of Adviser for Art and Drama to the Southern Arts.

Later when he was appointed Senior Adviser at the County Offices in Oxford, I followed him there and worked for him again. We had hilarious morning meetings before he went out on his 'touring' while I stayed behind carrying out the admin work.

Gerard has helped, supported and inspired a large number of people throughout his life. He is very dear to many, many people in all walks of life. They all share a part of him that is always generously given. It is hard to see him struggling with the degree of pain and the limiting effects of his immobility. However, he rarely allows himself any self pity and always tries to have time for any one in need. I hope that between us all we can, in some measure, portray the very precious person whose story we are trying to tell."

Gerard resumes his reminiscences, and amplifies what Nick Woolfrey has already told us about the Quatercentenary Performance.

G "In the same year that we went on tour, I had to do something else for Lord Williams's School's 400th Anniversary.– I did another first performance   - 'The Lion and the Unicorn'. Clemence Dane, the author, came to the first night and loved seeing it produced.

Here I include an excerpt from Gerard's reflections on his years at LWS.

"Before the end of the summer term we presented the world premiere of a play by the famous author Clemence

Dane. The great theatrical producer C.B. Cochran had commissioned 'The Lion and the Unicorn', the story of Queen Elizabeth's reign and, in particular, her passionate relationship with the young Earl of Essex, for the Festival of Britain, and he had already contracted the famous Dame Sybil Thorndike to play the Queen. Unfortunately, Cochran died before he could realise this project. Meanwhile, I had come across the play during a Drama Training Course. It captured my imagination, not least because some of the characters appearing in the play were connected with the School, as, for example, Lord Williams, our founder. This was too good to miss. Clemence Dane was thrilled that somebody had expressed an interest in the play and was most supportive, even turning up at rehearsals.

The cast list was enormous, and I recruited Sixth Form students, old boys, colleagues and their wives, and for Elizabeth a professional actress, with whom I had worked, agreed to join us. For Essex I persuaded Nick Woolfrey, who was such a memorable Falstaff, now on officer training in his conscription service, to come back. This meant intensive week-end rehearsals. Nick found it difficult to play the young toyboy, Essex, but the moment he could put on a beard and become the popular military commander, who dares oppose his Queen, he brought the intelligent, handsome, aristocratic young man to life. 'The Lion and the Unicorn' was a great community drama occasion. My wife Eileen designed the play; our lawns took on all sorts of colours with fabric printing drapery drying out. The Old Tamensians helped to finance this expensive enterprise, and, because it was a world premiere, critics from London expressed an interest."

Now follows a Review from 'The Tamensian', the school annual magazine.

'THE LION AND THE UNICORN'
By Clemence Dane

An occasion needs a fanfare. The trumpet blast, ringing out in an Elizabethan peal of silver, on the occasion of the four-hundredth anniversary of Lord Williams's School, was Mr Gerard Gould's production of 'The Lion and the Unicorn', by Clemence Dane. This was a first performance, a world premiere of a play about the first Elizabeth, performed by a School that was established when Elizabeth was queen.

'The Lion and the Unicorn' (1959)

The achievement in capturing the play at all for Oxfordshire was great. Nothing could have been more suitable for the occasion. The ancestors of people in and around Thame walked again on the stage in the flesh of the young players.

Scene after scene, excellently designed by Mrs Gould, and excellently produced, glittered before us, and, as they glittered, built up a story that is as British as the story of the foundation of the Grammar Schools. Statecraft and education, the local land around us, and all the high seas, seemed to mingle curiously, by association of ideas, as we watched the play and as we thought of all the struggles and circumstances that had resulted in our watching this particular play with these particular players on this particular occasion.

Perhaps the performance could never have equalled, in achievement, the actual capture of the play for Lord Williams's School. This capture had meant, on Mr Gerard Gould's part, waiting patiently over years. It meant the siege of agents' offices - waiting, arguing, planning. It meant the happy strategy of meeting the distinguished writer of the play, and of talking back-stage with Dame Sybil Thorndike and Sir Lewis Casson. Finally, it needed the courage to take the chance when it came, and then to rise to the occasion when this lion and this unicorn had been captured for this occasion.

In performance, the elements fought the play. Heat, humid heat, soggily invaded the hall of Wheatley Secondary Modern School. Blankets to keep us in theatrical darkness closed the heat in above the dripping, grease-painted heads of the players, and around the sweltering heads of the audience. Players and audiences had to fight! Still success was won. It was lucky that after such a battle for the play, that it was. Such an achievement, such an occasion, deserved success.

Oliver Wilkinson.

288

Gerard now continues.

G "There was no time for Oxford Theatre Players any more for me. I gave that up. There had been a bit of a split there – a trade union element had broken in and I can't work under trade union regulations. So I left them and with me came some of their best actors. It was unfortunate. But I couldn't have done much in any case. The school took up a lot of time – the drama work, taking them to the theatre – I loved it all. I was really totally involved in it. After this I produced 'Cyrano de Bergerac' in school. Tom Hassall made an excellent Cyrano."

Tom Hassall – an excellent Cyrano – with Mary Stokes (1961)

Here I include the extensive acting notes provided for Tom by Gerard to ensure that his performance was indeed 'excellent'. They show how much time, thought and care Gerard put into his productions.

CYRANO

On the credit side; you are building up to a strong performance of course. Cyrano must dominate the play throughout even when he is absent from the stage. You are holding yourself well (movements are still a bit stiff, stride a bit more, put your feet more firmly on the ground). Voice clear and resonant. You are also giving the impression (very important) that you are thinking of what you are saying. The pathos is convincing; you are making us believe that there is a tremendous battle raging within him.

Debits; Panache and more sheer devilry in eyes and general attack. More unashamed playing to the gallery - mock-heroism - facial expression. USE YOUR EYES. To help you, try to build up to a climax in every act somewhere.

ACT ONE: Superb command of the stage upon entrance, completely relaxed, bland and mischievous. Build up to the big speech with Valvert - make it big, panache your way through that speech. Do not underplay scene with Le Bret; if you reread it, you will find a lot is mock stuff - mocking himself, deprecating himself, because he cannot believe that anyone would ever take him for what he really is - "I love" is serious, most of the rest is spoken in a deprecatory tone - his thin skin is showing through every pore. Do not be too serious or sincere in this. Keep all this up your sleeve for the third act.

ACT TWO. Build up to big speech to Le Bret and the story telling. In the former TREMENDOUS PRIDE delivered flamboyantly (panache again) and story bit sheer comedy, sweat more, more visible forcible restraint. Be much more ill at ease with Roxane at first; you should play this scene as a grotesque lover dwindling into a sugar-daddy and let us see it. But show us that your moment of being alone with her is almost unbearable to you. You have looked forward to it so much that it is bound to be a flop. But again keep lyricism and sincerity up your sleeve.

ACT THREE: Build up to scene with Roxane. Now show us for the first time that we are dealing with a highly intelligent, imaginative poet. Let yourself be carried away by the atmosphere and let the voice do most of the work. More MUSIC in the lyrical scene. Later back to panache with de Guiche, but show your feeling when Roxane is married.

ACT POUR: The soldier, brave, loyal, reassuring (I am not too happy about your nose flap in the helmet).The big moment is when you are about to tell Roxane. Make more of it.

ACT FIVE: Here you must combine panache with poetry and sincerity and switch from one to the other. Remember to feel week and dizzy, make yourself. Think of flu feeling.

If you act with concentration and projection and remember to build up to the scenes mentioned and use every part of your body esp. eyes, you will give a really outstanding performance. I have every confidence you will. This is one of the great parts. Good luck - you have rehearsed conscientiously, now reap your harvest."

Mary Stuck, formerly Stokes, was imported from Holton Park, the sister school, to act at this time. She now takes her place on stage to share her fond memories of Gerard with us.

M.S "I remember a vital, energetic man, directing high quality school productions at Thame, demanding much from young actors in action, voice production and passion in performance. He introduced me, an immature and inexperienced seventeen year old, to drama, and to a community of boys – 'chemistry', his word! In 'Cyrano' 1961, I had no idea what I was doing, but Gerard conjured some spark. He introduced me to drama in Oxford and in so doing was responsible for Paul (now my husband) and me meeting in 'Blood Wedding' in 1963.

I remember his partnership with Eileen, her serenity and practicality providing the setting (and wonderful sets) for his imagination and drive.

I remember his productions for the Theatre Guild in Oxford, the meticulous notes in Gerard's script, finding a key word to get at the essence of a character, encouraging one to go further. All the frustrations and the laughter, people we encountered, friendships made, cold rehearsal rooms, rainy college gardens, and magic.

I think of him as educator, giving back. As a teacher, as Adviser for the county, as coach to all those young hopefuls.

I think of his love of literature and the way in which he communicates his enormous interest and knowledge with passion and humour.

I think of his espousal of England as his adoptive home; his gratitude for what he has received; his courage and generosity – personally to me in terms of time, advice and encouragement and to all those other individuals who have received the same hospitality.

I think of him chairing our coffee gatherings at his house, discussing theatre and dissecting plays and players.

I remember that he bore the loss of Eileen with great fortitude, the strength of a survivor as he described himself to a close friend.

I remember how he began to tell us the story of his youth and of his coming to England. I see and admire his fortitude now in the face of pain and decreasing mobility.

He has been in my life for almost fifty years. He is part of the fabric of our lives: mine, Paul's, Laura's and Helen's - a courageous, generous man to whom I am deeply grateful."

Gerard resumes his reminiscences about school productions.

G "Gradually, I gave up the open-air performances. The weather was unreliable and it's not theatre to me, open-air. We had a new hall and stage in the early 60s, so it meant I had a choice when to do the school play. As I told you, Nelson, the Head, had no time for drama. His attitude was, 'Get it over and done with so you stop disrupting the whole school!' Ha, ha! When we got the new hall, I took the October slot so we could start the new school year with it.
But meanwhile, I had brought drama in as a teaching method. The basis of that lay in improvisation. Now this was a very complex subject that was just beginning to come in. At that time

a big national survey was being done on the arts in schools and by that time we had an H.M.I. for drama called John Allen. I knew him and he asked me if I would like to become his chief assistant on this survey. My immediate answer was, 'Yes, but how?'

'Well, you've never had a sabbatical, have you?'

'No. That doesn't exist in our world!'

'Oh, I can arrange that.' He did. I had a sabbatical.

Now, the professional theatre by that time had become interested in setting up educational drama groups. But there was a big squabble – would it be better to have a separate team of professional actors who would only do work for young people, or ask the existing repertory companies - there were a lot of them at that time - to take on that work. Well, I didn't know the answer, and I thought it would make a wonderful topic for my sabbatical. John Allen agreed to it immediately. So I wrote round to all the companies that had been doing it and it was really half having a separate company and half their own. Coventry, Bristol, Manchester, Liverpool, Newcastle and Southampton – I toured round – I was on tour! (*We both find this tremendously funny!*) I **loved** being on tour! And everywhere I went, I was known as the man from London! Ha, ha! I had a wonderful time. It was quite hard work – I had to write up all my notes, etc. But it was very interesting. It was very difficult to come to a conclusion, but on the whole my sympathies were with – guess what."

M "Just have the one company."

G "Yes. Coventry was the first company to set up and they chose to have a separate company. I could see what was happening. There would be a division between professional theatre and educational drama. The latter became the step-child. Whereas, the whole policy at the Oxford Playhouse was ... you see, the director, Frank Houser, had all of these wonderful actors and he could have the pick of the bunch. They all had to do some work for young people. Can you imagine me taking young Ian McKellan, Judi Dench and Ian McShane out to schools in the wilds?"

M "You did?"

G "Yes! The local authority formed a policy for the arts and I was asked to administer it as part of my job. By this time I was already part-time adviser to help struggling teachers. I said to the Director of Education that I would do this on the understanding that it would be English as well – I did not want drama divorced from English. Now it has become divorced."

M "Yes, it has."

G "And it hasn't done either side any good. In some of the schools, particularly in private and public schools, the English department is still doing the school play, but they've employed a drama specialist, who is not interested in staging a play – they do drama as a subject. We were so lucky here. I agreed totally with Frank Hauser's policy – it worked. All these big names, I took them into schools. There was a sum of money involved – I could give them a little bit of money. It wasn't much, but actors look at every ten shillings! They are so badly paid. And they loved actually sitting in a circle of young people. It worked wonderfully - theatre's magic.
Frank had asked me if I would form a young Playhouse association, but only supporting. He didn't want it to turn into another youth theatre.
I said, 'It won't. If I do any more directing, I want to do it with adults'.
The Young Playhouse Association was an appreciation group and we met before the Saturday matinee. As many of the company as were willing to come turned up. It was very successful. It meant that the youngsters must see the play before

they came so they had something to talk about. There were about fourteen different productions a year. It was fascinating for me – I learnt so much. You never know what seeds were sown. Someone came up to me the other day at the reunion and told me that I'd changed his life. I was thrilled to bits by that. The chances are I didn't even teach him – he was Sciences, but he came on all the theatre outings."

Here, to prove just this, is a tribute from an old pupil, Ian Waite.

I.W. "I was a rather lost and unmotivated boarder at the school in the late 60s. Gerard Gould never taught me English, but for the first year of my French A Level course he taught the literature component. In that short year Gerard Gould changed my life. He opened my eyes to the meaning of civilisation and to the 'Consolation of Literature'. He would appreciate this nod to Boethius, I am sure. To that year under his wing, I owe my subsequent studies at the Warburg Institute, my academic and military career, and now, my current position at the European Commission.

Let me give you the measure of the man. I once mentioned to another teacher that I had never read anything by Dickens. The unhesitating response was to issue a detention for ignorance of a great writer. We all know what Gerard would have done in a similar situation. He would have lent me one of his personal editions of Dickens and explained why he believed that I should read it. And that is why he touched the lives of those who were taught by him and why he could turn the basest of lead into Gould's gold."

Gerard continues to speak about the far-reaching effects of the Youth Association.

"These were the Frank Hauser glory days! One of his great actresses was Barbara Jefford, and, when I met her a while back, she told me that Frank was very high in her estimation. We were so lucky for twenty years. We were so lucky to have him. Tish Francis, who ran the Playhouse for many years, told me that it was through me she became fired into theatre and the Young Playhouse Association."

Tish Francis, former co-director of the Oxford Playhouse, comes forward to make her tribute.

T.F. "There are two or three people without whom I wouldn't have ended up at the Playhouse – and Gerard is one of them. My taking on the job of Director – with Hedda Beeby – was very influenced by my past association and memories of going to the theatre as a teenager – and he was responsible for that – along with my drama teacher of course! It was as a member of Gerard's YPA that I had my first encounter with Pinter's work, so when Douglas Hodge asked if he could direct 'Dumb Waiter' and six other Pinter short plays, I couldn't refuse.

From the moment we were appointed, Gerard has been one of our / my "constants" – helping, introducing, challenging. He engineered a memorable fundraising evening when the wonderful Barbara Jefford did a reading of 'Chéri' with the then relatively unknown Ralph Fiennes.

Running a theatre like the Playhouse is a daily exercise in plate spinning. Gerard was there to make sure we kept our eyes on the most precious one – which of course is the performance. What a programme the theatre would have had if he been at the helm! It might have been challenging in terms of audience numbers but thrillingly European nevertheless.

I have about 18 of what must have been about 50 of his unsolicited critiques of one season – which however damning or praising would be awaited with eager anticipation. We might not always agree but what we share is a passion for the theatre and this one in particular. Gerard's knowledge about theatre, past and present, is encyclopaedic. He watches and responds to talent – particularly voice – which of course makes sense when you think of the resonance of his own! It is that voice – that laughter – that I would listen out for in the stalls – and then less eagerly in the foyer lest – as on some occasions he should bark a condemnation of the performance within close earshot of the great director!

At least once a year Hedda and I would have tea with Gerard to hear his appraisal of the programme in person and chat about our hopes for the future. Several never materialised – the idea of a European Theatre Festival being one, (which of course he could have programmed ten times over,) but some did, such as the Youth Theatre set up by the wonderful director, Frank Hauser. Years later I found out that a very elderly Frank was living in a nursing home in south London and I asked Gerard to come with me to visit him. Frank didn't register who I was, but, with Gerard there, they both animatedly reminisced about the Meadow Players!"

Gerard continues speaking about his work in Lord Williams's School.

G "Then drama began to become a really important subject at Lord Williams's. It became a timetabled subject and, while I was there, I jolly well made sure it was closely linked with English. At interviews, when I had to enlarge the English Department, the key question always was, 'Are you willing to do drama?' If they were not ... ! They were so much better teachers by doing drama – **that's** what I was looking for. The

298

new Head, Geoffrey Goodall, was totally for it and he continued to be supportive and appreciative in the years we worked together.

As is right and proper, Geoffrey Goodall is now given an opportunity to speak for himself!

G.G. "Gerard Gould was a remarkable Head of Drama and Head of English at Lord Williams' School, Thame, in the nineteen-fifties, sixties and seventies. Each year he would direct a school play of staggeringly high quality. These included three premieres by well established playwrights: viz. "The Lion and the Unicorn" by Clemence Dane; "Post Mortem" by Noel Coward (a world premiere with the author's full blessing) and "King Eric the 14th" by August Strindberg (English Premiere). He took several of his Shakespeare productions - received with acclaim on tours of German cities and schools. An astonishing number of his pupils have gone on to be successful, professional actors and actresses, and he has kept in touch with them all. At School he wrote and Blackwell's published a seminal book, entitled "Dramatic Involvement".

He was also a brilliant Head of English. His pupils regularly won Scholarships and Exhibitions to Oxford University Colleges. He gathered around him three outstanding young English teachers, who all became school authors in their own right, but while at LWS, they produced, under Gerard Gould's guidance, a four part series of textbooks, published by Macmillan, for UK schools called "Explore and Express". This series was taken up by hundreds of schools. It embodied Gerard's educational philosophy, namely that creative, original writing and thinking should be fostered intensively by a whole range of classroom activities, (long before the writings of Howard Gardiner and Daniel Goleman) which drew upon the pupils' vivid emotions, their imaginations and their ideas. This included wherever possible first-hand personal experiences, the highest quality literary and drama stimuli, active and sometimes unusual improvisations, extensive role play, followed by discussion (often heated), and finally essay, short story and/or poetry writing.

They say "you never forget a good teacher". None of Gerard's pupils ever forget him, especially those whose later lives he so deeply influenced. I count myself privileged to have been his friend and colleague. He is in my view a great man."

Gerard continues speaking about the support he had at this time from other staff members.

The Heads of History and French were equally enthusiastic. My physics college, Norman Lilley, gave me the practical support that I much needed! He generously put in a lot of time backstage, especially with the lighting and with producing excellent, professional photographs of our performances over the years."

At this point I ask Norman to put down his wires, screwdriver and camera and come out from behind the scenes.

N.L. "As soon as Gerard came to Thame he contacted our local builder, Harry Howland, to get a house built opposite mine – it's conveniently near school. Harry's wife, Betty, was one of the key players in the Thame Dramatic Players group, so there was a lot of affinity there. The Goulds were absolutely marvellous neighbours. As soon as Gerard walked into school he effectively took over not only the English, but drama as well. Gerard's reputation soared as far as schools' drama was concerned in the county. We had enormous successes and got so much pleasure out of his productions, most of which, to start with, were done out of doors.

I remember being roped in. Gerard was expert in what I call 'exploiting people's interests', as it were. I was involved in the electrical side of it, and one day Gerard and I went up to the Old Vic where we had a contact. They supplied us with their throw-out electrical lights – spotlights and floodlights that we started off with had actually come from the Old Vic!

Gerard was absolutely brilliant – literally – at picking out pupils with talent and at that point – pre 1971 when the first girls came – very clever in managing to get female leads from good schools around. As a colleague he was incredible – bubbling with enthusiasm. He was always remarkably, charmingly polite. He knew what he wanted and he got it, in the nicest way. He was persuasive with staff and pupils - and some of the boys he had taking part took some persuading - but once he got them there they were hooked. Very simply, they adored him. He got the disciple in the classroom and on stage by sheer dint of his personality, not through instilling boys with fear. He was respected. I think his voice too was part of it – it was a warm, loving type of voice.

He was a very private person. None of us in the school knew very much about his family history and it was years before I knew his original name. But this reserve did not stop him being great fun as a neighbour. I remember at Christmas, he and Eileen would come to us and he would fool around and smoke a cigarette just for fun. He'd pull faces and he didn't mind dressing up. There was a little bit of the born actor in him, but it didn't come out in public – he just brought it out in other people. He was always very interested in our three boys and very generous with them, whatever age they were. I have never seen an unpleasant side to Gerard and I have known him for over fifty years. Basically, I admire him."

Peter More, another colleague of Gerard's, who taught Geography, now takes his place on stage.

P.M. "I have known Gerard for 52 years. As well as being colleagues we have always been friends and my wife Audrey was very fond of Eileen. We all got on extremely well together. But in spite of our closeness, it was many years before Gerard told us anything about his early years – where he was born and what his original name was. He wasn't ready to follow up his family until a few years ago when he went to Israel.

I remember a time when Gerard opened up to me. It was in 1973. As a family we went to Czechoslovakia. We told him that we were going to Marienbad and he told us that he had been there as a child. He described some special biscuits or cakes he used to love and we bought some to bring back for him. When I gave them to him he nearly broke down. It was such a tangible reminder of a life that had been lost.

I remember the do at the Oxford Playhouse. Gerard was quite unaware. When he came into the theatre he was thunderstruck seeing the place full of people that he knew. It was a lovely moment. He let out one of his great loud giggles. That's one of his features that people remember – his laugh. He's got a very good sense of the ridiculous. No time for pomposity."

Gerard now recalls the time when he returned from his sabbatical.

G "During my sabbatical – while the cat's away – the others in the department got together and wrote an English textbook based on the school's method and presented me with it when I got back. I was delighted with it – I really was. This is what it should be. I had sown the seeds. I turned my back and they produced it – all three were Oxford academics and years ago they wouldn't have even dreamt of doing drama! And there they all were doing it. I was thrilled. I then began to get commissions to write.

My first book was a school book called 'Introducing Shakespeare'. Then I got commissions from Longmans who had new play versions coming out, which would be used in schools, not for acting, but as a reader. Having developed this drama method, it was meant to be done in the drama way. I did three or four for them. I wish I'd had time to do more writing, but you can't do it all."

M "No, you can't. You've crammed in about ten lifetimes' worth already! Tell me a bit more about this method – it seems quite revolutionary."

G "Oh, it was! I introduced a completely new and alien teaching method where you begin with a text – a scene from a play for example – and it's just words, words, words. Now I couldn't stand there in front of the class and do all the work myself – they wouldn't learn anything. So after having read the scene, you divide the class of thirty plus into groups and give them a few minutes to talk about it. You ask them to appoint a writer who logs what's difficult to understand, what they got out of it, what they thought was the theme of it. They then have to work out an improvisation on one of the themes. It could be very far removed from the original text, but it must follow the theme. This takes two weeks and then each group presents their improvisation to the rest of the class. Then there would be what I call 'interpretation' where they must get back nearer to the original text. They were improvising again, but closer to the text, using a few key words from it. The final thing is reading the original text again with much greater understanding. It was a method which worked **extremely** well."

M "And through your books it was used in other schools."

G "Yes! My best customer was Eton! There was a huge royalty from Eton! Ha, ha!"

I now include extensive excerpts from Gerard's article, 'What Drama Means to Me', because, although it was written decades ago, he is making some very astute points here that could well be extremely relevant for us today. The problems we are currently experiencing with bullying and violence amongst young people has to be addressed. Here, Gerard is spelling out a modus operandi that would help in the field of prevention as well as cure. My hope is that someone in drama education will have the sense to pick up on it.

What Drama Means to Me'

'To dialogues of business, love, or strife;
But it will not be long
'Ere this be thrown aside,
And with new joy and pride
The little actor cons another part;
Filling from time to time his 'humorous stage'
With all the Persons, down to palsied Age,
That Life brings with her in her equipage;
As if his whole vocation
Were endless imitation.'

These lines of Wordsworth's admirably sum up children's natural tendency to play. It is unfortunate that 'shades of the prison house' may later remove this natural tendency only to return, in adult life, sometimes in a form somewhat removed from reality - a desire to find some fulfilment in amateur drama.

Wordsworth's essential theory 'how Nature educates man' through the heightening of the senses, the arousing of feeling and the awakening of the intellect does not only refer to the 'Growth of a Poet's Mind.' It is basic to the growth and development of the Imagination and is everybody's birth right. I happen to believe that, through Drama, we can achieve such growth.

Drama means Action - doing. Its virtue in Education is that it helps children to feel and understand by doing rather than sitting and being passive, although LISTENING is important training.

Drama may begin with Imitation. Fair enough. The greatest minds have borrowed and imitated (cf. Shakespeare's plots). Imitation often implies close OBSERVATION. Small children imitate their elders. The Primary Teacher should never be afraid of letting her children imitate her or their parents, but she should watch for that extra bit of originality they may bring to their imitation. That is the moment to encourage. Thus Drama, even at that level, makes us AWARE of the uniqueness of man - that little bit which makes each one of us different from the other. There is a slightly worrying tendency for this quality to be lost in later, secondary group work.

What stimulates small children? One never-failing source, of course, is the STORY that is read to them. Let them act it out afterwards. That is how they will remember it.

I cannot see why MOVEMENT should not be accompanied by SPEECH if the children wish it so. It is unnatural to keep moving without speaking. MUSIC does not always act as a stimulus for exploratory work. To many imaginative children 'The Sorcerer's Apprentice' remains 'The Sorcerer's Apprentice' and nothing else. But certain objects that can be identified with famous deeds, achievements or stories can act as a stimulus. A piece of material can become a cloak for a king or the only garment for a beggar. Human skeleton bones can become all sorts of fascinating objects. Let them respond to a stimulus, become absorbed in the work and then share it with other people.

In fact, RESPONSE, ABSORPTION and COMMUNICATION are the three stages of dramatic involvement, at all levels. Begin by letting the class RESPOND to all sorts of sounds, sights, smells, tastes, and touch. Let them learn to guide a 'blind' person across space - empty and crowded spaces. Let them explore together confined spaces while undergoing some stress.

ABSORPTION levels will differ from child to child, from group to group. The more stimulating the source has been, the more absorbed the exploratory work will be and bring to each person greater awareness.

COMMUNICATION does not always mean showing one another's work to the rest of the form. This can be tedious and time-consuming. It means talking within your group, tolerating other people's view points, being able to explain simply what you are trying to do. By all means, and again if the class strongly wishes to do so, time may be found to let them see, occasionally, some of each other's work.

IMPROVISATION is the basis of such creative drama work. It allows children to discover fresh areas of experience hitherto undreamt of. Here, again, much depends on the context within which this work is done. Stanislavsky used improvisation to give his actors the opportunity of discovering new areas of experience within the parts allotted to them; Joan Littlewood, when producing the prison play 'The Quare Fellow', made her actors improvise for weeks in order to get the feel of confined prison life. In Drama lessons we are not concerned with training actors or preparing pupils for a performance. We use IMPROVISATION to give them an opportunity to freely explore their own world and their relationships with other people or the world of books they happen to be reading or other areas of school studies. For instance, a study of the Factory Acts in History would become much more relevant if the class were allowed to improvise scenes of child and woman-labour exploitation with a confrontation with the factory owners. French may become a much more relevant subject if the class is encouraged to create their own French 'days': a breakfast scene with the children rushing off to school and the parents trying to make them eat their breakfast in peace and reminding them of all their books and duties for the day; going shopping in the market; buying a record; going to the cinema etc,

Much criticism is levelled at IMPROVISATION, because the children's vocabulary is so poverty-stricken, and it does not seem to extend their command of language. It is true, of course, that much of the work of this kind we see is banal, trite, monosyllabic and would not stand up to a sceptical ear. However, if one remembers the hours and hours of often tedious silence that were spent just sitting passively in classrooms pretending to listen without ever having an opportunity of saying anything oneself, then, surely, this attempt to allow children to talk is an improvement. However, there are some measures that can and should be taken to make improvisation a worthwhile exercise for all concerned. So much, once again, depends on the 'sparking off' point. Go back to your sources. A very simple story by William Saroyan called 'And Man' about a boy who went for a walk before breakfast to sort things out for himself and thus caused the rest of his family to tease him and later played truant from school (a typical story about adolescence) caught the imagination of a third year secondary class of boys, many of whom could perfectly well identify themselves with the boy. They 'improvised' a number of family and school scenes, all based on this theme, and all of which had the authentic ring of truth about them. There was no trouble about inadequate vocabulary. If improvisation leads to banal work, isn't it often the result of banal or ill prepared sources?

Many senior pupils badly need some training in gaining confidence, poise and understanding of themselves. Drama should not be used as a therapy merely, but it is most valuable in helping young people to face the demands of life. For instance, the First Day at Work is a necessary and valuable theme. This could be started by asking a former pupil to come and talk to the class on his own experiences. This could lead to some improvisation work on the theme. 'What happens if I am asked to make tea for an entire office staff and take it to them?' A very interesting (and revealing scene) could be developed here. Some enterprising school may even invite a Works Official to see some of this work and discuss it sensibly with the class.

There is no reason why, in senior secondary classes, the study of Drama should not be allied to the more specialised subject of Theatre Arts. After all, the Theatre has proved, throughout centuries, one of the most enriching experiences for some people, and, surely, it is desirable that it should be made available to more people. This study can take various forms: it can take the form of studying decor, costumes through Art or its technical resources like lighting and sound. But, above all, one hopes that it will lead to greater appreciation of plays and acting.

In senior forms, students might be encouraged to arrange their own workshop sessions which could well be shared with other students, either from the same school, or from elsewhere. Such workshop sessions can be arranged in 'THEMES' ('Boy meets Girl') and can include rehearsed scenes from plays, improvisation dance dramas, mimes and even filmed material. Many larger schools possess their own film unit, and its use in drama is just beginning to be realised. These workshop sessions give a much-needed edge to some Drama work. Within such context, the school play or the polished performance of a play has its rôle.

In a school, where Drama plays a serious, educational function, it is noticeable that the pupils become more tolerant of and towards one another, less inhibited in their attitudes, more communicative and more articulate. That, surely, is sufficient justification for its existence in the curriculum.

Gerard is not all theory and no action. Back in those early days before anyone ever spoke about 'drama therapy,' he had the foresight and perception to realise that as well as being an excellent media for the development of awareness, imagination and understanding of the world, drama could also be a useful tool in the field of behaviour modification. When there was a spate of nasty bullying in the school, he produced a play which deals specifically with this issue, 'Unman, Wittering and Zigo'. It was performed before the whole school with very effective results.

A scene from 'Unman, Wittering and Zigo' (1969)

Gerard now talks about some exciting premieres that he produced in school.

G "Now, apart from doing Shakespeare plays at Lord Williams's School, I also pursued another road, which was directing plays by famous playwrights which they had not presented before in public for various reasons. And they would nearly always produce something of interest. (*'Something of interest' is quite an understatement, in that the next character to enter the stage and find himself in the spotlight is Noel Coward, who enjoys the moment immensely.*) I discovered that Noel Coward in 1930, which was the height of his theatre life, had written a play called 'Post Mortem', but would not allow a public performance of it.

M "Do you know why?"

G "Well, usually, when playwrights do this it's because they find, on reflection, that the work is – do you know the expression 'jejune'. (*I shake my head.*) 'Immature', when they've already made a success in a totally different direction. By 1930, Coward had already done 'Private Lives', 'Cavalcade' – all the great ones. I had a copy of 'Post Mortem'."

M "How did you get it?"

G "Oh, it was published in the collected works. It was a wartime edition and I reread it in 1962 or so. I thought it would do very well indeed for the top end of the school, so I wrote to Coward, not hoping in the slightest that he would break his oath, as it were – particularly as it was Coward. I did say in the letter that this play would have a lot of meaning for Sixth Form students. At the time I wrote to him, Coward felt that he'd been left behind and was no longer in vogue – we were hearing about Pinter, Osborne, etc. - all the modern movement in theatre. I had no immediate reply and I forgot all about it.

One morning I went to my pigeon-hole after morning assembly. There was a conspicuous blue envelope waiting for me.
I thought, 'Who writes to me at the school in blue envelopes?'
I opened the letter and looked at the wonderful signature of Lorn Loraine. It meant nothing to me, but suddenly the penny dropped.
I thought, 'This is Noel Coward's personal representative'.

The letter went something like this: 'Mr Coward will be willing to give you permission to present the first public performance of 'Post Mortem'.
The royalty fee was very low – deliberately low. I couldn't believe it! The world première of a Noel Coward ... (*pause for dramatic effect here and it is effectual – I gasp*) ... at Lord Williams's School."

M "What on earth possessed him to say 'yes'?"

G "I think I touched him by saying it would have a lot of meaning. I can imagine Lorn Loraine saying, 'You have nothing to lose.' I took the letter and ran along the corridor – long, long corridor at the end of which was the Headmaster's room. Knocked at the door! (*I am laughing during this lovely performance and he is lapping it up.*)
'Geoff, Geoff! We're going to have a world premiere at Lord Williams's!'
I'd told him earlier of course that I was writing to Coward, and he'd said, 'No hope'! Ha, ha!
I said, 'Geoff, **all** the critics will be descending on us.'
He was as thrilled as I was.

M "What aplomb you've got!"

G "The first scene of the play is in the trenches, 1917. A young lieutenant is wounded and dying, and during the waiting period he goes forward in time to 1930, not back. He visits family and friends twelve years later, his mother, his fiancée who is now one of the bright young things, and then his best friend who is utterly world weary. The most powerful scene in the play is the annual reunion dinner of those who survived in his unit. There are four officers at dinner and their younger selves stand behind them. He goes to visit them there. Wonderful scene! Wonderful! The last scene is back in the trenches and the young officer is dying. Good play, marvellous play. It was wonderful to do.

David Tomlinson, the actor, had a son at our school and when he heard about all this he went **dotty**.
'Oh, you must meet Coward! You must interview him! You must get publicity!' etc. etc.
He got hold of Coward – they were friends.
'Oh, all right,' I said. (*Gerard says this in the very begrudging way Coward himself might have answered.*)

In due time I got a call. At that time Coward was in London, at the Queen's Theatre, about to give his very last performance. I got a call for seven o'clock – curtain up at eight. I was terrified. I'd heard of Coward interviews – **he took charge**. (*It surprises me that Gerard makes this comment, given that, seemingly, he is full of confidence and can stand up for himself admirably.*)
I thought, 'Whatever can he say to me? He probably feels that I should be very grateful that I've been given permission.'

Well, Eileen came with me to give me moral support, but not into the theatre. I presented myself. I arrived ten minutes early and sat by the porter's lodge. On the dot of seven, a dapper little sun-tanned man in a very smart Italian summer suit turned up and took one look at me. 'Follow me.'

I followed him into dressing-room number one, which was a very long room and all along the length of one wall was a fixed table with mirror over. On the table was a complete array of potions and lotions. Then there was a chintzy little settee, which was positioned so that you looked into the mirror when you sat on it.

He said, 'Sit down... take no note of me.' Silence. (*Here, Gerard takes Coward off to a tee and chuckles.*) So I sat down – taking no note was more difficult than I'd imagined. He knew that perfectly well, and I was supposed to talk to the mirror if I said anything at all! I'd thought he would do all the talking, so I hadn't fully prepared. He started to strip. I wondered where he would stop. Well, he stopped at the briefest of briefs. There was no talking – complete silence, and I thought, 'Well, somebody must begin.'

So I did, and I could hear myself sounding like a young apprentice with his guru! Oh dear, I was so embarrassed and ill at ease.
I said something along the lines of, 'Thank you very much for giving us permission.'
'Yes.'
Whatever I said, was either 'yes' or 'no' or 'certainly not' in reply. It was totally different from what I'd expected.
I thought, 'How do I get out of here?' That's what was uppermost in my mind – it was useless, utterly useless. I just kept on nattering about the play and then it dawned on me that he'd forgotten about it – he couldn't remember. We were talking about something he'd written years ago and he'd never seen it acted, of course.
I thought, 'I must change these stupid questions that I'm asking'.

In the middle of all this there was the most explosive bellowing from him, '**DANNY, DANNY!**' In came a very hunky, hip-rolling personal servant/chauffeur kind of man, who took a good look at me!"

M "Oh, no! That would make you want to escape even quicker!"

G "He wanted his special make-ups got ready. I hadn't been there very long and I thought I couldn't just go like that, although he would probably be glad to be shot of me. I thought I must link it up with what's uppermost in his mind – the play he was doing that evening. I'd seen it, fortunately, and one of the characters in 'Post Mortem' was very similar to the one he was playing in the current play. It was the only time in the whole meeting that he came to life.
He swivelled round on his chair and said, 'Oh, do you think so?'
He had some degree of animation in his voice.
I thought, 'Well, I woke him up. That's enough now.'
I said, 'I really mustn't disturb you any longer', and I swept out.
I really couldn't get out quickly enough. Would you believe it!"

M "He was weird. He obviously had personality problems." (*It does not do Gerard any good to be rejected and snubbed – he had more than enough of that in Germany in his formative years.*)

G "There's a follow up – well, two follow ups. First of all, he wouldn't be able to come to the First Night, because as soon as that play was finished in London he was off on holiday to Jamaica. But we did get a lovely telegram from him on the first night – he remembered – very, very warm."

M "Strange, very strange. Have you still got it?"

G "No. Oh, wait a minute, it might be in the special folder."

M "Oh do try to find it –it's just the sort of thing to have in the book!" (*We have searched high and low for this, but it has not come to the light of day. What we do have is a letter that*

315

Coward sent to Norman Lilley to thank him for sending the original photographs he took of the first night.)

BLUE HARBOUR
PORT MARIA
JAMAICA
W.I.

27th February, 1967.

Dear Mr. Lilley,

Thank you so much for your letter

of the 31st. Also my particular thanks for

so kindly sending me your excellent photographs

which I was most interested to see.

All my good wishes.

Yours sincerely,

316

G "Now the other follow up was some years later. The Radio Times featured an article on an interview that somebody quite well known had had with Coward. It was word for word the same as mine, which reassured me. It wasn't just for me."

M "No, the man had problems."

G "The funny thing was David Tomlinson came back to me and reported that his friend Coward had said to him that Gerard Gould was a frightfully clever fellow! I thought I'd been stupid, utterly dumb and stupid! So it was extraordinary, wasn't it!"

M "Put it this way, Freud would have had a tremendous time with him!"

G "Well, on the day of the First Night, ITV came to the school and took quite a lengthy excerpt for that evening's news – I couldn't see it, because I was in the school, of course.

Gerard being interviewed about 'Post Mortem' for ITV News

It was shown during the main news – fame! All the critics came. First Night was all dress up in dinner jackets, as it was a Noel Coward first performance. The 'New Statesman' critic was hilarious!
He said, 'It was an extraordinary experience to sit in the school hall of Lord Williams's Grammar School, Thame, with all those stuffed shirts in dinner jackets and to have England railed against.'
It is. It's a play that attacks the government of that time."

M "Oh it's all so wonderful! You must be so pleased with yourself for having pulled it off!"

G "I pulled it off! I loved the play, I really did and David Tomlinson came in and rehearsed the scene with the fiancée for me, in a real West End fashion. The girl who played the fiancée, Meg Davis, became a well-known actress. It was a very successful production. It had a very good cast."

Review from the Guardian.

Coward revived by schoolboys

'Post Mortem' is an unknown play by Noel Coward, wilfully shelved since it was written in 1930 but taken down and acted by schoolboys last night as something of a revelation. What it reveals is a furiously unfamiliar Coward: looking back in blazing anger at what the 1914-18 World War hadn't taught people. It is written in a tremor of youthful indignation, and much overwritten in places. But its rage is authentic, the fury fresh, and the feeling in the writing very considerable.

318

Why it has been shelved for so long is a mystery: something to do, perhaps, with the author's reputation at the time for brittle light comedy, and the play also treads familiar ground. The debt to 'Journey's End' is admitted. All the same, it's very odd that such a vigorous piece should have been held back by its author for so long. And odder still perhaps that its first British production should be left to the Lord Williams's Grammar School at Thame, near Oxford.

The explanation is clear, however, when you see it. Their sincerity matches the author's. Professional gloss or polish would seem out of place amid so much personal indignation.

A scene from 'Post Mortem' (1966)

M "What an honour for those young people to be in it and for the school to have had all that publicity! Did you have girls in the school by then or did you have to import?"

G "No, we got them from our sister school. And I was right, you see – the play had a lot to say to sixth-formers. It was very powerful. There were quite a number of unperformed plays by well-known writers. It was a gold mine. 'The Lion and the Unicorn' - I mentioned that before - Oh! A Strindberg – 'Erik the Fourteenth' who was a Swedish King – a very powerful play. When we did that it was a British premiere. Again, it was very suitable for bright seniors. Nigel Cooke played an admirable King Erik.

Nigel Cooke at King Erik XIV (1973)

The parents weren't all that struck by that play though. **But I was!** Ha, ha! It all took a lot of time – it doesn't come down from the sky."

Review by Karen Bowles

ERIK THE FOURTEENTH

It is a wonder that August Strindberg's 'Erik the Fourteenth' has never before been seen on the English stage. Pupils of Lord Williams's Upper School, Thame, proved it to be a stimulating and captivating piece of theatre on their British premiere night, last Wednesday March 13.

The play outlines a part of Swedish history, but even more, it is a searching study of the human character. The play's producer, Mr Gerard Gould, who is head of the English and Drama department at the school, cast the play very well, with Nigel Cooke giving an outstanding performance as Erik the Fourteenth. Nigel's command of the part made the king's temperamental ways very real. He both moved and spoke well, and fine entrances made with great gusto.

The surprise opening of the play was most effective, with the assembled cast (with the exception of the king) in 'frozen' positions, being introduced by a narrator in modern day clothing (Ashley Goodall), complete with clipboard. It helpfully acquainted the audience with a large cast and the historic setting in which the play takes place. It also set off the first spark of excitement and expectation of what was to come - which was certainly fulfilled.

The scene changes themselves were extremely effective - with stage hands moving props to a background of music and a pale green light. The splendid costumes were provided by the Royal Shakespeare Company, and additional costumes were made by Allison Rogers.

This, the school's fourth premiere by a major playwright since 1959, was an undoubted success. As the producer, Gerard Gould, notes - the school is lucky indeed to have been able to present for the first time a work of such a major playwright as Strindberg. For they have the unique opportunity of exploring drama which a professional company could, or would not do, and cannot, therefore, be accused of being a mere copy of another production. Lord Williams's faced the challenge admirably, and with successful results.

We continue to talk about Gerard's productions at LWS.

M "When you decided to produce plays, what were your motives? Was it because you wanted to do them or because you wanted to get your pupils interested?"

G "Wanting to do it was secondary. The first point always was, 'Will this work?' But when it came to 'War and Peace', it was 'this **must** work!' Ha, ha! My motive was to give the boys an opportunity they wouldn't get otherwise. It goes back a long, long way as I told you."

322

A scene from 'War and Peace' (1964)

Gerard does not give particular mention to every play he produced during his time at LWS. To give a flavour of how prolific it was some reviews and pictures have been included here.

From the Oxford Times July 22nd 1960

A THAME SHREW OF QUALITY

Lord Williams's Grammar School, Thame, has acquired a growing reputation for its high dramatic quality. This reputation has, to a considerable extent, been helped by the polished direction of Mr Gerard Gould, the senior English master at the school.

323

This year's choice of play is 'The Taming of the Shrew', which it is hoped to present for at least one performance in the open-air. The hallmarks of Mr Gould's skill are stamped firmly upon the production. The grouping is decorative but meaningful, and the general pace is commendably brisk.

'The Taming of the Shrew' (1960)

Review of 'Antigone' and 'Scapin' from the Thame Gazette 23rd July 1958

Anouilh and Moliere at Lord Williams's School

It would be difficult to find two more different plays than Anouilh's 'Antigone' and Moliere's 'Les Fourberies de Scapin'. Farce is always an easier matter for boy actors than tragedy. Our sense of the ridiculous develops earlier than our understanding of the tragic, and it is only the exceptional boy that can appreciate the Agamemnon

324

whereas 'The Frogs' is everyone's cup of tea, from the sixth form to the first. It is the exception that tests the validity of the rule, however, and the rule obviously did not apply in the present case. Both plays were extremely well cast and in each play the cast knew exactly what they were doing, and had clearly been most admirably coached,

'Antigone' is an impressive play. The theme, a modern version of the ancient Greek legend, is the resistance of the individual to dictatorship - or, rather, to the Juggernaut of Establishment, or System, with its cry, 'No deviation'. Like the admirable costumes, the characters are stylized.

'Antigone' (1958)

Moliere's farce 'That Scamp Scapin' is terrific fun. It was brilliantly dressed and was a magnificent foil to 'Antigone.' The highlight of the play was undoubtedly the scene in which Scapin hides the unfortunate Geronte in a sack and acts the parts of assassin and defender alternately, with truly professional aplomb.

'That Scamp Scapin' (1958)

Oxford Times Review of 'Electra' and 'The Ridiculous Young Ladies' (1967)

Tragedy and farce join forces

A constant care for standards of achievement, and for the correct stylistic approach in presentation and performance, are unfailing attributes of Gerard Gould's productions at Lord Williams's Grammar School, Thame. These qualities are maintained in Mr Gould's direction. The experience of acting in two such plays, which represent (in tragic and comic form) two facets of the vanity of human wishes, gives pupils the means of imaginatively extending their appreciation of literature and life.

'Electra,' in Eric Spencer's warm-toned classical setting (very well-lit, by the way) and the costumes of Angela Fletcher, with their fine sense of both line and colour, is directed by Mr Could with a commendable insistence on clarity and, where possible, musicality of speech.

F.W.D.

I now ask Gerard about a play that he wrote himself.

M "You gave me the play you'd written yourself to read – the one about Rupert Brooke."

G "Oh, yes, my Rupert!"

M "Was it ever produced?"

G "Yes, yes it was, but not till after I'd retired. And the first night was in Rugby, Rupert's home ground! I remember, when I was interviewing for the part of Rupert, one lad came along with his parents and they stayed throughout the interview!"

M "Oh no! How embarrassing!"

G "Well, we were great friends. But I immediately thought, 'he's no Rupert.' He was nervous, and I was nervous!
I said to him, 'Look, are you coming home in the week at anytime?' I took him out to a pub lunch without the parents.

That was a much better do – I began to realise he had great charm, as Rupert had, and I thought I could work on him."

M "That's one of the many things I like about you, you have a flexible mind and you can see potential in others that might not be very obvious on first meeting."

He now launches into a very amusing anecdote about introducing this young gentleman to the lady playing his mother. This meeting took place at the boy's house, but the parents had the good sense to disappear this time.

G " Well, I made a big mistake – they had a large sitting room, like mine, and he sat one end and I planted myself next to my leading lady, Val, at the other. I don't know why I did that."

M "Because you enjoy sitting next to a lady, I expect!" (*He chuckles.*)

G "Yes! Yes! Anyway, he read badly – but that never worries me. So, it wasn't an easy morning at all. We got through it. I drove Val back ... silence in the car! I didn't speak. She didn't. I knew her so well. I knew damn well what she was thinking. We got almost home, when a little voice in the upper region piped up.
'Do you think he'll do?' (*He mimics her tone and we both explode with laughter!*)
I could have strangled her at that moment! So I stopped the car.
I said, 'Look, Val, it's like this ...'
Well, to cut a long story short, guess what happened?"

M "You had him, and he was very good."

G "Excellent – and Val fell for him, hook, line and sinker! Which is just what I wanted, of course, because Mrs Brooke was absolutely devoted to her son. That was a play and a half!"

We now hear from Hal Fowler, Gerard's Rupert.

H.F "Within moments of hearing the name, Gerard Gould, I find myself sporting a grin before a sea of happy memories come flooding in. It was the summer of 1987. I had just finished my first year at Guildford School of Acting before embarking on my first professional engagement, a Gerard Gould play for the Mayfly Theatre Company. 'Rupert My Son' is a play about the relationship between the poet, Rupert Brooke and his mother, written by Gerard to commemorate the birth of Brooke in 1887.

'Rupert My Son' was a serious play although I found myself the victim of uncontrollable corpsing. (*This is a theatrical term, meaning the spoiling of a scene by either forgetting lines or by uncontrollable laughing.*) Even thinking about it now brings tears to my eyes. Laughter had never been a problem for me before. In fact it always came perfectly naturally to me and the slightest thing would often set me off. Worse perhaps, I managed to find innuendo in everything and subsequently would often be in hysterics. It became a serious problem when such laughter met a serious play.

The scene was duologue with Rupert and girl. The setting was a riverbank and, if my memory serves, the dénouement was a kiss. So, there was enough to be dealing with without the added pressure of schoolboy giggles. In the scene Rupert talks about John Keats's love of a young Miss Brawne (Fanny) from whom he was separated when he left for Rome following advice from his doctors. The line went something like this – *he just couldn't go on without his dear little Fanny.* From the very first reading of the line I was on the floor. Trying to hold in the laughter was hopeless often resulting in bizarre noises akin to the symptoms of Tourettes. However, the innuendo had eluded Gerard and, when he questioned me about the corpse, I couldn't bring myself to confess to the cause of it. This had the effect of making the corpse worse and worse with each run-through until my only option was to come clean. Gerard howled with laughter when he realised what had been going through my mind since the start of rehearsals.

On a more serious note, I am eternally thankful to Gerard for his enthusiasm, the opportunities he gave to me as he has done for so many other young people with a passion and love for theatre."

We return now to speak about those later years.

M "When did you retire, Gerard?"

G "Well, after I left Lord Williams's there was the time I worked for the Local Authority. I finally retired from full time employment back in 1984, but just when I was about to retire completely the police gave me the public appeal they had put out for linguists to come in and interpret! Oxford was just beginning to get a lot of people with little or no English. I discussed it with Eileen, because I really wanted to do something useful and put my French and German to some use. They came to the house to give me a very stiff interview and that was it. My goodness, I got a lot of calls – mainly needing my French. I had to be ready anytime. A lot of the calls were at night, especially on Saturday night. I did that for twelve years or so."

M "Did you retire from directing too?"

G "Oh no! I directed quite a bit in those years after retirement. I think the last one was in 2004 – 'The Merchant of Venice' in the college gardens. " (*My maths being a bit slow, I leave it till later to work out that he is in his eighties at this point!*)

Here, Belinda Beasley takes the stage, to remember those days with fondness.

"I first met Gerard when I was brought in to produce Hamlet, which he directed for the Oxford Theatre Players. We became firm friends and I went on to work with him as Stage Manager on several productions which he directed for the Oxford Theatre Guild – 'Pygmalion' at the Oxford Playhouse in1998, 'Twelfth Night' in New College Gardens in 2000 and 'The Mysteries' at the Old Fire Station in 2002.

I chose to work with Gerard for many reasons, not least because he is such good company (I always love going to Gerard's for tea and a gossip), but also because he takes the business of directing theatre seriously. As I wanted to learn everything I could about directing, it was clear to me that I could learn more from Gerard than from anyone. Later, when I went on to direct shows myself, he gave me lots of useful, practical advice and insights but, more importantly perhaps, he encouraged and motivated me and made me feel that anything was possible. I now work full-time for Sheffield Theatres and I have Gerard to thank for giving me the courage to follow my dreams."

Here is a review of the 2000 production of 'Twelfth Night', which Gerard directed in the Fellows' Garden, New College.

'Twelfth Night': New College Garden

A chilly evening with more than a hint of rain, a lot of pollen in the air and the threat of biting insects – this was the first night of the City of Oxford Theatre Guild's production of 'Twelfth Night' in the garden of New College, where it runs until 15 July. But audiences who flock to 'summer' Shakespeare are a hardy lot, and with blankets for hire at £1 a go thoughtfully provided by the organisers and spiced wine available in the interval, we all had a thoroughly good time.

Under Gerard Gould's direction, this is a 'Twelfth Night' in traditional style, set in an intimate corner of the garden which is well endowed with trees to help the wicked purposes of Sir Toby Belch and friends. In the absence of staging, a creative use of music and costume results in a pleasantly harmonious and unified production, which begins and ends with the whole cast joining in singing Feste's songs. Quite apart from their other strengths, these actors would make a very acceptable choral group.

The cast is predominantly young, and of high quality, evidenced by the fact that a number of them are about to embark on professional training. The comedy scenes are executed almost flawlessly. With the actors on the first night undeterred by chiming clocks, passing sirens and shrieking revellers on the other side of the wall, the City of Oxford Theatre Guild is set to notch up yet another success with this, its 46th consecutive production of summer Shakespeare.

Paula Clifford

I can see that Gerard is looking tired. I ask him whether there is anything further he wants to say at this point. He smiles gently and shakes his head.

G "I don't think so."

M "A cup of tea?"

G "Yes, a cup of tea and some of that nice cake."

I leave him and make a leisurely cup of tea while he takes a nap and dreams of theatre.

The Grand Finale

Refreshed by tea, Gerard is refuelled and ready to direct his 'Grand Finale'.

M "Gerard, tell me about the special surprise evening they gave you."

G "Yes, it was a few years ago. Nick Rawlinson and Nigel Cooke organised an evening at the Playhouse all behind my back."

He stops here to find a scrapbook and hand it over to me. It was an evening of celebration of and tribute to Gerard given by actors, friends, family and members of the Theatre Guild, held at the Oxford Playhouse, October 2005.

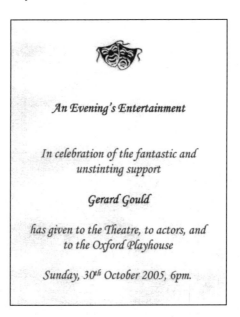

An Evening's Entertainment

In celebration of the fantastic and unstinting support

Gerard Gould

has given to the Theatre, to actors, and to the Oxford Playhouse

Sunday, 30ᵗʰ October 2005, 6pm.

M "Ah, it's lovely! Really lovely! Eileen would have been so proud of you, wouldn't she? I'm sure she was there!"

G "She was there, she was there, yes."

M "Absolutely there."

G "They even wrote to my nephew and niece to send something in."

M "Yes, I can see. It's lovely. It's like 'This is Your Life'."

G "Yes, exactly. It was 'This is Your Life'. "

M "Oh yes, I can second this tribute someone's written here - 'Thank you for your honesty, generosity and wisdom'. What a compliment! 'You are an inspiration'. This is so lovely! Oh, it must have been so moving."

G "Yes, I was overwhelmed – I was totally overwhelmed you see. It was a complete surprise. They couldn't believe my face when I came into the Playhouse – I'd no idea what was going on."

M "Where did you think you were going?"

G "Well, you see, Nick Rawlinson and his wife, Tanya, had arranged to take me out to supper and I was told that Nick was doing a talking books recording. Tanya came by herself to collect me and told me we were going to meet Nick in Oxford. We drove down by the Playhouse and saw it all lit up.

Photo taken by Nick Holmes

That was very unusual for a Sunday evening.
I think I said, 'Oh, there must be something on in there.'

Ha, ha! And then I saw somebody rushing across the street, which turned out to be Nigel Cooke's wife. I asked her what she was doing there. She took my arm and said, 'Come on!'

Ha, ha! We entered the theatre and it was full and I suddenly saw faces I knew. I couldn't believe it. There's a photograph that shows I stood there, mouth wide open!

Gerard Gould – This Is Your Life

'What's going on?' Then it dawned on me!

I said, 'Oh no!' Ha, ha!"

336

Tributes follow from actors, who appear one by one from the wings to take their place downstage. The first is Martyn Read. Martyn is a former pupil of Gerard's who was inspired to take up acting as a career. He takes his place centre stage.

Martyn Read

M.R "I was a pupil at Lord Williams from 1956 to 1963 and I believe Gerard joined in 1957. Gerard **immediately** impressed me and a lot of other boys. I was about eleven at the time and I'd never met anyone like him. He then still had a slight accent and some of the boys mimicked him. He had and still has the most wonderfully infectious laugh which could stop traffic. He had very, very wavy black hair that some of the boys quite envied.

He came to LWS at the same time as Norman Lilley and Peter More. There was a new head too, Nelson. It seemed like a breath of fresh air. But Gerard had quite a run in with the Head, because I was cast as Henry V in an excerpt from the play and Gerard wanted me to grow my hair! In those days it was short back and sides. I was brought into Nelson's study, actually.
'Read, your hair's too long.'
'I'm playing Henry V, Sir.'
'No excuse.'
'But Mr Gould wanted it, Sir.'
'Humph!'
Anyway, I kept my hair! But better than that, I do remember this headmaster saying, 'Do we need a school play?' and Gerard alone upheld the flag. He was determined to do at least one Shakespeare play a year.

And then, this must have been 1958, Gerard, who had not been back to Germany since the war, organised a trip for us to take this production to schools in Germany. At the time, it never occurred to me to wonder how Gerard felt. Years later I wrote a one man play about Dr. Watson. It played at the Oxford Playhouse and was acted by Nigel Stock. It attracted quite a bit of international press and my agents sent me a review from a German theatrical paper. I took it to Gerard for translation – this would have been about twenty five years ago. And he looked slightly bashful.
He said, 'I'm not sure I can do it.'
I said, 'What do you mean?'
He said, 'Well, when I left Germany I made a point never to speak the language again, never to think in it again.'
He did make a cursory translation of it, but it was obviously the first time.

It's curious to think, he eventually ended up at Lord Bills' teaching no German. We have a German teaching English Literature and French to the older groups and I think he's far more in touch with French and France than he is with Germany.

His theatre was an inspiration. We had to perform in open air space as we had nothing indoors, but Gerard made sure we did the Shakespeare and also some plays such as 'Antigone'. He just inspired the most unlikely boys either as actors, set builders or anything. And his lessons were always electric. They were never, 'You will read three pages of Pope,' you know. It was always much more inventive and joking. I remember once we were studying Wordsworth and Gerard was reading it aloud to us. A great friend of mine, Martin Harris, was in the class – he wasn't the world's greatest literary expert. Gerard read this piece and the word 'intercourse' came up, meaning between man and nature. I'll paraphrase it.
'And man has intercourse with great nature and Harris well done for not smiling and giggling on the word 'intercourse'!'
Then he seamlessly went on with the poem! He was great – he didn't turn a hair!

There was a chap called Ellis in my class. Ellis's father was in the R.A.F. and Ellis was **completely** obsessed with aeroplanes. He was a dreamer, and there was no way Ellis was going to become an academic. And Gerard could see out the corner of his eye that he'd lost the point of what we were discussing. Suddenly, out of nowhere, came, 'Flight E double L 1 S come in to land! Please, come in to land!' The way he said this you'd have thought it was the whole theme of what we were discussing.

I think he also released a flare in pupils - well certainly in boys like me who were naturally interested in literature, acting and theatre – he absolutely opened the gas valve on that. I think Gerard recognised that I had some sort of talent for it. It might not have happened at all otherwise, especially with the then Head's attitude towards drama.

His caring for us didn't end when we left school. He was always very loyal to his ex-pupils, especially when he was younger. He went to see all of us as much as he could in our productions. In my case, it was six years after leaving school that I decided to go to into drama. The first person I thought of was Gerard, and he helped me to choose the right school and get into it.

He gave me so much, so I was glad when I had the chance to do something for him. He's passionate about French Theatre and about ten years ago I was into radio. There was a lovely, eccentric radio producer called John Theocardis. I introduced him to Gerard, who wanted to do a feature on Radio 3 about French Theatre. So they went off to France together and he was thrilled to bits with it, talking in French to people involved in theatre – his idea of heaven!"

As Martyn retires into the wings, his place downstage is taken by Cate Fowler. Like Martyn, she was a pupil at the school and went on to become a professional actress.

C. F "The irony is I was never, ever directed by Gerard. I was only at the school for two years, in the Lower Sixth and then Upper Sixth. During that time I did operas, which were directed by Colin Brookes. I did 'Murder in the Cathedral' which was directed by Richard Adams, but it was a two year break for Gerard from directing! So I was in that window when he didn't produce anything. Nevertheless, he means everything to me.
I did English A-level and I was in his English group. You know, I still remember the texts we studied at A-level. I think possibly it's because of the way Gerard taught them and because of the understanding and the insight he gave me. I guess he used to

keep quite a close eye on what was going on. I was having voice and acting classes with Isobel Van Beers and doing a lot of dance with Jackie Kiers. So Gerard always knew who was in his scene, as it were. I think I warmed to him because of the passionate way he talked, and how he brought his subject to life. I'd seen productions of his when I was at another school. He had a reputation.

Cate Fowler

When I first came to the school I was intending to become a dancer. From the age of six to about sixteen I knew exactly what I wanted to be, and then suddenly, at seventeen, I didn't know anymore. I grew too tall for ballet and went off the whole idea. Gerard came into my life at that time and gave me direction. Then I knew what I want to do. He was there at the right time. I always remember, when I got into drama school, there was the question of a grant and my parents obviously weren't au fait with grants, drama schools, or anything like that. I remember Gerard taking the afternoon off and driving me into Oxford to the Education Offices. He sat outside while I did my interview to get my grant. Now that was a parental role, not just a teaching role.

He used to take us on the most wonderful trips to the theatre. They were not like school outings, although I'm sure there was a coach involved somewhere – you know, it was so thrilling to be taken to the West End and be given that experience when you come from a small market town in Oxfordshire. I remember we went to the RSC one evening and he nudged me and pointed and said, 'That's one of the greatest actresses of our time', and there a few rows in front of us was Dame Peggy Ashcroft. I don't know which of us was the more excited! He was part of that world and I was drawn to him like a magnet, because that was the world I wanted to inhabit. He was the key, I guess - the key to opening that door. Often when actors are interviewed, they talk about a teacher who was instrumental in their careers. But Gerard has touched the lives of many other pupils who didn't go on to work in theatre, who nevertheless, through him, have acquired a love of the arts, literature and poetry.

Then I went to drama school and since then there has never been a time when I haven't been in touch with Gerard. I would call him when I got an audition and we would talk about how to approach the part, the language and the background and often I would receive pages of handwritten notes from him. He would often come to my opening nights or otherwise be there at some other point during the run and always be honest and constructive in his criticism. When he came to first nights, he would always come to the first night party and by the end of the evening everybody in the room would know him, because he loves theatre, he loves actors, and that radiates out of him. They just warm to him – everybody adores him – including me!

I do very much regret that he never directed me. It would have been lovely to have had the opportunity to have worked with Gerard on the text as well as on the acting. I just wish I could tell you firsthand what he was like as a director. But certainly, watching his productions, they were not school productions – they were more like professional shows – they even went on tour!

His love of the theatre is absolutely palpable, his knowledge is extraordinary. He was inspirational in every connection that I had with him. And he had total faith in me – encouraging me when I wasn't working. 'Have you tried this? Why don't you try that? What you need to do is ...' - always full of ideas, enthusiasm and energy. And Eileen, his wife, was lovely. She is much missed. They were great together. I know I'm not the only ex-pupil who keeps in touch – there are many, many more. He is instrumental in what I'm doing now. He gave me direction at a time when I could have lost my 'raison d'etre.' I feel very privileged and very lucky to have had Gerard in my life – I really do. Dear man, I love him. You know, I seriously considered failing my A-levels so I could stay on another year and be directed by him!"

Cate moves into the wings and the spotlight is now on another actor, Nick Rawlinson, who has taken his place centre stage to make his personal tribute.

Nick Rawlinson

N.R "I came to know Gerard through the Oxford Theatre Guild when I applied for the part of Richard III. I had been heavily involved in drama at Oxford and was wanting to continue living in the Oxford area. I saw the audition advertised in the local paper and thought it sounded exciting. I got the part, and then had a regular series of meetings at Gerard's house with him and, of course, Eileen. She was the constant sounding board. She had enormous resources of calm. As soon as I met her, I realised she was someone wonderful – the still centre of the turning wheel of their life. She would be able to summarize things beautifully and Gerard would work on her comments.

It was incredibly exhilarating – I had never met a director as intelligent as Gerard and as sensitive in all the best possible ways, who really wanted to explore the entire experience of the play, rather than just ending up focussing on the mechanics. With Gerard, he really wanted to go deeply into what it meant to **be** those characters and also what it meant as part of our national consciousness to be involved in a Shakespeare play. So we had some wonderful conversations and I learnt a great deal.

When Gerard came to England as a young man he saw a performance of Gielgud, and a production of 'Hamlet' in Oxford and he talks about walking home from them absolutely reeling. Those things left a deep and lasting impression on him – it is almost as if he is just absorbing everything about England that is good. He has understood us, and absorbed our history, our culture and our language in a most extraordinary and sensitive way. He's become part of the fabric of our country. Gerard is one of the truly great teachers. His ability to look at people, to understand what makes them tick and to help them become better people is amazing. He's worked with incredibly wonderful actors, helping them to become what they are now, but he's still prepared, when a spotty seventeen year old boy knocks at his door and says, 'I want to do some acting,' to open it and say, 'Come in.' It is not hyperbole to make the comment that Gerard is an alchemist – he has shown us so many times that he can take base metal and turn it into gold."

As Nick joins the others upstage, his place is taken by yet another pupil who became an actor with Gerard's encouragement – Nigel Cooke. Just as he did on the evening of tribute at the Oxford Playhouse, he stands now, centre stage to draw the performance to its close.

Nigel Cooke

N.C "According to the theatre director Max Stafford Clark, having anyone watching rehearsals other than people directly connected to the production is a bit like having a third party in the bedroom: dangerous. On that basis, aged eleven, I was a proper little Peeping Tom. I would spend many an after school hour spying on Gerard's rehearsals, confident in the belief that, from behind a curtain, I hadn't been seen. Wrong. Years later, Gerard told me he'd spotted me and had said to himself, 'Ah, jolly good, I have a willing recruit in the making there.'

Willing recruit I certainly became. Apart from my parents, Gerard has been the single most influential person in my life. When I was first there in 1969, Gerard cut a very distinctive figure about the small, market town Grammar School that was Lord Williams's. Amongst the rich brew of the teachers, he was in a league of his own. A classroom's ability to savagely expose anything that was remotely different about a teacher was, looking back, quite terrifying. Not so with Gerard. Yes, he had his nicknames, Chunky and Greasy. (The former alluding I think to his solid build, the latter to his skin quality which had an enviably natural shimmery glow.) Yes, we imitated (mostly inaccurately) his very precise, clear but subtly different intonations and inflections of speech. Above all, we made merry with his extremely full blooded, idiosyncratic laugh. Gerard knew all this, but never seemed in the least bit troubled by it. Why not? Our mimicry had not the slightest hint of maliciousness behind it. He took such delight and interest in us as individuals. We in turn delighted in his individuality.

I was a very mediocre academic student. A very good friend and contemporary of mine, Tom, was even more mediocre. Neither was he a willing drama recruit. His prowess was on the rugby field, an activity which at best perplexed and at worst exasperated Gerard. 'What's the point of it all, what are they trying to do to each other? That boy has to play Mark Antony this evening - it's all so barbaric!' At a parents' evening Tom and his parents traipsed from teacher to teacher receiving only negative reports.

What music to their ears must Gerard's appraisal have been - 'I like Tom very much and if I was stranded in the Sahara desert he is the person I would most want to have with me.'

Imaginative, generous and honest, Gerard's positivity shone wide and far. When he first came to our house, I remember silently imploring my Dad (an outspoken maverick true blue Tory) not to pick one of his "for fun" fights with Mr Gould (whom Dad had down as a well meaning, but nonetheless, progressive trendy leftie). I needn't have worried. They got on famously. They playfully argued the toss over certain issues, but found absolute unanimity in their gratitude to and admiration for Winston Churchill. Odd details of Gerard's first years in this country emerged. Everything he said expressed his gratitude and admiration - eyes twinkling, positive, delighted. Not for one minute was he out to evoke sympathy. Dad's verdict, when Gerard had left?
'What a super bloke that Gouldilocks is, absolutely bloody marvellous fellow!'

If England has been Gerard's security, France is his mistress. Its language, gastronomy, theatre and ... Paris. 'Just to get a whiff of that magical city.' Probably the biggest treat he'd give himself would be a four night stay in Paris when he'd watch an average of six hours of theatre per day. I have never been to Paris with Gerard, but I was lucky enough to be invited by his beloved Eileen and him to spend the Easter holiday (prior to my A level exams) with them in their recently acquired holiday home in the Dordogne. The deal was that Gerard would give me three hours a day French tuition and I would help Eileen with the odd bit of unfinished work on the conversion of the building. I'm sure this reciprocity had been devised to - a) assuage my parents' desire to pay something towards the trip and b) make me feel I had a role.

The deal was done, Gerard valiantly tried to help me with my French, but it was a bit like shutting the stable door after the horse had bolted. I duly knocked up the odd mix of cement for Eileen.

There was much more besides. Gerard's fluent French and interest in people ensured there was great fraternising with the locals. They loved him. A visit from the le Professeur Anglais always merited getting out the best homemade pâté and a glass of wine or eau de vie. Market day in the nearest town, Riberac, was a must - smelly cheeses, chickens flying around! It was astonishing how many people Gerard knew, with whom he would strike up the most animated conversations. We even went to a couple of lycées where Gerard, ever eager to spread the wonder of William Shakespeare, would talk to a class and then get me to recite a bit of Romeo.

Driving around the countryside he'd ask mischievously what the time was.
'Five to four Gerard.'
The car would come to an abrupt stop and he'd gleefully exclaim,
'Ah, Pâtisserie Time.'
We'd pile into a cafe and plough our way through rum ba-bas and the like. He loved his bit of pâtisserie.

The trip was a huge education for me, in all sorts of ways. Not least, because I was given an insight into Gerard and Eileen's remarkable relationship. It was definitely a marriage of opposites which worked as a team. A particularly memorable example of that teamwork was when one afternoon Eileen sat me down for a talk. Very calmly, she gave me an account of how and why Gerard had come to England, and who and where his remaining relatives were. He thought I ought to know, but also thought that the information would be less disturbing or burdensome for me coming from Eileen. The way Eileen gave me Gerard's history, it was as if she was entrusting me with a precious gift. And it was a gift that demanded absolutely nothing in return.

Thinking of everything Gerard has given and continues to give me, the spirit in which it is given stays the same: totally unconditional. I do know that he draws great pleasure from my career, my family and their careers. Only today, his voice was brimming with excitement over the fact that my wife and I had each received good notices in the newspapers for the plays in which we are currently appearing. He was also very excited by his new television and the man who came to install it.
'If I have a problem I can phone him at ANY time I want: people are really very helpful you know.'

Ever dependable, ever consistent, he never ceases to surprise as well. One occasion was when, as a pupil, I'd responded a little too airily to something he'd generously proposed. No 'how dare you behave like that' or losing of his temper, (though I'm sure he was angry) no punishments, just a few very well chosen words and briskly off on his way leaving me feel two inches tall and (here's the clever bit) with the space to reflect on my rude behaviour.

His view and opinions, on whatever subject, can often be totally unpredictable. He had praise for plays or productions I was convinced he'd loathe. One of the biggest surprises of all came in 2003 when he telephoned saying 'Nigel, I've just watched England win the Rugby World Cup and I found it deeply moving.'

I asked what on earth had induced him to watch it in the first place and what could he have possibly found moving about it. 'Well, it was an important national event, so I should have an interest. And Jonny Wilkinson - his composure, quiet determination and his modesty. It was lovely to behold. So utterly, utterly English.'

Gerard's gratitude, again.

Will he ever believe the extent of my (and many, many other people's) gratitude **to him**? As he becomes increasingly housebound, maybe this book will go some way towards convincing him. With all my heart and love, I hope so."

At this point all the actors in the finale of our grand production, 'Making an Entrance', return to the stage, together with the shady figures from his boyhood time in Germany and post-war rural England. With them are all the unknown players whose lives have been touched by Gerard's magic for well over sixty years. We see the children from Wheatley, who were given a chance to shine and the WI ladies and villagers alongside all the professionals. Joining them now are the critics, who have come down from London, in full evening dress for this world premiere! It causes a stir. Their coming up on stage is quite without precedent.

They move forward now, as a chorus, pronouncing their review:

"'Making An Entrance' is another stunning production from Gerard Gould. He has, as ever, his finger on the pulse of the play, the players and the audience. He has the ability to lead us into hell, where we weep with anguish, and with a quick flick of his magic wand, he has us out into the light again and helpless with laughter. The man has style, panache, and charming audacity, coupled with a keen intellect and profound understanding of the human condition. His life as a director, writer, teacher and adviser is a precious and unique gift to the world. We now ask you to rise and give him the standing ovation he deserves."

*The entire cast now turns its back on the audience to welcome the director onto the stage. Gerard enters from the wings and makes his way to centre stage front. We see the actors break ranks to give him space. He glows his way through, with his head held high. He is **making an entrance!***

The ovation is long and shows no sign of ending. When he reaches centre stage, there is a roar of approval and a crescendo in the applause as he steps forward. This performance has brought the house down! The attention of the whole auditorium is focussed on this figure. At a signal from Gerard, the ecstatic audience seats itself again, as one. There is a pregnant pause – the tension is electric. The only movement in the whole theatre is the stage lighting.

Slowly the cast is put into shadow as the spotlight falls on Gerard Gould, bringing to everyone's notice the four figures that are gathered in an arc around his back. Three adults are dressed in pale grey. The older lady, in a 1930s' hat and jabot, is Gerard's Mother and the man beside her is his Father. The younger lady is Eileen. The fourth figure is that of a young boy who is also dressed in 1930s' style German clothes. He is Günter Goldstein. He steps forward to be at Gerard's side. Immediately, Gerard gives him a welcoming and unhurried hug before he addresses his audience.

G "Unlike Prospero at the end of Shakespeare's play, 'The Tempest', I am not about to lay down my 'magic' and say 'Goodbye'! On the contrary, I am here to introduce myself to you all.

As he speaks the next sentence he turns to Günter and makes an arc over him with his arm, which extends over all those gathered behind him and then back to himself.

Here ... (*he makes the arc*) ... **is Gerard Gould**.

There is total silence in the theatre.

I would like to finish with some words that are very meaningful to me from Wordsworth's 'Prelude'.

> 'Many are our joys
> In youth, but oh! what happiness to live
> When every hour brings palpable access
> Of knowledge, when all knowledge is delight,
> And sorrow is not there.'

The curtain closes to tumultuous applause.

Appendices

Appendix 1

Plays produced by Gerard Gould

The key to the organisation performing the play is at the end of the table

Year	Play	Playwright	Venue	Org
1945	The Mask	Harwood and Jesse	Watlington	WYS
1946 1948	Dance Mime		Rotherfield Peppard School	
1947	Saint Joan	Shaw	Rotherfield Peppard School	RSM
1950	The boy with a cart The Red Velvet Goat	Fry Niggli	Peppard Memorial Hall and Shiplake Memorial Hall	RSM
1950	The Browning Version Harlequinade	Rattigan	Peppard Memorial Hall	PDS
1951	The Would Be Nobleman	Molière	Drama festival	SWI
1951	The Romantic Young Lady		Headington	OTP
1952	The Ideal Husband	Wilde	Headington	OTP
1953	You never can tell	Shaw	Headington	OTP
1953	Asmodee	Mauriac	Headington	OTP
1954	The Young Idea	Coward	Headington	OTP
1955 or 56	Village Wooing Candida	Shaw	On tour	PP
1956	The Romantic Young Ladies The Bells Dance Mime	Molière	Wheatley	WSM
1957	The Merry Wives of Windsor	Shakespeare	LWS	LWS
1958	Separate Tables	Rattigan		TP
1958	Antigone	Anouilh	LWS	LWS
	That Scamp Scapin	Molière	LWS	LWS

Year	Play	Playwright	Venue	Org
1959	The Lion and the Unicorn *World premiere*	Dane	Wheatley Secondary school	LWS
	Twelfth Night	Shakespeare	Thame, Abingdon, Rotherfield Greys and tour of West Germany	LWS
1960	Under Milk Wood	Thomas	Thame Town Hall	TP
1960	The Taming of the Shrew	Shakespeare	Thame Town Hall	LWS
1961	Cyrano de Bergerac	Rostand	Thame Town Hall	LWS
1962	'A Range of Passions' love scenes	Shakespeare	LWS	LWS
1963	In Good King Charles's Golden Days	Bernard Shaw	Josca's Little Theatre	OTG
1964	War and Peace	Neumann and Piscator	LWS	LWS
1965	Hamlet	Shakespeare	LWS	LWS
1966	Hamlet	Shakespeare	Tour of Germany	LWS
1966/ 1967	Post Mortem *World premiere*	Coward	LWS	LWS
1967	Electra	Sophocles	LWS	LWS
	The Ridiculous Young Ladies	Molière	LWS	LWS
1967	The Way of the World	William Congreve	The Kenton Theatre Henley and The Oxford Playhouse	OTG
1968	Julius Caesar	Shakespeare	German tour	LWS
1969	The Browning Version	Rattigan	LWS	LWS
	Unman Wittering and Zigo	Cooper	LWS	LWS
1971	Macbeth	Shakespeare	LWS	LWS
1973	Erik XIV *UK premiere*	Strindberg	LWS	LWS
1974	Romeo and Juliet	Shakespeare	LWS	LWS
1976	Comedy of Errors	Shakespeare	St John's College	OTG
1976	Cavalcade	Coward	LWS	LWS

358

Year	Play	Playwright	Venue	Org
1981	Much Ado About Nothing	Shakespeare	The Sheldonian	OTG
1985	The School Mistress	Wing Pinero	The Oxford Playhouse	OTG
1986	Hamlet	Shakespeare	Christ Church	OTG
1993	Richard III	Shakespeare	Oxford. Playhouse and Magdalen College	OTG
1998	Pygmalion	Bernard Shaw	The Oxford Playhouse	OTG
2000	Twelfth Night	Shakespeare	Fellows' Garden, New College	OTG
2002	The Mysteries	Denys	The Old Fire Station	OTG
2004	The Merchant of Venice	Shakespeare	Fellows' Garden, Exeter College	OTG

Key to name of organisation performing the play

LWS	Lord Williams's School
OTG	Oxford Theatre Guild
OTP	Oxford Theatre Players
PP	Phoenix Players
PDS	Peppard Dramatic Society
RSM	Rotherfield Secondary Modern School Dramatic Society
SWI	Sandhills Women's Institute
TP	Thame Players
WSM	Wheatley Secondary Modern School
WYS	Watlington Youth Centre Amateur Dramatic Society

Appendix 2

Books published by Gerard Gould

Title	Author	Publisher	Year
Dramatic Involvement	Gerard Gould	Blackwell	1970
Learning and Language in the Classroom: Discursive Talking and Writing Across the Curriculum	Peter Chilver and Gerard Gould		1982
Into Shakespeare: An introduction to Shakespeare though Drama	Richard M Adams and Gerard Gould	Ward Lock Educational	1982
Sisterly Feelings	Alan Ayckbourn and Gerard Gould	Longman Study Texts	1982
Pygmalion	Bernard Shaw Gerard Gould	Longman Study Texts	1983
Absurd Person Singular	Alan Ayckbourn and Gerard Gould	Longman Study Texts	1989